The GREATEST DETECTIVE, the GREATEST CITY...
the GREATEST CHALLENGE!
SJ FICTION
DEATH NOTE
デスノート
ANOTHER NOTE: THE LOS ANGELES BB MURDER CASES
LOS ANGELES AUTHORITIES ARE TRACKING A SERIAL KILLER WHOSE CLUES ARE SO COMPLEX THAT EVEN L, THE WORLD'S MOST DECORATED DETECTIVE, CAN'T DECIPHER THEM. ENLISTING THE HELP OF FBI AGENT NAOMI MISORA, CAN L CRACK THE CASE —AND PRESERVE HIS REPUTATION— BEFORE THE VICTIMS OUTNUMBER THE CLUES?
DEATH NOTE
ANOTHER NOTE
THE LOS ANGELES BB MURDER CASES
FIND OUT IN ANOTHER NOTE: THE LOS ANGELES BB MURDER CASES—NOVEL IN STORES NOW
GET THE COMPLETE DEATH NOTE COLLECTION—BUY THE MANGA, PROFILES BOOK AND ANIME TODAY!
SHONEN JUMP ADVANCED
On sale at deathnote.viz.com
Also available at your local bookstore and comic store.
DEATH NOTE - ANOTHER NOTE LOS ANGELES BB RENZOKU SATSUJIN JIKEN -
© 2006 by NISIO ISIN, Tsugumi Ohba, Takeshi Obata/SHUEISHA Inc.
RATED T+ FOR OLDER TEEN ratings.viz.com
viz media
www.viz.com

DEATH NOTE
デスノート
HOW TO READ
Story by
Tsugumi Ohba
Art by
Takeshi Obata

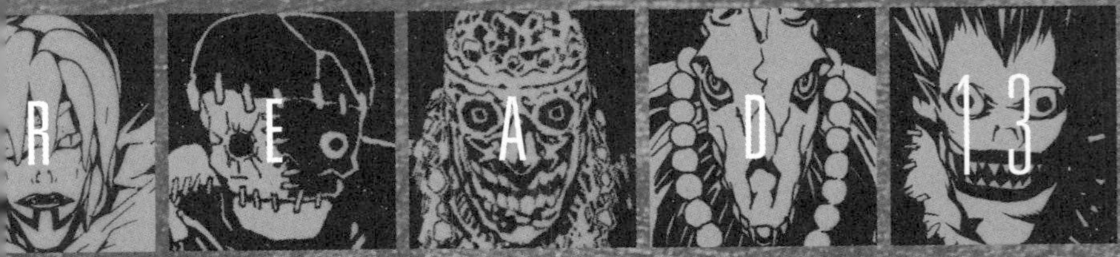

CONTENTS

HOW TO READ -STORY- 083

115 HOW TO DRAW -TAKESHI OBATA-

HOW TO READ -RULES & TRICKS- 141

HOW TO CREATE -TSUGUMI OHBA x TAKESHI OBATA-

201

HOW TO PLAY -RYUK'S NOTEBOOK-

HOW TO READ
CHARACTERS

Main Character Profiles

The Forces Involved in the Kira Case

Kira Case Participant Relationships

Complete Shinigami File

Shinigami Observation Diary

A complete analysis of Light, L and all the main characters who play a role in this fierce battle of minds.

Light Yagami 夜神月

■■■Personal Data

Birthday	02/28/1986
Deathday	01/28/2010
Height	5'8"
Weight	119 lbs.
Blood Type	A
Likes	Justice
Dislikes	Evil

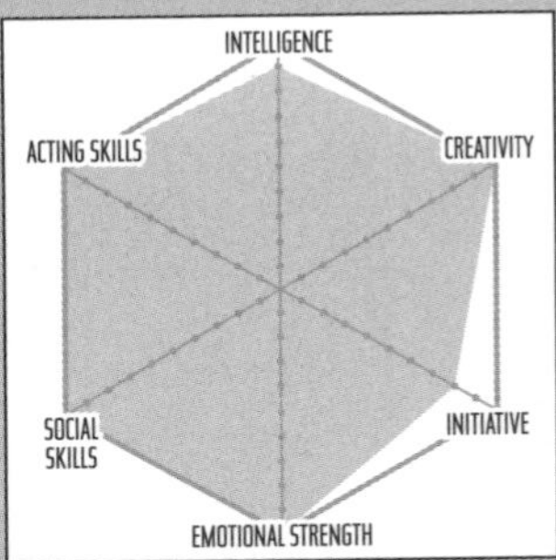

BASIC DATA The Haughty Murderer Who Tries to Become God

A young man who tries to make the world a better place by using the Death Note. Combining his innate intelligence with the power of a Shinigami, he secretly tries to take over the world as Kira, the God of the New World.

I'M GOING TO MAKE THE WHOLE WORLD KNOW I'M HERE...
THAT SOMEBODY IS PASSING RIGHTEOUS JUDGMENT ON THEM!!

🡅 Light joyfully explaining his ideals. His life would change greatly from this point on…

L'S HEIRS ...
SO I'M STILL FIGHTING AGAINST L...

🡆 Kira's power could control the governments of even the largest countries, but he could never escape L's curse…

CHARACTER FILE 01

PERSONALITY Pure Yet Extreme

Light was uncompromising when it came to achieving his ideals. He sullied himself by using the Death Note, but his extreme actions may have been the result of the purity within him before he got his hands on the notebook.

← Overtaken by evil, Light even takes advantage of love to achieve his goals.

ABILITIES L's Rival with Both Pen and Sword

Light is a genius who never stops working hard. By combining extensive planning with his already brilliant mind, he was able to go head to head with L. If you had to identify a weakness, it could be that he never doubted his own ability.

↑ Light is always one or two steps ahead. Even facing the greatest danger in his life, he escapes with a brilliant plan and turns the tables on L.

↑ Light fools everyone around him by fulfilling the roles of both L and Kira.

CAREER From Kira to the Second L...

Having defeated L, Light names himself as the Second L and takes control of the Kira investigation. With this ultimate cover, Kira continues to influence the world while playing the part of L.

Light Yagami Quotes

"I will reign over a new world!" (Volume 1, Page 49)

Light's favorite line. It's a line that shows how intoxicated with power he became.

"Let's catch Kira…together!" (Volume 5, Page 45)

Words from Light after he lost his memories of the notebook.
Light's original fate may have been as someone on L's side…

"Exactly as planned." (Volume 7, Page 24)

Everything he had prepared goes exactly as he had intended…
His expression when he's confirmed his own victory is shocking.

"A bunch of hopeless fools…" (Volume 12, Page 145)

The arrogance that came with Kira's power caused him to completely lose sight of who he used to be.

L エル

■■■Personal Data

True Name	L Lawliet
Birthday	10/31/1979
Deathday	11/5/2004
Height	5'8" (estimated)
Weight	110 lbs. (estimated)
Blood Type	Unknown
Likes	Sweets
Dislikes	Socks

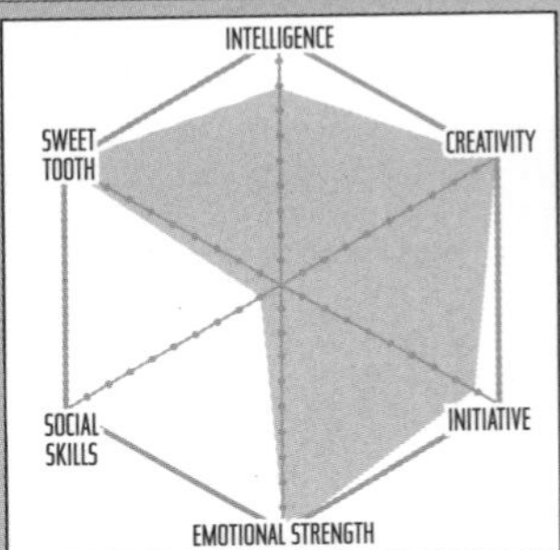

BASIC DATA Kira's Pursuer: The World's Greatest Detective

He's the most respected detective in the world, but his identity is shrouded in mystery. With the Kira case, he stands on the stage of history for the first time. But the results are…

...I SUSPECT THAT YOU MAY IN FACT BE KIRA.
IF YOU STILL WANT TO ASK ME, KNOWING THAT, GO RIGHT AHEAD.

➡ L takes the upper hand using surprise and is able to press Light with his strategies.

⬆ L may have lost to Kira, but he does solve the case at the very end.

CHARACTER FILE 02

PERSONALITY Competitive and Childish

As L himself acknowledges, he has a childish personality and hates to lose, no matter how small the contest. Very suspicious by nature, he'll use any method he can to track down the truth until he's completely satisfied with the answer. As such, he's often misunderstood.

➡ Somehow he's mastered the Brazilian martial art, capoiera. It seems he's been in a few serious fights.

TASTE Odd Eating Habits

L has a sweet tooth and is never seen eating a regular meal during the investigation. Everything he eats is either candy or some other kind of sweet. Staying healthy on this sort of diet requires a lot of skill. Misa was jealous.

⬆ L snacking during an important meeting. He doesn't seem to be taking anything seriously, but this is his style.

ABILITIES A Brilliant Mind and Daring Moves

L is the best detective in the world not only because of his brilliance but also because of his daring actions. From watching a monitor for days to planning the capture of a suspect, he can do it all.

⬆ L blends into the crowd and steals Misa's cell phone. He'll even commit a crime to solve a case he's working on.

L Quotes

"So, come on! Kill me if you can!!" (Volume 1, P. 75)

A very daring move, but L's confident he won't be killed.

"That the good guys always win." (Volume 2, P. 87)

Does the fact that he can say such a cheesy line indicate the strength of his commitment, or…?

"…Light-kun is my first-ever friend." (Volume 4, P. 132)

Even while fighting him as an enemy L establishes a weird friendship with Light. They make a good team during the Yotsuba investigation.

"I could fall for you, you know?" (Volume 6, P. 49)

This is directed toward Misa. It's hard to tell from his expression, but it's probably a lie. He doesn't seem to have much experience when it comes to women.

Mello メロ

■■■Personal Data

True Name	Mihael Keehl
Birthday	12/13/1989
Deathday	1/26/2010
Height	5'6"
Weight	114 lbs.
Blood Type	A
Likes	Chocolate
Dislikes	Those better than him

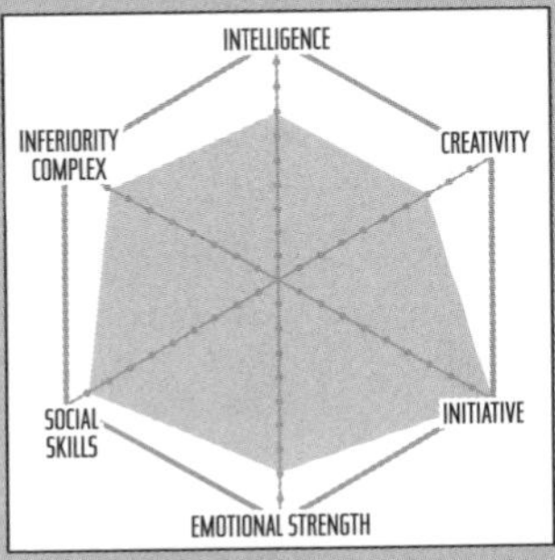

BASIC DATA No. 2 Candidate to Be the Next L

One of the children raised as a possible heir to the L name. After L is killed Mello acts on his own to capture Kira. He uses any means available—even teaming up with the mafia.

...IS TO GET YOUR HANDS ON THE NOTE-BOOK TOO. RIGHT?
AND YOU WANT IT BEFORE ITS EXISTENCE GOES PUBLIC.

↑Threatening to kill the president of the United States in order to procure his cooperation.

THIS WOMAN... SHE'S CON-NECTED TO KIRA...
UNLESS I DO THIS...

➔With no other options, Mello forces the issue.

ABILITIES
Swift Action and No Conscience

Mello often disregards the law. Despite his inferiority to Near, Mello finds a way to be a major threat to Light.

KIDNAP SOICHIRO YAGAMI'S DAUGHTER, SAYU, NEXT!

⬆A hostage is the quickest way to get what you want. While incredibly risky, Mello's plan fools both Light and Near.

AMBITION
Get Rid of Those in My Way and Be the Best

Mello has always been obsessed with defeating Near. By capturing Kira before Near can, he's hoping to wrestle away the title of No. 1 for himself.

PERSONALITY
A Strong Desire to Be the Best and an Inferiority Complex

Although he has an excellent mind he sometimes lets his emotions get in the way. His hatred of Near, for example, has created a flaw in his personality. Realizing that he will never be the best, Mello becomes a criminal in order to reach his goals.

⬆Overcome by the desire to beat Near, Mello takes drastic action. These reckless moves eventually cost him his life.

I WANT KIRA'S HEAD ...
AND I'LL KILL ANY-ONE WHO GETS IN MY WAY. I'LL BE NUMBER ONE.

⬆Mello is always obsessed with being the best. His final objective is to dispose of Kira and use the notebook to rule the world for himself.

Mello Quotes

"No matter what I have to do, I will get it before Near…" (Vol. 7, P. 183)

Due to his jealousy of Near, he has to be the first to solve a case that even L couldn't solve.

"I'll kill anyone who gets in my way. I'll be number one." (Vol. 7, P. 198)

His "kill anyone in my way" mentality is actually closer to Kira's than to L's.

"I'm not a tool for you to use to solve the puzzle." (Vol. 9, P. 136)

Mello explodes when he discovers he's merely a pawn in Near's plans. To him this is the worst humiliation he could suffer.

"Matt… I never thought you'd be killed… Forgive me…." (Vol. 12, P. 15)

Mello apologizes to Matt for getting him killed. He doesn't intend for Soichiro to die either. Mello is not purely evil.

Near ニア

■■■Personal Data

True Name	Nate River
Birthday	8/24/1991
Deathday	--
Height	5'
Weight	88 lbs.
Blood Type	B
Likes	Toys, puzzles
Dislikes	Kira

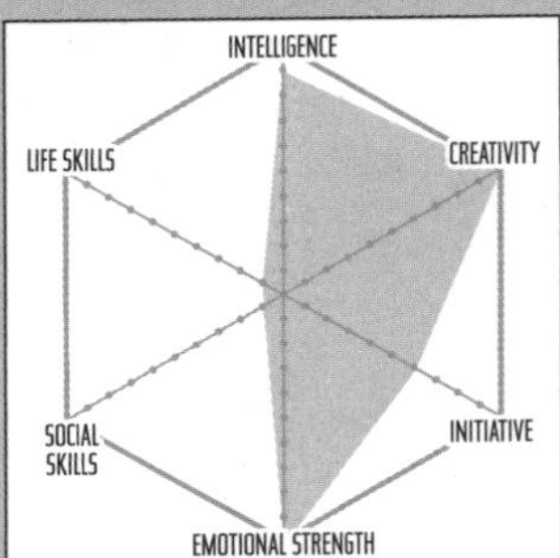

BASIC DATA
The Genius Who Inherits the L Name

A prodigy said to be the closest to L in terms of ability. He's the leader of the anti-Kira team, SPK, and controls the FBI as he sees fit. He challenges Kira directly and pushes him to the brink.

RIDICULOUS!
ACCEPTING KIRA IS OUT OF THE QUESTION.

⬆Near is angry when he hears how America responds to Kira. His feelings against Kira are even more intense than L's.

➡The final battle, where he pins down Light with irrefutable evidence.

LIGHT YAGAMI. YOU ARE KIRA.

CHARACTER FILE 04

PERSONALITY
Better Than L at Keeping His Cool?!

Is he just following the beat of his own drum, or does he, like L, simply lack basic social skills? He doesn't hesitate for a second when he finds himself in legal grey areas. For Near, the ends justify the means.

➡ Near takes control of a situation through verbal domination. At times he even gets the best of Light.

AH...
...SO YOU'VE SEEN HIM.

NEAR, WHY DON'T YOU COME OUTSIDE FOR ONCE?
FORGET HIM, LINDA.
NO THANK YOU.

ABILITIES
His Mind Is Brilliant but...

His gifts of reasoning and insight are equal to L's, but because his social and basic living skills are even lower than L's he can fully utilize his abilities only when he's surrounded by support.

⬅ Near rarely goes outside and keeps human contact to a minimum. It doesn't seem as if he had any friends at Wammy's House.

⬆ He doesn't seem to have much loyalty to a particular type of toy, but he does take his favorites with him when he escapes his base.

HOBBY
A Love for Blank Puzzles and Toys

Near is always surrounded by toys, as if he were a child. Even while playing he'll start putting together a blank puzzle, which shows just how talented he is.

Near Quotes

"If you can't solve the puzzle, you're nothing but a loser." (Vol. 7, P. 193)

Near is obsessed with the end result. If you lose the battle, nothing else matters.

"If you're wrong, you just have to say 'sorry.' " (Vol. 9, P. 97)

This line is in response to a question about his tactics.
Although very unreasonable, this way of thinking is similar to L's.

"Together we can surpass L." (Vol. 12, P. 121)

Had Near and Mello worked together, they may have eclipsed even the great detective L.

"You are just a murderer." (Vol. 12, P. 140)

This is how Near responds to Light's impassioned Kira speech.
No matter his ideals, a murderer must not be accepted.

Misa Amane 弥 海砂

■■■Personal Data

Birthday	12/25/1984
Deathday	2/14/2011
Height	5′
Weight	79 lbs.
Blood Type	AB
Likes	Light Yagami
Dislikes	Light's enemies

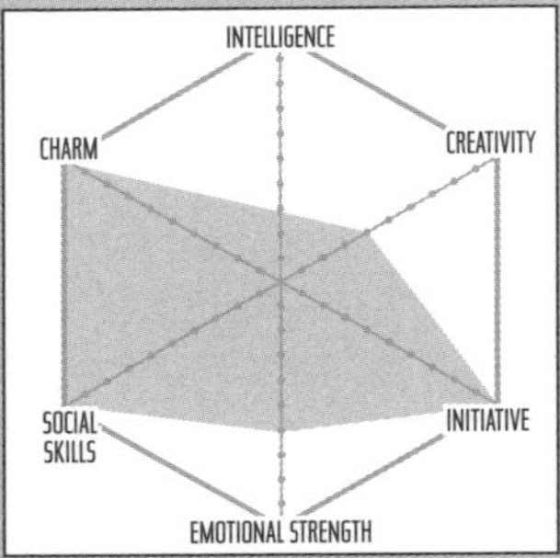

BASIC DATA

The Second Kira, Who Loves Light

A beautiful girl who works as a model and actress. With the Death Note given to her by Rem, Misa becomes the Second Kira. Having fallen in love with Light, she tries to help him.

THANKS TO YOU, LIGHT REALLY DID BECOME MY KNIGHT, REM.
LOOKS LIKE IT.

←↑ With her Shinigami Eyes, Misa is an asset to Light and helps him in various ways.

CHARACTER FILE 05

CAREER From Idol to Actress

She was just a model for a popular magazine until she heard about the Kira case. That's when she started using her own Death Note. Because of her acting talent she's able to help both the police and Kira. She's a pretty good actress and has entertained many offers for movie roles.

I'M MISA-MISA!
I WON'T DO ANYTHING INVOLVING NUDITY, BUT SWIMSUITS AND LINGERIE ARE FINE! THANK YOU FOR CONSIDER-ING ME!

↑ Misa has a great screen presence and doesn't wilt under pressure. Her talents are very helpful during the Yotsuba investigation.

PERSONALITY Presumptuous and Stubborn

Like most young girls, Misa is very passionate about love. She's completely loyal to those she falls in love with, but when she becomes emotional she doesn't back down. Her cheerful and open demeanor gives her the ability to charm just about anyone.

↓ Misa is very jealous and possessive of her lovers. If other women become involved with Light, she'll have to kill them.

THERE'S NO WAY I'LL STAND FOR YOU SEEING OTHER GIRLS.
IF I SEE THAT, I'LL KILL THEM.

MAKE THE EYE TRADE WITH ME!
!

FATE A Life Saved by Death

Misa's life was saved by a Shinigami named Rem. If things had stopped there, she probably would have lived a happy life as a normal girl. However, with the appearance of Kira and the Shinigami her life changed dramatically.

← Because she makes the "eye trade" twice, Misa's lifespan is greatly reduced. Even though she's only being used by Light, Misa seems happy.

Misa Quotes

"What a wonderful way to kill." (Vol. 4, P. 40)

Misa thinks a death caused by love is wonderful. She must be a romantic.

"Yeah but…to me, Light is more important than the world…" (Vol. 4, P. 112)

She always thinks of her lover first. It's hard to tell if Light is happy being the object of her affection.

"Motchi and Monchichi." (Vol. 10, P. 72)

Misa uses friendly nicknames for everyone. Her bubbly personality helps her greatly in the entertainment industry.

"You'll probably get the death penalty." (Vol. 11, P. 82)

It's probably supposed to be a joke, but part of her wants it to happen. A fight between two jealous girls can be a scary thing…

Teru Mikami 魅上照

Personal Data

Birthday	6/7/1982
Deathday	2/7/2010
Height	5'7"
Weight	123 lbs.
Blood Type	A
Likes	Order
Dislikes	Chaos

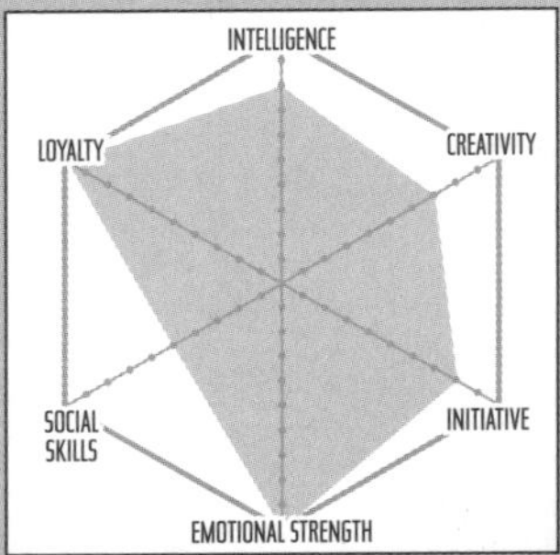

CHARACTER FILE 06

BASIC DATA — A Young Prosecutor Who Adores Kira

Mikami is the new Kira proxy whom Light chooses. He worships Kira and faithfully carries out any order from him. Mikami possesses a sharp mind and frequently acts on his own judgment as well.

FATE — Despair and Death in Prison

After seeing Light struggle pathetically against Near, he quickly comes to the painful realization that Kira is not the god he envisioned. While in a state of disillusionment he is captured as a suspect in the case.

← Mikami being arrested by the SPK. He dies in prison, but mysteries remain.

UPBRINGING — Warped Morals

Mikami is a smart young man with a strong sense of justice. But his intense love of justice manifests itself as an extreme hatred for evil, and this makes him sympathetic to Kira.

The deletion of the people he rejected...
...happened all at once.

↑ After seeing evildoers "deleted," just as he had wished for, Mikami starts to believe that evil is meant to be punished.

Kiyomi Takada 高田清美

■■■Personal Data

Birthday	7/12/1985
Deathday	1/26/2010
Height	5'4"
Weight	97 lbs.
Blood Type	AB
Likes	Smart men
Dislikes	Stupid women

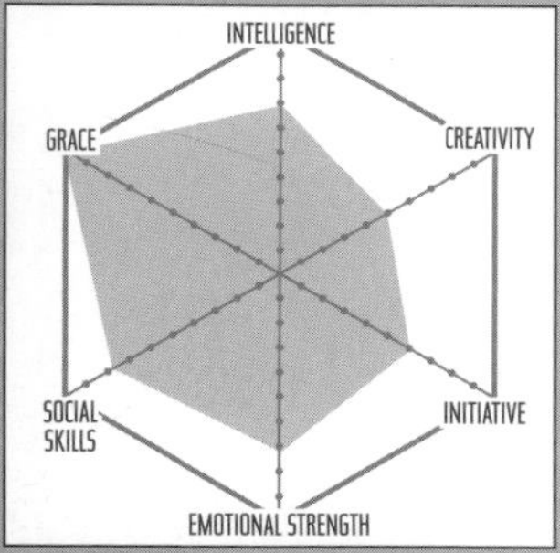

BASIC DATA — The Goddess of the Kira Worshippers

A popular anchorwoman who is revered as Kira's representative. She was a classmate of Light's during their college days and even dated him. As an adult she is reunited with Light and helps him.

CHARACTER FILE 07

CAREER — Popular Female Anchor on NHN

Already a well-known news anchor, when she's elevated to being Kira's representative her popularity skyrockets. Always surrounded by guards, she's treated like royalty.

➡ She's comfortable spreading Kira's message through the media.

PERSONALITY — Royal Pride

A beauty since her days as a student, Takada takes a job in the limelight as a news announcer. Already used to being the center of attention, she's treated like a goddess by the Kira worshippers, which further inflates her ego.

➡ Confident in her own intelligence, Takada doesn't think the feeble Misa is deserving of Light.

Soichiro Yagami 夜神総一郎

■■■Personal Data

Birthday	7/12/1955
Deathday	11/11/2009
Height	5'9"
Weight	150 lbs.
Blood Type	A
Likes	His family
Dislikes	Crime

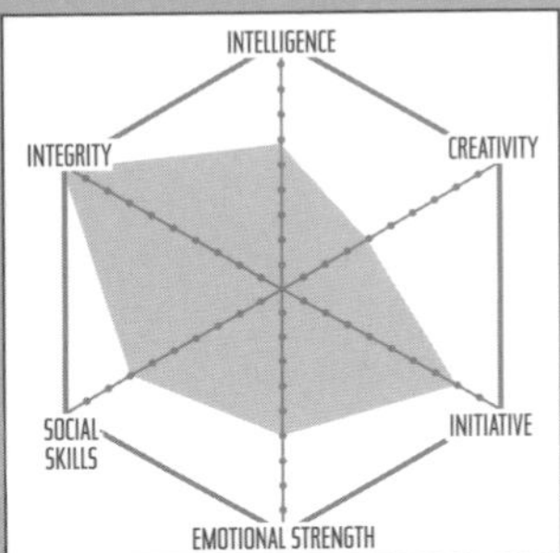

CHARACTER FILE 08

BASIC DATA — Light's Father and a Strong Believer in Justice

Soichiro is Light's father and a member of the Japanese police force. Soichiro leads the Kira investigation not knowing that his son is behind the killings. A serious and responsible individual, he's respected by everyone.

FAMILY — A Family Destroyed by a Shinigami

Because of his involvement with the Kira case his daughter is kidnapped and in the end he even loses his own life. These events are all the more tragic since Kira is his own son.

I... I'M SORRY... I COULDN'T KILL HIM AFTER ALL...

⬆ Shot by the mafia, Soichiro continues to believe in his son's innocence.

⬇ Brilliant acting done to erase the suspicion cast on his son. Even L has to agree to release Light after this.

CONVICTION — Risking His Life to Capture Kira

After the police back off the case Soichiro continues to risk his life for the investigation. His youthful spirit is of great help to L.

Touta Matsuda 松田桃太

■■■Personal Data

Birthday	12/14/1978
Deathday	--
Height	5'7"
Weight	130 lbs.
Blood Type	B
Likes	What's fashionable
Dislikes	Slow and steady work

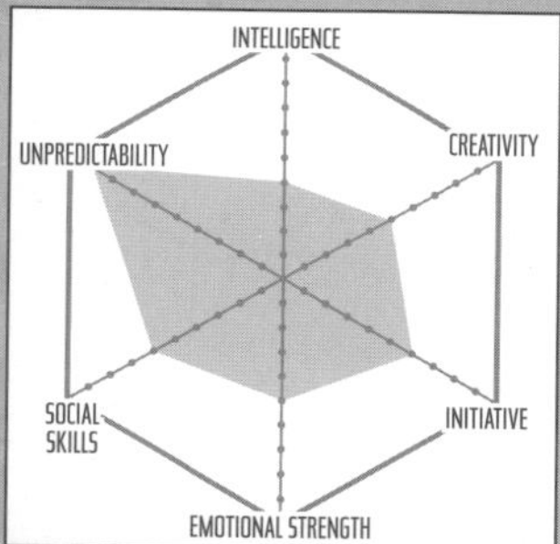

BASIC DATA — The Task Force's Troublemaker

The youngest officer on the team of Japanese investigators. He has the drive, but his lack of experience sometimes hurts the investigation. He likes Light and believes in his innocence, but...

CHARACTER FILE 09

ABILITIES — Hasty Actions Lead to Unexpected Results?!

Matsuda has an inferiority complex, possibly because he's always surrounded by talented people. He gets himself into trouble with some risky moves, but he also aids the investigation with quick thinking.

⬅ Matsuda in big trouble after being caught eavesdropping. He then brilliantly follows L's plan and saves himself.

PERSONALITY — A Fickle Young Man of the Times

Matsuda is a pretty typical young man. He gets very excited about trends and gossip and is easy to get along with. He seems like the black sheep on the task force, but this allows him to appear less suspicious to the Yotsuba members.

⬅ Matsuda getting all excited over the selection of Takada. Those around him are often annoyed by his behavior.

© Main Character Profiles

Shuichi Aizawa 相沢周市

■■■Personal Data

Birthday	5/11/1969
Deathday	--
Height	6' (including his hair)
Weight	154 lbs.
Blood Type	B
Likes	His daughter
Dislikes	Insincerity

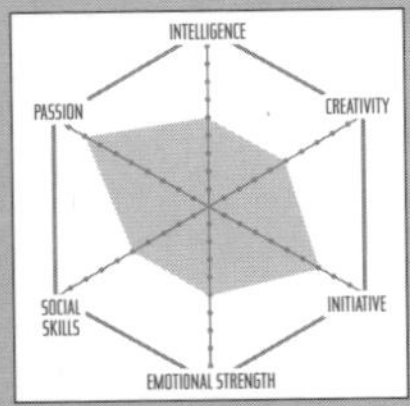

BASIC DATA

A detective for the NPA and a very serious and passionate officer. At one point he quits the investigation for the sake of his family but later returns. He comes to suspect Light and tries to help Near solve the case.

ABILITIES

He's a talented detective but is nowhere near the level of Light or L. While he's not able to dramatically aid the investigation, his achievements are acknowledged afterward.

➡ He realizes Light is secretly passing notes, but he can't secure the evidence.

CHARACTER FILE 10

Kanzo Mogi 模木完造

■■■Personal Data

Birthday	7/12/1973
Deathday	--
Height	6'2"
Weight	179 lbs.
Blood Type	O
Likes	Food
Dislikes	Expressing himself

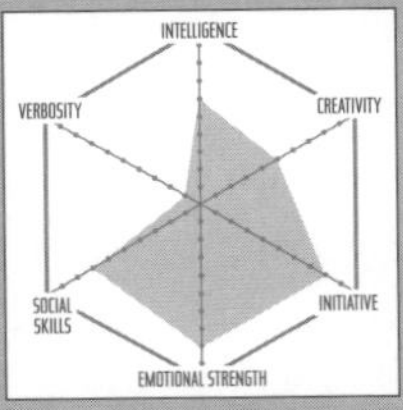

BASIC DATA

A detective with the NPA and a very quiet guy. He's not flashy, but he's talented and tough. He's a valuable member who supports the investigation by doing a lot of the heavy lifting behind the scenes.

ABILITIES

From gathering information to acting as Misa's manager, Mogi fills various roles. He's big but also skillful—he's even good at cooking!

➡ Even Near is impressed with Mogi's mental toughness.

CHARACTER FILE 11

Hideki Ide
伊出英基

■■■Personal Data

Birthday	9/29/1969
Deathday	--
Height	5'6"
Weight	137 lbs.
Blood Type	B
Likes	Literature
Dislikes	Variety shows

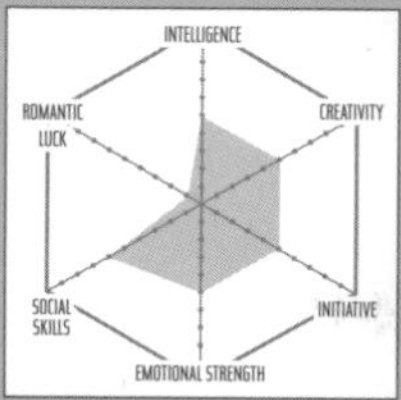

A member of the NPA who disagrees with L's methods and decides to investigate on his own. Later, he rejoins the team and sees the case through to the very end.

← He and Aizawa have a strong bond of trust.

CHARACTER FILE 12

Hirokazu Ukita
宇生田広数

■■■Personal Data

Birthday	11/9/1977
Deathday	4/18/2004
Height	5'3"
Weight	112 lbs.
Blood Type	A
Likes	Cigarettes
Dislikes	Waiting

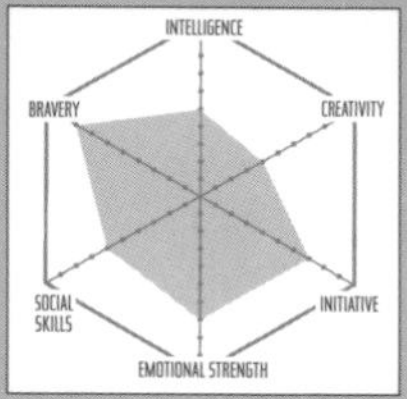

A young and brave NPA detective killed by the Second Kira during the Sakura TV incident. He was a pretty heavy smoker.

→ He's the first member of the team to be killed by the Death Note.

CHARACTER FILE 13

Relationship to Police Department

Eriko Aizawa
相沢恵利子

Yumi Aizawa
相沢由美

Aizawa's wife and daughter. The family faces issues due to Aizawa's busy career. There is also a baby in the family.

Kanichi Takimura
多貴村管一

Head of the Japanese police. He's kidnapped by Mello as a bargaining chip but is ultimately killed by Kira.

Koreyoshi Kitamura
北村是良

NPA deputy director and Soichiro's boss. He buckles under Yotsuba's pressure, but he isn't a bad guy.

Sayu Yagami 夜神粧裕

■■■Personal Data

Birthday	6/18/1989
Deathday	--
Height	4'8" (junior high), 5'3" (college)
Weight	84 lbs. (junior high), 99 lbs. (college)
Blood Type	O
Likes	Idol singers (junior high), shoes (college)
Dislikes	Difficult things (junior high), alcohol (college)

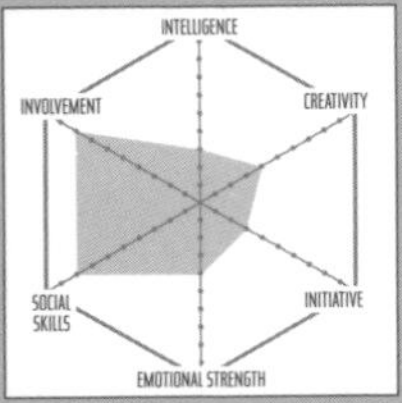

BASIC DATA The Pure Girl Whose Brother Is Kira

Light's sister is a kind-hearted girl who looks up to her older brother. During junior high she seems younger than her age and relies a lot on her brother's help, but by college she grows into a mature woman. After she's kidnapped by the mafia under Mello's orders, the emotional trauma causes her to withdraw from the world.

⬆ The high amount of stress affects her greatly. She takes time off from school to recover.

CHARACTER FILE 14

■■■Personal Data

Birthday	10/10/1962
Deathday	--
Height	5'2"
Weight	110 lbs.
Blood Type	O
Likes	TV dramas
Dislikes	Salesmen

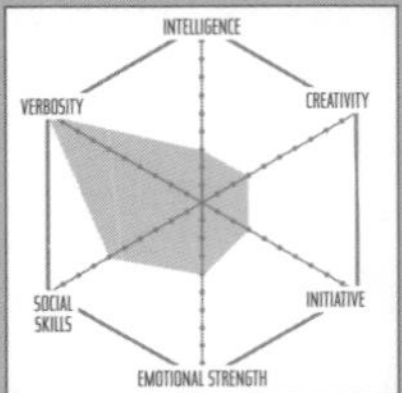

Sachiko Yagami 夜神幸子

A strong woman who stays by Soichiro's side and supports him through thick and thin. She's a dutiful wife and does her best to keep her family from falling apart during the Kira investigation.

DON'T BE SILLY. I'M GOING TO BE WITH YOU ALL THE WAY.
NO MATTER WHAT...
...YOU DECIDE FROM NOW ON, I'M GOING TO BE RIGHT BEHIND YOU.

➡ Worn out by the stressful fight with Kira, Soichiro receives encouragement from Sachiko until the very end.

CHARACTER FILE 15

Raye Penber レイ=ペンバー

■■■Personal Data

Birthday	12/31/1974
Deathday	12/27/2003
Height	5'9"
Weight	152 lbs.
Blood Type	O
Likes	Naomi Misora
Dislikes	Overtime

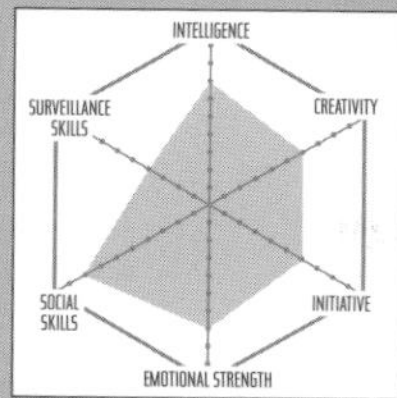

BASIC DATA A talented FBI agent working under L to monitor the Japanese police. Because he's assigned to watch the Yagami family, he ends up being used as a pawn in Kira's plan and loses his life.

LOVE He and Naomi Misora were planning their wedding when he died. Her existence was a vulnerable point that Light took advantage of.

➔ From time to time Raye would have to remind Naomi to stop acting like a cop.

CHARACTER FILE 16

Naomi Misora 南空ナオミ

■■■Personal Data

Birthday	2/11/1976
Deathday	1/2/2004
Height	5'6"
Weight	101 lbs.
Blood Type	A
Likes	Leather jackets
Dislikes	Skirts

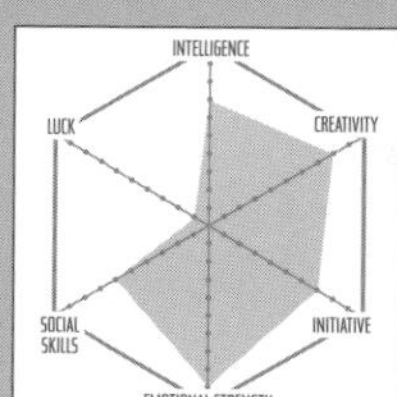

BASIC DATA Raye's fiancée and a former FBI agent. She realizes that Raye's death was caused by Kira but then hits a run of bad luck and is killed by Light. Because her body is never found, she's still considered a missing person.

ABILITIES During her career, she was a first-rate agent who earned the trust even of L. She shows a remarkable investigative ability by closing in on Kira's identity with only a few clues. But that very skill ends up being what kills her.

MY FIANCÉ... AND THE CONVENIENCE STORE ROBBER... AND THE BUSJACKER...
WERE ALL USED BY KIRA IN ORDER TO MURDER THE FBI AGENTS IN JAPAN. I'M CONVINCED OF IT.

⬆ She's the first to realize the true scope of Kira's power.

CHARACTER FILE 17

Aiber アイバー

■■■Personal Data

True Name	Thierry Morrello
Birthday	7/17/1969
Deathday	4/7/2005
Height	6'2"
Weight	165 lbs.
Blood Type	O
Likes	Conversations
Dislikes	Violence

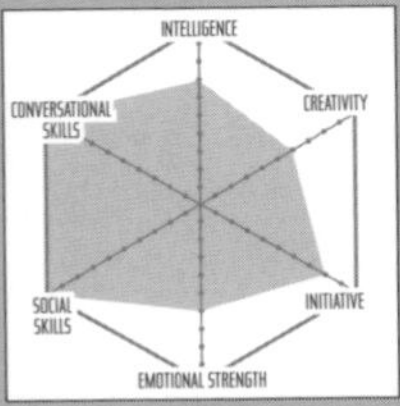

BASIC DATA

A worldly con artist and professional mobster who sometimes helps L do his dirty work. He assists L in solving the Yotsuba case but is later disposed of by Light.

ABILITIES

Aiber can speak numerous languages and often assumes false identities. He's supposedly very talented in using his good looks to get information out of women.

➡ He loves life on the edge: swindling people gives him the biggest thrill.

CHARACTER FILE 18

Wedy ウエディ

■■■Personal Data

True Name	Mary Kenwood
Birthday	11/2/1974
Deathday	1/10/2005
Height	5'6"
Weight	106 lbs.
Blood Type	B
Likes	Bikes
Dislikes	Cops

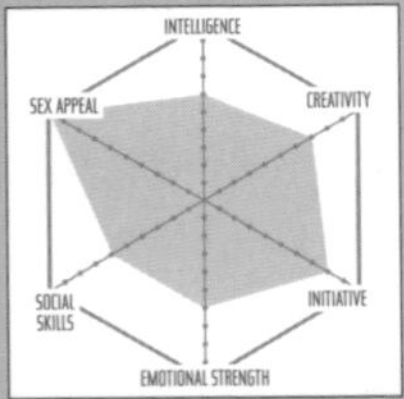

BASIC DATA

A thief and an expert at breaking and entering. Trusted by L, she uses her skills to assist in the capture of the Yotsuba Kira. She dies in a motorcycle accident: the accident is, of course, Light's doing.

ABILITIES

A professional thief, she's more knowledgeable than L when it comes to decoding modern security systems. She also has great athletic ability.

➡ She can easily get through an average security system.

CHARACTER FILE 19

Watari ワタリ

■■■Personal Data

True Name	Quillsh Wammy
Birthday	5/1/1933
Deathday	11/5/2004
Height	5'7"
Weight	112 lbs.
Blood Type	B
Likes	Earl Grey tea
Dislikes	Dirty rooms

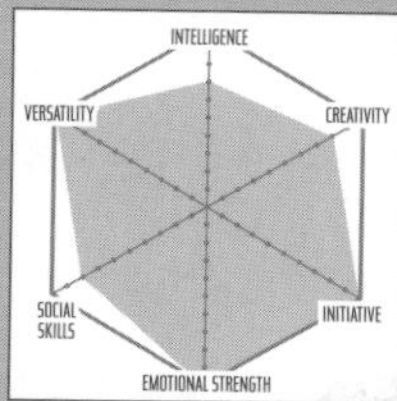

An older gentleman who provides support to L under the name "Watari." Using the fortune he amassed as an inventor, he built an orphanage that teaches children with special talents and sends them out in the world.

➡ Watari's talents include assisting L and marksmanship.

CHARACTER FILE 20

Matt マット

■■■Personal Data

True Name	Mail Jeevas
Birthday	2/1/1990
Deathday	1/26/2010
Height	5'5"
Weight	115 lbs.
Blood Type	O
Likes	Video games
Dislikes	Going outside

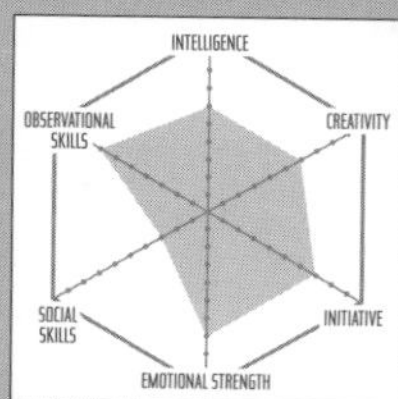

A young man from Wammy's House. At the orphanage he was the smartest kid after Near and Mello. He agrees to help Mello but is killed when he's unable to get away from a group of angry Kira worshippers.

➡ Monitoring multiple screens. His cockiness leads him to make a few mistakes...

CHARACTER FILE 21

Roger Ruvie ロジャー=ラヴィー

■■■Personal Data

Birthday	4/29/1939
Deathday	--
Height	5'5"
Weight	108 lbs.
Blood Type	A
Likes	Insect books
Dislikes	Kids

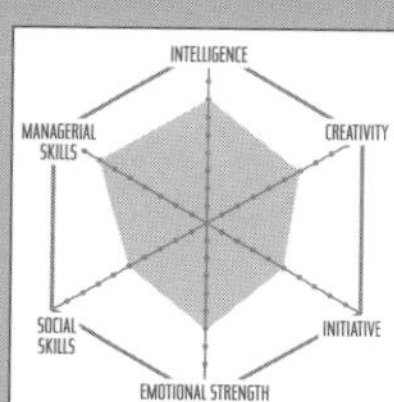

The manager of Wammy's House when Watari isn't around. When something happens to L or Watari, he will know about it. Later, he serves Near as a second "Watari."

➡ His job is to assemble talented kids and raise an heir to the L name.

CHARACTER FILE 22

Kyosuke Higuchi 火口卿介

■■■Personal Data

Birthday	6/6/1972
Deathday	10/28/2004
Height	5'5"
Weight	130 lbs.
Blood Type	AB
Likes	Authority
Dislikes	Demotion

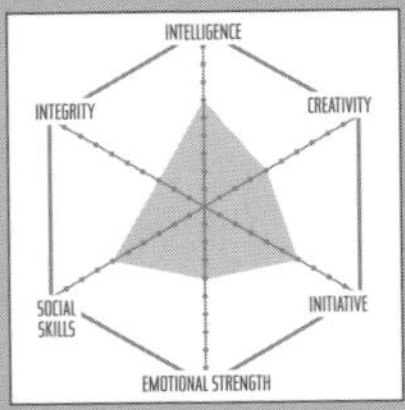

BASIC DATA The head of Technology Development for the giant international corporation Yotsuba. As part of Light's plan he's given the Death Note and plays the role of Kira, but his identity is soon uncovered by L and Light working together. He's killed by Light while being apprehended by the police.

ABILITIES A very greedy, forceful and selfish person, he uses the Death Note to try and achieve the status that eludes him. His stupidity eventually destroys him.

➜ Pushed to the brink, Higuchi trades for the Shinigami Eyes, but it's already too late.

CHARACTER FILE 23

Reiji Namikawa 奈南川零司

■■■Personal Data

Birthday	8/3/1974
Deathday	4/10/2005
Height	5'9"
Weight	141 lbs.
Blood Type	A
Likes	Shogi (Japanese chess)
Dislikes	Useless subordinates

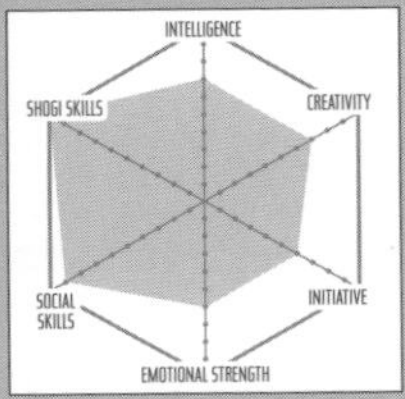

BASIC DATA Yotsuba's Vice President of Sales. At first he supports the Yotsuba Kira, but after a phone conversation with Light he backs off and merely observes the battle between Higuchi and the police. He could have had a bright future but he's killed by Kira.

ABILITIES He's the most talented of the eight members who participate in the "Meetings of Death." He has the potential to make it to the top even without Kira's help.

HA HA, SO EVEN L FALLS FOR STUFF. AFTER YOUR REACTION I'M NOW 100 PERCENT SURE IT'S HIGUCHI.

➜ Namikawa cleverly causes Light to misstep and thus confirm that Higuchi is Kira.

CHARACTER FILE 24

Takeshi Ooi
尾々井 剛

■■■Personal Data

Birthday	3/31/1961
Deathday	4/10/2005
Height	6'2"
Weight	170 lbs.
Blood Type	O
Likes	Model guns
Dislikes	Crowds

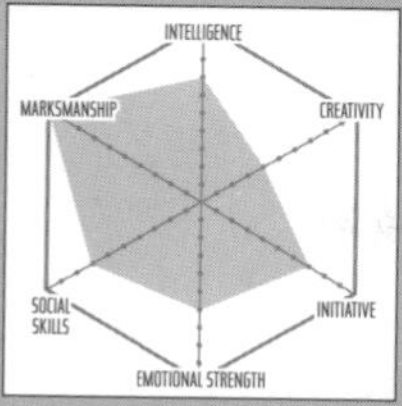

Yotsuba Vice President of VT Enterprises. He's the oldest member of the "Meetings of Death" and appears to control the meetings. He seems like a tough guy who doesn't sweat the details.

➡ The most influential participant in the meetings, he communicates with the members individually.

WHAT? A CALL FROM COIL? DID WE LEARN ANYTHING ABOUT L?

CHARACTER FILE 25

Shingo Mido
三堂芯吾

■■■Personal Data

Birthday	1/25/1972
Deathday	4/10/2005
Height	5'7"
Weight	132 lbs.
Blood Type	AB
Likes	Fencing
Dislikes	Finance

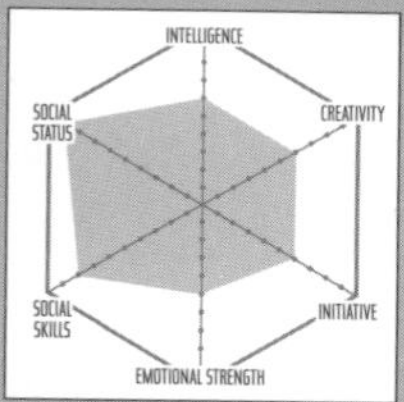

The VP of Corporate Strategy and Director of Financial Planning at Yotsuba. He has reservations about Kira and thinks about leaving the group.

➡ It seems he has a sense of appreciation for the company he works for.

WELL, IT'S A FACT THAT A YOTSUBA EMPLOYEE WAS KIRA. THERE'S NOTHING WE CAN DO ABOUT THAT.

CHARACTER FILE 26

Eiichi Takahashi
鷹橋鋭一

■■■Personal Data

Birthday	12/19/1963
Deathday	4/10/2005
Height	5'9"
Weight	161 lbs.
Blood Type	B
Likes	Surfing
Dislikes	Being teased

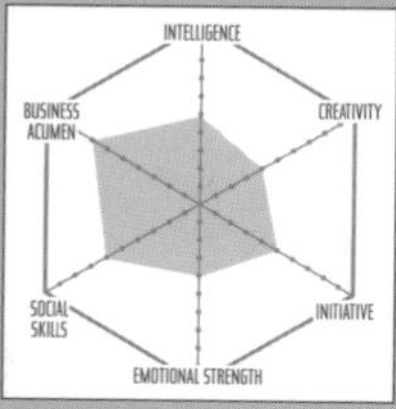

VP of the Yotsuba Material Planning Division and Yotsuba Homes. He never had what it takes to be a true leader. He was chosen for the meetings to make Higuchi look good.

➡ Because he doesn't seem to put much thought into his comments the others often see him as foolish.

SHE'S REALLY CUTE IN PERSON...

CHARACTER FILE 27

Suguru Shimura
紙村 英

▪▪▪Personal Data

Birthday	7/21/1968
Deathday	4/10/2005
Height	5′6″
Weight	126 lbs.
Blood Type	AB
Likes	Rugby
Dislikes	Gambling

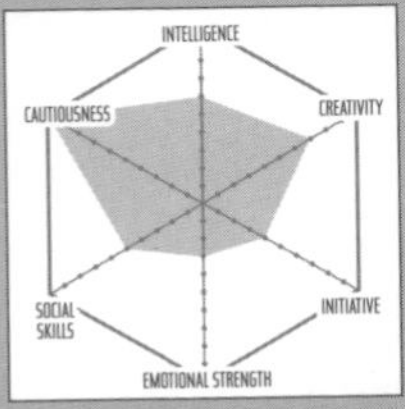

Head of Personnel at Yotsuba. Very nervous and paranoid, he's always keeping a close eye on people. That attention to detail is what gets him into the meetings, which wasn't something he wanted.

➜ He doesn't miss even the subtle changes in expression on the poker-faced Namikawa.

CHARACTER FILE 28

Masahiko Kida
樹多正彦

▪▪▪Personal Data

Birthday	10/20/1971
Deathday	4/10/2005
Height	5′5″
Weight	132 lbs.
Blood Type	O
Likes	Glasses
Dislikes	Contact lenses

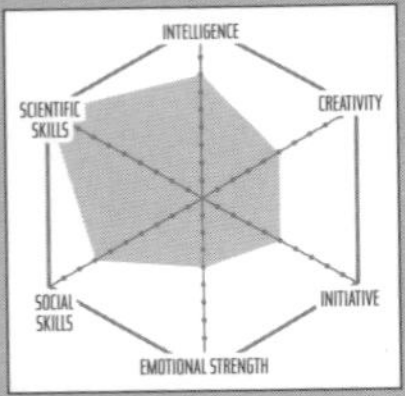

Yotsuba VP of Rights and Planning. Calm and collected, but very calculating. He's in charge of the meeting's finances and is the one who contacts Coil, which is what first brings L's attention to the group and leads to the Yotsuba Kira's arrest.

➜ Kida panics and shows a lack of ability to deal with surprises when Coil asks for a fee increase.

CHARACTER FILE 29

Arayoshi Hatori
葉鳥新義

▪▪▪Personal Data

Birthday	3/22/1971
Deathday	10/13/2005
Height	5′4″
Weight	121 lbs.
Blood Type	A
Likes	Ceramics
Dislikes	Vegetables

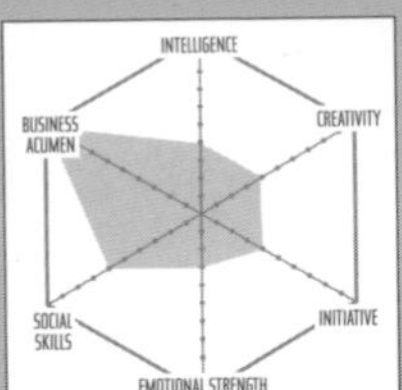

Yotsuba's VP of Marketing. He's the company president's illegitimate son and uses that to his advantage. He appears to be something of a lightweight and is unable to take the pressure of the "Meetings of Death."

➜ A careless outburst causes him to become a victim of Yotsuba's Kira.

CHARACTER FILE 30

Anthony Rester

アンソニー=レスター

■■■Personal Data

True Name	Anthony Carter
Birthday	1/6/1968
Deathday	--
Height	6'3"
Weight	185 lbs.
Blood Type	O
Likes	Haiku
Dislikes	Traitors

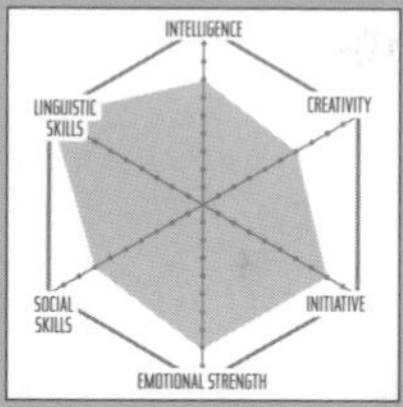

BASIC DATA

The SPK's number-two man and the lead crime scene investigator. Except for emergency situations, he stays by Near's side. Near trusts Rester and sometimes reveals the truth only to him.

ABILITIES

In terms of intellectual ability he's far below Near, but his quiet personality and physical strength make him a very useful member. You could say he acts as Near's guardian.

I TRUST YOU...BUT, PLEASE DON'T TELL ANYONE ELSE MORE THAN THAT A MURDER NOTE-BOOK EXISTS. KEEP ALL IMPORTANT INFORMATION IN YOUR MIND ONLY.
ALL RIGHT...

➡ Near comes to rely on Rester to stop information from leaking out of the SPK.

Stephen Gevanni

ステファン=ジェバンニ

■■■Personal Data

True Name	Stephen Loud
Birthday	9/1/1982
Deathday	--
Height	5'10"
Weight	134 lbs.
Blood Type	A
Likes	Ships in bottles
Dislikes	Unreasonable superiors

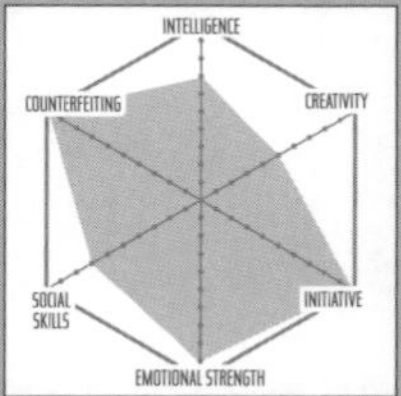

BASIC DATA

Part of the SPK. Even after numerous SPK members are killed by the Death Note, he never backs down and stays aboard until the case is finally solved. He plays a major role in Near's plan.

ABILITIES

Gevanni is highly skilled at tailing and monitoring suspects and also is very crafty at jobs like picking locks. The Kira case couldn't have been solved without him.

TAILING HIM IS STRANGELY EASY... IT'S NOT LIKE HE'S MAKING A MOVE TO GO INTO HIDING OR ANYTHING, AND HE'S BEEN LIVING AT THE SAME PLACE FOR THE PAST 4 YEARS, LEADING AN ORDINARY LIFE.
HE'S VERY ACTIVE WITH HIS JOB AS WELL...

➡ Gevanni's thoroughness in the Mikami investigation helps solve the case.

Halle Lidner ハル=リドナー

■■■Personal Data

True Name	Halle Bullook
Birthday	2/18/1980
Deathday	--
Height	5'9"
Weight	115 lbs.
Blood Type	B
Likes	Bathing
Dislikes	Moths

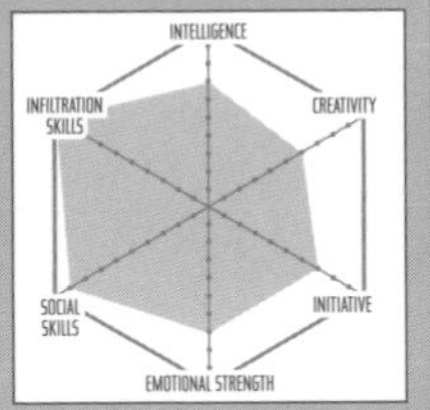

BASIC DATA

The only female member of the SPK. One of the Yotsuba Kira's victims was an acquaintance of hers, which was one of the reasons that led her to join the SPK. Unlike the other members she's in the odd situation of helping Near while also passing along information to Mello.

ABILITIES

Lidner is an excellent officer who once worked in the Secret Service protecting the president of the United States. An individual thinker, she assists both Near and Mello during the Kira case. Her skills as a bodyguard are also first-rate.

MISSION

Besides her regular duties as an investigator, she's also an information source for Mello. She uses her position as a female agent to become a bodyguard for Takada in order to uncover the connection between Takada and Kira.

← A flashy bodyguard, she becomes popular with the public.

CHARACTER FILE 33

Members of the SPK

Ellickson Gardner エリクソン=ガードナー

True Name: Ellickson Thomas

A member of the SPK. Becomes a victim of the Death Note because of the SPK leak.

John McEnroe ジョン=マッケンロー

True Name: Larry Conners

An FBI officer and SPK member. It's assumed he died when most of the members were purged.

Ill Ratt イル=ラット

True Name: Shawn Dunleavy

A member of the SPK and also a spy for Mello. He's killed by the Death Note.

■■■Personal Data

True Name	Dwhite Gordon
Birthday	4/13/1968
Deathday	11/10/2009
Height	6'2"
Weight	187 lbs.
Blood Type	B
Likes	Tequila
Dislikes	Soccer

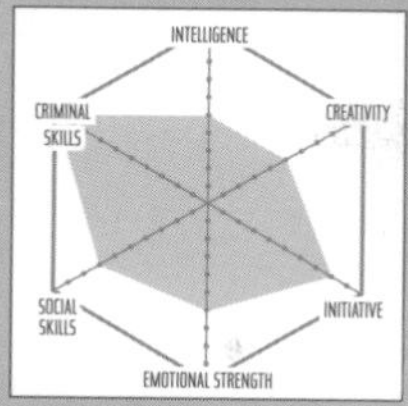

Rod Ross

ロッド=ロス

The boss of an American crime syndicate. A big fish whom even the police can't take down. He teams up with Mello to get the Death Note. Because his identity is known, he is easily killed by Light.

WE JUST HAVE TO DO AS MELLO TELLS US. HAS HE EVER SAID SOMETHING WRONG IN THE YEAR AND A HALF HE'S BEEN WITH US?

➡ He places his trust in Mello's plans and follows his orders.

CHARACTER FILE 34

■■■Personal Data

True Name	Kal Snydar
Birthday	2/23/1973
Deathday	11/10/2009
Height	5'5"
Weight	110 lbs.
Blood Type	AB
Likes	*Anne of Green Gables*
Dislikes	Mello

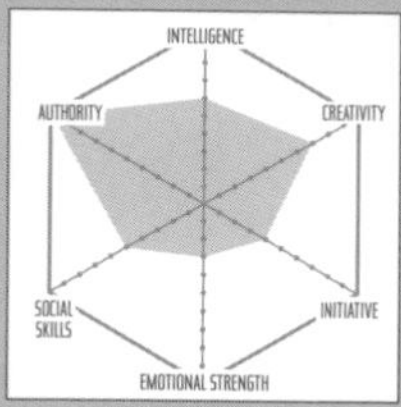

Jack Neylon

ジャック=ネイロン

He was one of Ross's low-ranking thugs until he acquired the Death Note. Light uses him to reveal the whereabouts of the gang's hideout.

➡ Threatened by Ross, he trades for the Shinigami Eyes and ends up saving the gang from danger.

CHARACTER FILE 35

Rashual Bid

ラシュアル=ビッド

True Name — Al Meem

Having been with the organization for a long time, he dies along with most of his cohorts when Kira wipes out the mafia members.

Glen Humphreys

グレン=ハンフリーズ

True Name — Ralph Bay

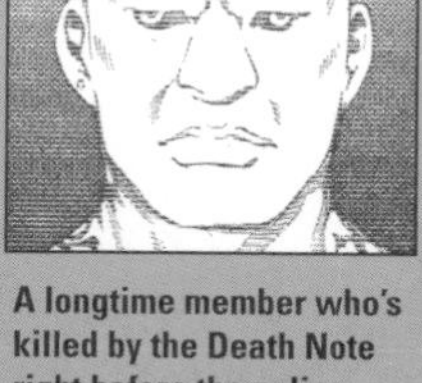

A longtime member who's killed by the Death Note right before the police storm the gang's hideout.

Zakk Irius

ザック=イリウス

True Name — (Same)

Used by the mafia to deal with the Japanese police at the airport: after guiding Soichiro to the right airplane, he's disposed of by the organization.

Mafia

Hitoshi Demegawa
出目川 仁

■■■Personal Data

Birthday	4/4/1966
Deathday	11/28/2009
Height	5'4"
Weight	163 lbs.
Blood Type	A
Likes	Money
Dislikes	Reading

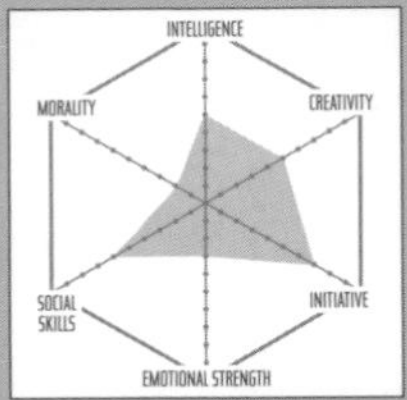

BASIC DATA

The director of Sakura TV. The police keep a close eye on him because of all the Kira-related programming he runs in order to get high ratings. He acts as Kira's representative but is killed by Mikami when he becomes too arrogant.

CONDUCT

A greedy person who readily airs any program, regardless of its value, to attract more viewers. He makes many ill-advised decisions.

➜ He gains a lot of attention because of Kira's power, but he makes the mistake of thinking it's his own.

NOW, LET ME INTRODUCE YOU TO THE EXECUTIVE MEMBERS, WHO I HANDPICKED MYSELF!

CHARACTER FILE 36

Takuo Shibuimaru
渋井丸拓男

An unfortunate man used by Light to test the Death Note. Because he isn't a criminal, Light feels a sense of regret and conflict.

Kurou Otoharada
音原田九郎

A criminal who takes hostages and barricades himself in a nursery school. He's killed when Light sees the news on TV and writes his name into the Death Note. He becomes Kira's first victim.

Kiichiro Osoreda
恐田奇一郎

A bank robber used in Light's plan to uncover Raye Penber's name. He touches a piece of the Death Note and flips out when he sees Ryuk, but this incident is treated as a drug-induced hallucination.

Lind L. Tailor
リンド=L=テイラー

Presented on TV as the famous detective L, he's really a death row inmate. Because of this ruse L is able to get closer to tracking down Kira.

David Hoope デイビット=ホープ

The president of the United States, he is threatened by Mello with the Death Note. He works unsuccessfully with L (Light) to infiltrate Mello's hideout. He's a strong leader but powerless against the decree of the Death Note.

← It's believed that Kira disposed of him after the special forces attack failed.

George Sairas ジョージ=サイラス

The U.S. vice president, he ascends to the presidency when David Hoope dies. He is weak-willed and clearly lacking as a leader. He easily falls for Kira's threats and passes along secret information about the SPK.

...HAVE DECIDED TO ACCEPT KIRA, AND WILL DO NOTHING TO STAND IN KIRA'S WAY.
I INTEND TO SUGGEST THIS TO THE OTHER WORLD LEADERS IN THE NEXT WORLD SUMMIT.

← Officially announcing support for Kira.

Steve Mason スティーブ=メイスン

The director of the FBI. He helps L investigate the Japanese police. At one point he withdraws from the Kira case but later helps Near create the SPK. He is killed by the Death Note.

← Because of his connection with L, Light is able to contact him as well.

Yitzak Ghazanin イサク=ガザン

True Name Joe Morton

IF WE CAN KILL, THIS JOB WILL BE EASY.
WE'LL BE FULLY EQUIPPED AND OUR FACES WILL BE HIDDEN. THAT NOTEBOOK WILL BE USELESS AGAINST US. EVEN IF THERE ARE A HUNDRED OF THEM, WE'LL STILL BE ABLE TO DEFEAT THEM.

Captain of a special forces unit stationed in the Middle East. His team raids Mello's hideout to retrieve the Death Note but is wiped out by the mafia with the help of the Shinigami Sidoh.

← His team is skilled, but helpless against the Death Note.

◎ Main Character Profiles

The Forces Involved in the Kira Case

The Kira Case is a worldwide phenomenon. This is an in-depth look at the organizations involved in the case.

↑ A technologically advanced headquarters building was created with L's wealth.

Japanese Task Force

MEMBERS: L, Light Yagami, Soichiro Yagami, Shuichi Aizawa, Kanzo Mogi, Touta Matsuda, Hideki Ide, Hirokazu Ukita

The Kira Case Headquarters Under L's Control

Set up after L determines that Kira is operating from within Japan, it's the only organization in the country pursuing Kira. Its existence is not made public and the members' names and personal information are kept secret. When L dies at Kira's hands the organization faces the prospect of being disbanded. Light Yagami takes over as the Second L and keeps the team going.

SPK (Special Provision for Kira)

MEMBERS: Near, Anthony Rester, Stephen Gevanni, Halle Lidner

The Secret Investigative Team That Carries on L's Will

After L's death, elite members of the FBI and CIA come together to form a new anti-Kira organization. Membership in the SPK is kept small to ensure secrecy. They prefer to work on their own, separate from the Japanese task force.

← The leader of the SPK, Near. He appears to be nothing more than a child, but he reveals extraordinary investigative skills that impress even the president.

↑ Those willing to risk their lives on the case are few. Many threaten to quit to avoid becoming further involved.

NPA

MEMBERS: Koreyoshi Kitamura, Kanichi Takimura

Authority Bowing to Kira

When Kira is revealed to be in Japan the NPA pursues him aggressively but is ultimately diverted by Kira's powers. After the Yotsuba Kira brings political pressure to bear against it, the NPA stops its investigation.

FBI

MEMBERS Raye Penber, Naomi Misora (former member), Steve Mason

Operating Independently on L's Orders, But...

Many criminals in the U.S. are thought to be victims of Kira. Because of that, the FBI agrees to help L. However, America backs off after a number of agents are killed.

↑ With the deaths of the American agents in Japan, the secret investigation of Japanese police personnel is revealed.

The Mafia

MEMBERS Mello, Rod Ross, Jack Neylon

Mello's Pawns in Gaining Kira's Power

An underworld organization in America that increases its influence by teaming up with Mello. The organization wants the Death Note and more power but is being used by Mello.

↑ A merciless and cold-hearted organization that would readily kill even its own members.

Wammy's House

MEMBERS L, Near, Mello, Watari, Roger, Matt

The Orphanage That Produces Genius

An orphanage financed by the wealth of inventor Quillsh Wammy. He assembles talented kids from all over the world and gives them specialized education. Graduates of the program work in various fields, including investigation and the arts.

↑ Due to L's sudden death his successors have to take over for him at a young age.

The Media

MEMBERS Hitoshi Demegawa, Kiyomi Takada

The Invisible Power That Controls Public Opinion

Never underestimate the power of communication. The media's broadcasts of information relating to Kira eventually create an ideological group of Kira worshippers. This group has the power to go up against even the police.

↑ With the media seeking approval from Kira, the world starts to change dramatically.

Kira Case Participant Relationships

The Kira Case is a worldwide phenomenon. This is an in-depth look at the organizations involved in the case.

Relationship with Kira
Relationship Between Organizations

JAPANESE TASK FORCE

The cooperation between L and the NPA results in only five members joining the team. Under L's command, the team captures the Second Kira and is close to solving the case. However, they end up being fooled by Kira's plan. With L's death, the team's situation changes dramatically.

↑ While not the most talented personnel, they're filled with a sense of justice and the drive to complete the job.

L closes in on Light, whom he suspects is Kira. Light uses that to his advantage and joins the task force. From a disadvantaged position, L pushes Light to the edge but comes up one step short.

SEPARATION

LIGHT

KIRA

With L as his only real adversary, Kira increases his support worldwide. He gains the help of Misa, the Second Kira, and uses Higuchi as a proxy.

Higuchi, the Yotsuba Kira, gains influence over the government and has pressure put on the NPA. With their country against them, the Japanese police have no choice but to back off the Kira case, exactly the result Light had planned.

← Soichiro is given the shocking news from his boss, Kitamura. The members of the task force decide to quit the police during this time.

JAPANESE POLICE

On the surface they withdraw from the Kira case and remain silent, but there are some who continue the investigation. They participate in the arrest of the Yotsuba Kira.

↑ Ide leads a group of members who covertly continue the investigation.

YOTSUBA

Through the use of Kira's power the company's fortunes continue to rise. This unnatural growth catches the eye of the Japanese task force and Higuchi is captured as Kira. Afterward, their stock tumbles.

LOOKS LIKE WE'RE ALL HERE. LET'S BEGIN OUR MEETING.

← Members of Yotsuba vying to lead the company hold "Meetings of Death" every week to plan out who to kill.

HELPS L IN CAPTURE

THE MEDIA

First spread on the Internet, Kira's ideals are soon broadcast around the world. Some TV channels use Kira's influence to increase their own popularity. Kira's existence can no longer be ignored.

← Sakura TV, which specializes in questionable programming, is being monitored by the police.

In order to deflect the suspicion that he is Kira, Light creates a new Kira. Rem set her eyes on the Yotsuba Group, and by cutting a deal with a high-ranking employee there makes Yotsuba into a Kira proxy.

The task force uses the media to communicate with the Second Kira. The media is also helpful during the Yotsuba Kira capture; they're not completely on Kira's side at this point.

HIGUCHI

MISA

FBI

Because Kira is located in Japan the FBI originally is not very involved in the case. It later sends agents to help at L's request, but after several agents are killed it quickly cuts off its relationship with L.

HMPH, HERE'S A PHONE CALL FROM THE JAPANESE TASK FORCE ALREADY...
I'M TELLING THEM THE FBI WAS THERE AT YOUR REQUEST, L... IS THAT UNDERSTOOD?

↑ With the safety of its agents in peril, the FBI quickly admits that it acted at the request of L.

With the FBI in pursuit, Light begins to kill all the agents. During this time L realizes that it is possible to uncover evidence that will help lead him directly to Kira.

LIGHT... YAGAMI!

← The deaths of the FBI agents mark the first time Kira goes after innocent people.

HELPS ON REQUEST OF L

Kira Case Participant Relationships

After L is gone Kira continues to strengthen his rule, but new challengers emerge.

Relationship with Kira
Relationship Between Organizations

JAPANESE TASK FORCE

The investigators continue after L's passing but with no new developments. Essentially, they are regarded as incompetent. After the loss of the Death Note to the mafia and Soichiro's death, the team begins to break apart. Some members start investigating on their own, but the team remains together in appearance only.

ELPING
ACH OTHER
EHIND THE
CENES

← Some members start to suspect Light.

DEMAND THE DEATH NOTE

KIRA

LIGHT

Kira's stronghold seems impenetrable, but in direct confrontations with the SPK and the mafia cracks slowly begin to appear...

Just as Light planned, Kira is now in the odd situation of being in control of the very team whose duty it is to capture him. By leading the investigation as he sees fit, Light controls the members and makes sure that Kira is never caught.

Light's plan to use the media to spread Kira's ideals is successful, especially after a representative of Kira is chosen to speak directly to the people.

↑ By manipulating Takada, who is pro-Kira, Kira gains the support of public opinion.

THE MEDIA (KIRA WORSHIPPERS)

By this time, the media have totally bowed to Kira and compete amongst themselves to support him. With public opinion on Kira's side, those who go against him are classified as evil.

↑ The television station is protected by a team of bodyguards—even the police can't get close.

SPK

America's anti-Kira team, created after L's death. While prodding the Japanese task force the SPK forcefully moves toward the truth. They also keep their eyes on Mello and look for opportunities to catch Kira in the act.

← All but a few key members are wiped out by the Death Note. The SPK is later placed in the difficult position of being told to disband by the U.S. government.

→ The SPK shares some information with Mello. They put their hostilities aside to get closer to Kira.

As the most powerful force to go after Kira, the SPK sacrificed much to take the fight to Kira. With assistance from Mello, they are able to turn the tables on Light and end the case for good.

↑ Near finally secures the evidence that Light is Kira.

MIKAMI

MISA

Mello upstages Light to take the Death Note and later sits in the advantageous position of gaining help from Sidoh. But his location is uncovered with Misa's eyes and he loses all of his men.

The U.S. ends up seeking the help of Kira. With new information on Mello in his hands, Light makes plans to retrieve the notebook.

THE MAFIA

His whereabouts unknown for years, Mello reappears with the mafia and sets in motion his plan to take the Death Note for himself. He initially succeeds, but Kira wipes out his organization. Mello is then forced to go after Kira alone.

← Using the mafia, Mello tries to get his hands on all the notebooks.

ATTACKS WITH SPECIAL FORCES

SECRET DEALS

THE U.S. GOVERNMENT

After being threatened the president teams up with L to go after the mafia. But Mello outsmarts them and the president is killed. All authority is lost...

↑ The president's resolve to go after Kira is strengthened.

◎ Complete Shinigami File

FILE No. 01 リューク

Ryuk

■■■DEATH NOTE

■■■ Observation Data	
Shinigami Rank	6
Gender	Male
Likes	Apples, games
Dislikes	Boredom

■■■ DEATH CHART	
Intelligence	☠☠☠☠☠☠
Inquisitiveness	☠☠☠☠☠☠☠☠☠☠
Initiative	☠☠☠☠☠☠☠☠☠
Empathy	☠☠☠☠☠
Kills	☠☠☠☠☠☠☠

The Radical Shinigami Who Hates Boredom

The Shinigami who dropped a Death Note into the human world to escape boredom. It's no exaggeration to say that this act is responsible for bringing chaos to the human world. Ryuk possesses no empathy for humans, watching intently as the human whom he possesses, Light Yagami, continues his crime spree. Actually, it seems that he rather enjoys it.

←↑Ryuk showing his many sides. At times he's calm and cold like a Shinigami should be, while at other times he panics and even begs.

HEY LIGHT, SINCE NOBODY SEEMS TO BE HOME, HOW ABOUT WE PLAY A GAME OF MARIO GOLF?
BAM
...

↑ Ryuk enjoys many facets of human entertainment. Video games seem to be his favorite. He also likes martial arts.

PERSONALITY Adaptable and Full of Curiosity

Ryuk is full of curiosity, a rare trait for a Shinigami. He's also very adaptable; he'll accept new things as long as he finds them entertaining.

FEATURES Like a Beast with Long Limbs

Ryuk has a very tall and slender body. Black feathers sprouting from his shoulders conceal wings and other things—like apples, for example. On his hip is a holster-like accessory that holds his Death Note.

↑ Being super flexible, Ryuk is able to contort himself in odd poses impossible for any human.

PURPOSE Momentary Escape from Boredom

Bored with the monotonous Shinigami realm, Ryuk comes down to the human world seeking excitement. In the end, it appears he got a lot of pleasure out of the humans.

▪▪▪ IMPORTANT PEOPLE TO ACHIEVE HIS GOAL

Light Yagami

The central character—and biggest victim?—in Ryuk's adventure in the human world.

Soichiro Yagami

Ryuk possesses him on Light's request; does he comply simply to alleviate his boredom?

Teru Mikami

Another person whom Ryuk uses to entertain himself.

DEATH COLUMN / The Worth of an Apple to Ryuk

MUNCH

PHEW... LIGHT, I THINK I'VE FOUND ALL THE CAMERAS.
DIDN'T KNOW SHINIGAMI COULD GET THIS WORN OUT...

Apples are invaluable to Ryuk. Obviously he doesn't need them for the nutrients, but without them he suffers from withdrawal symptoms. Ryuk may unconsciously equate the "red" of an apple with the "lifeblood" of humans and thus always needs them...

← He quickly tosses aside his Shinigami pride for an apple. He also first learns fatigue at this point.

◎ Complete Shinigami File

FILE No. 02 レム Rem

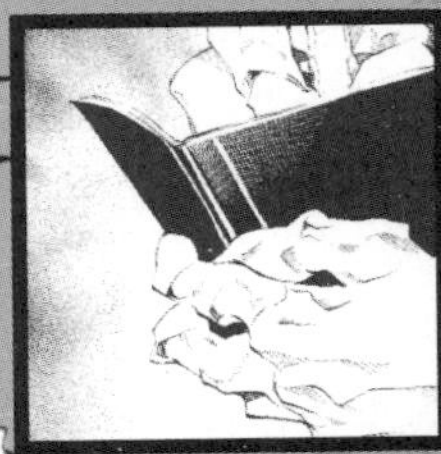

■■■DEATH NOTE

■■■ Observation Data	
Shinigami Rank	4
Gender	Female
Likes	Love
Dislikes	Light Yagami

■■■ DEATH CHART	
Intelligence	☠☠☠☠☠☠☠
Inquisitiveness	☠☠☠
Initiative	☠☠☠☠☠☠☠☠☠☠
Empathy	☠☠☠☠☠☠☠☠☠
Kills	☠☠☠☠

One of the Few Who Knows How to Kill a Shinigami

This serious female Shinigami possesses Misa, the Second Kira. Unlike Ryuk, Rem does not come to the human world looking for fun. However, she doesn't necessarily respect humans and at one point even calls their lifestyle "ugly." Had she not known Gelus, Rem would probably never have descended to the human world.

⬆Unfortunately, Rem and Gelus share the same fate.

⬆Even though she knows Misa is being used, Rem continues to follow her orders.

IF YOU DON'T SAVE MISA, I'LL KILL YOU.
HYUK HYUK ...

PERSONALITY Calm, Quiet, but Full of Emotion

A clever creature who always keeps her composure. When it comes to Misa, however, Rem sometimes lets her emotions get the best of her.

← Always going after those who could harm Misa. These kinds of actions show the warmth buried deep inside Rem.

PURPOSE Carrying Out the Will of Gelus

It all started when she became curious about Gelus's human watching. Feeling pity for Gelus, Rem decides to go down to the human world and give Misa his notebook.

IT'S TODAY, ISN'T IT? HER LAST DAY OF LIFE.
BUT SHE LOOKS SO HEALTHY ...WHY TODAY?

→ Had she never been fascinated by Gelus's actions, Rem never would have died in the human world...

IMPORTANT PEOPLE TO ACHIEVE HER GOAL

Misa Amane

The reason for Rem coming to the human world. In some ways, she's the person who changes Rem's fate.

FEATURES A Female Form Built from Bones

Her body appears to be constructed from white bones. Wings emerge from her shoulders when she needs to fly. Because of Rem's smooth head and white body, she appears more feminine than Ryuk.

YOU KNOW REM? THE WHITE, SPONGY, FEMALE SHINIGAMI.
NOPE...

↑ Ryuk describing Rem as "spongy." Does he think this because she's white?

DEATH COLUMN / The Love That Moves Rem

I DON'T KNOW.
THEN WHY DID HE STOP KILLING AND LEAVE IT TO SOMEONE ELSE?

I AM ON YOUR SIDE.
ON MY SIDE...? THIS THING...? EWW...

Most Shinigami mind their own business and lack any sort of emotion, but Rem is different. She carries out Gelus's wishes, helping Misa more than necessary, and she really cares about those whom she has strong feelings for.

← She reveals many Shinigami secrets to Misa. Her attitude toward Light and Higuchi is vastly different.

◎ Complete Shinigami File

FILE No. 03 シドウ

Sidoh

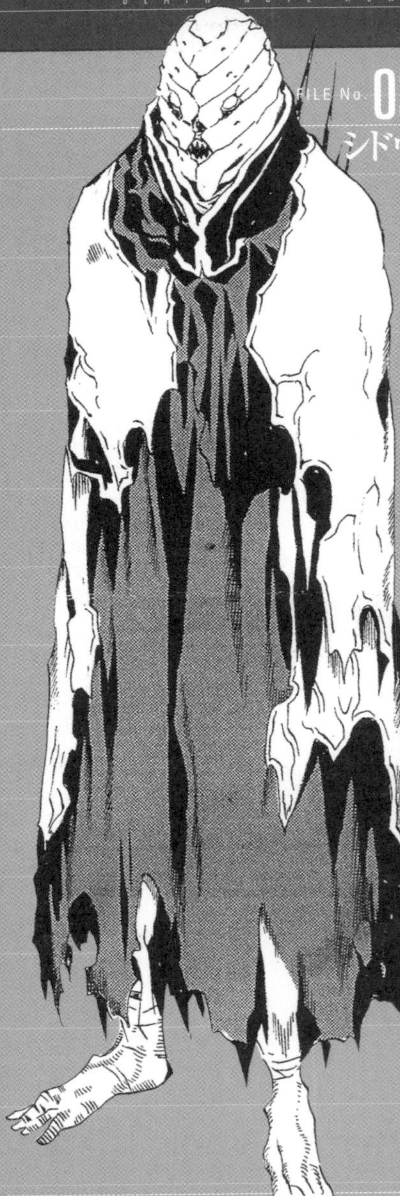

■■■DEATH NOTE

The True Owner of Light's Death Note

The Death Note that Light initially uses is actually Sidoh's. Sidoh is not very bright; in fact, he can barely remember the names of his fellow Shinigami. What appears to be tattered cloth around his shoulders are really his wings.

COME ON, IF YOU FIND HIM FOR ME, I'LL GIVE YOU ALL MY WINNINGS.

➜ In order to find the human who has his notebook, Sidoh passes out fliers in the Shinigami world. Obviously, this does not work.

■■■ Observation Data	
Shinigami Rank	8
Gender	Male
Likes	Chocolate
Dislikes	Ghosts

■■■ DEATH CHART	
Intelligence	☠☠
Inquisitiveness	☠☠☠☠☠☠☠☠
Initiative	☠☠☠☠☠☠☠☠
Empathy	☠☠☠
Kills	☠☠

PURPOSE — Recovering His Death Note

Sidoh must have been very lazy in filling out his Death Note, because his lifespan is nearing its end! He rushes down to the human world to get his notebook back from Ryuk as quickly as possible.

YIKES... SECOND-DEGREE IS AFTER FIRST, ISN'T IT...?

⬆ Trembling in fear over the punishment of the Shinigami realm. Sidoh is always afraid of something!

PERSONALITY — A Timid Shinigami

Sidoh possesses a certain charm that makes him hard to hate. He is, unfortunately, cowardly and afraid of one particular human. Sometimes it's hard to believe he's really a Shinigami...

FILE No. 04
ジェラス

Gelus

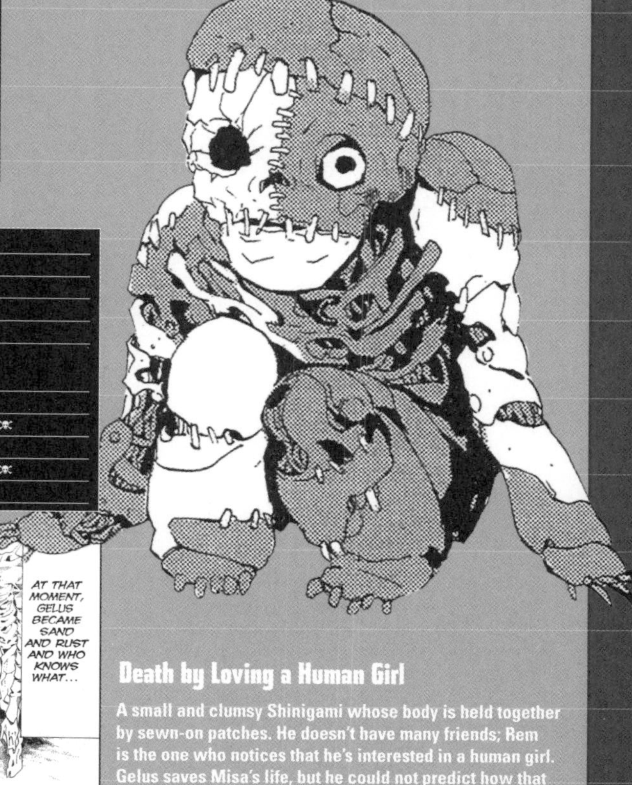

■■■ Observation Data	
Shinigami Rank	13
Gender	Male
Likes	Misa Amane
Dislikes	Writing

■■■ DEATH CHART	
Intelligence	☠☠☠
Inquisitiveness	☠☠☠☠☠☠☠
Initiative	☠☠☠☠☠☠
Empathy	☠☠☠☠☠☠☠
Kills	☠☠☠

Death by Loving a Human Girl

A small and clumsy Shinigami whose body is held together by sewn-on patches. He doesn't have many friends; Rem is the one who notices that he's interested in a human girl. Gelus saves Misa's life, but he could not predict how that would lead to his own death...

⬅While he probably does not intend to do so, Gelus is the one who shows Rem how to kill a Shinigami.

⬇ In a desperate attempt to save Misa, he does something without thinking.

HEY ...
GELUS THEN DID WHAT A SHINIGAMI SHOULD NEVER DO.

PURPOSE — The Desire to Help the One You Love

Whether or not he knows of the rule against helping humans, Gelus wants to protect Misa. He is able to successfully lengthen Misa's lifespan, but...

PERSONALITY — A Quiet and Kind Heart

Gelus has a rare and perhaps improper personality trait for a Shinigami: he cares deeply for humans.

Armonia Justin Beyondormason

FILE No. 05

アラモニア＝ジャスティン＝ビヨンドルメーソン

▪▪▪ Observation Data	
Shinigami Rank	2
Gender	Male
Likes	Jewels
Dislikes	Crows

▪▪▪ DEATH CHART	
Intelligence	☠☠☠☠☠☠☠☠☠
Inquisitiveness	☠☠☠
Initiative	☠
Empathy	☠☠☠
Kills	☠☠☠☠☠☠☠☠☠

The Shinigami Realm's Advisor

An important member of the Shinigami realm, he knows the rules well. The Shinigami King places great trust in him, and because of this he is often asked for advice by many of the inhabitants of the Shinigami realm. He is sometimes seen smoking.

FILE No. 06

ダリル＝ギロオーザ

Daril Ghiroza

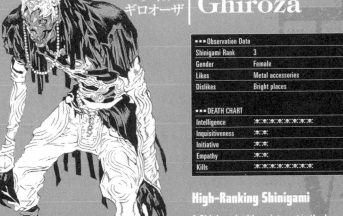

▪▪▪ Observation Data	
Shinigami Rank	3
Gender	Female
Likes	Metal accessories
Dislikes	Bright places

▪▪▪ DEATH CHART	
Intelligence	☠☠☠☠☠☠☠☠
Inquisitiveness	☠☠
Initiative	☠☠
Empathy	☠☠
Kills	☠☠☠☠☠☠☠☠

High-Ranking Shinigami

A Shinigami with no interest in the human world. She's comfortable in the Shinigami realm, where she enjoys gambling. She has an Asian appearance and is known for having a goofy laugh. Her rank is just below Justin's.

FILE No. 07

Deridovely
デリダブリー

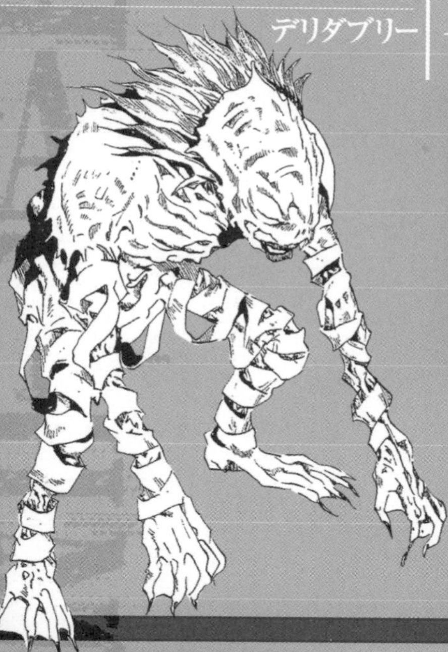

▪▪▪ Observation Data	
Shinigami Rank	10
Gender	Male
Likes	Gambling, naps
Dislikes	Work

▪▪▪ DEATH CHART	
Intelligence	☠☠☠
Inquisitiveness	☠☠
Initiative	☠☠☠
Empathy	☠☠
Kills	☠☠☠☠☠☠

Gambling to Kill Time

A humanoid Shinigami who wears a mask that appears to be made of bone. Because he carries a large sickle, he's pretty close to what many humans think a god of death looks like. He spends every day gambling with Gukku.

FILE No. 08

Midora
ミードラ

▪▪▪ Observation Data	
Shinigami Rank	9
Gender	Female
Likes	Humidity
Dislikes	Dryness

▪▪▪ DEATH CHART	
Intelligence	☠☠☠☠☠
Inquisitiveness	☠☠☠☠☠
Initiative	☠☠
Empathy	☠☠
Kills	☠☠☠☠☠☠☠

Giant Size That Commands Respect

A Shinigami who keeps it simple by wearing no accessories. Because of her size, her tail and her spotted body, she is well known in the Shinigami realm.

FILE No. 09 グック Gukku

■■■ Observation Data	
Shinigami Rank	7
Gender	Male
Likes	Gambling, naps
Dislikes	Work

■■■ DEATH CHART	
Intelligence	☠☠☠
Inquisitiveness	☠☠
Initiative	☠☠☠
Empathy	☠☠☠
Kills	☠☠☠☠☠☠

A Slacker Who Loves to Gamble

A friend of Ryuk's who watches as he heads to the human world. Gukku also gets along with Deridovely. The two are often seen gambling but... supposedly he's not very good.

FILE No. 10 ゼルオギー Zellogi

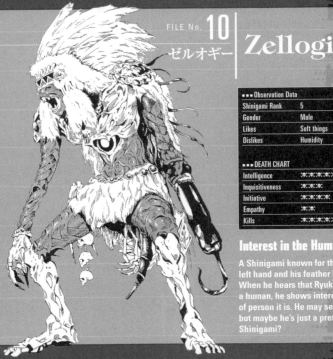

■■■ Observation Data	
Shinigami Rank	5
Gender	Male
Likes	Soft things
Dislikes	Humidity

■■■ DEATH CHART	
Intelligence	☠☠☠☠☠
Inquisitiveness	☠☠☠
Initiative	☠☠☠☠
Empathy	☠☠
Kills	☠☠☠☠☠☠☠☠

Interest in the Human World

A Shinigami known for the hook on his left hand and his feather headdress. When he hears that Ryuk has possessed a human, he shows interest in what kind of person it is. He may seem boorish, but maybe he's just a pretty curious Shinigami?

FILE No. 11

カリカーチャ

Calikarcha

Known for the numerous eyes along the sides of his head. Perhaps this is a rare type of Shinigami?

■■■Observation Data	
Shinigami Rank	11
Gender	Male
Likes	Blueberries
Dislikes	Direct sunlight

■■■DEATH CHART	
Intelligence	☠☠
Inquisitiveness	☠☠
Initiative	☠☠
Empathy	☠☠
Kills	☠☠☠☠☠

FILE No. 12

キンダラ＝ギベロスタイン

Kinddara Guivelostain

Stitches on her head, sharp teeth… She appears to be very violent.

■■■Observation Data	
Shinigami Rank	12
Gender	Female
Likes	Being violent
Dislikes	Thinking

■■■DEATH CHART	
Intelligence	☠
Inquisitiveness	☠
Initiative	☠☠☠☠☠☠☠☠
Empathy	☠
Kills	☠☠☠☠☠☠☠☠☠

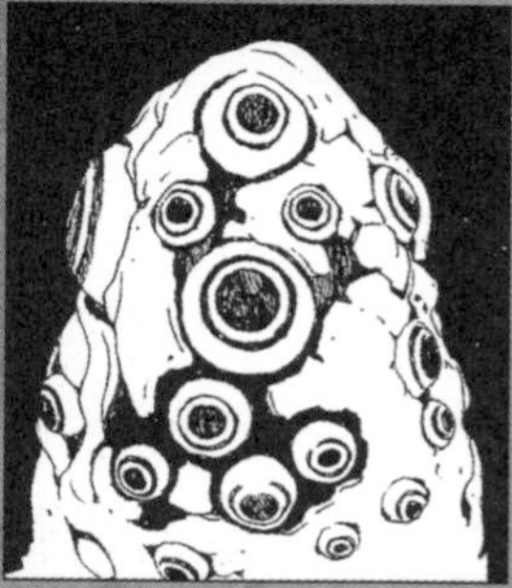

FILE No. 13

ヌ

Nu

Known for the eyes that cover her body. Supposedly only the Shinigami King is more powerful than she.

■■■Observation Data	
Shinigami Rank	1
Gender	Female
Likes	Repentance
Dislikes	Sound

■■■DEATH CHART	
Intelligence	☠☠☠☠☠☠☠☠☠☠
Inquisitiveness	—
Initiative	—
Empathy	☠☠☠☠☠☠
Kills	☠☠☠☠☠☠

FILE No. 14

死神大王

King of Death

■■■Observation Data	
Shinigami Rank	None
Gender	Unknown
Likes	Unknown
Dislikes	Unknown

■■■DEATH CHART	
Intelligence	Immeasurable
Inquisitiveness	Immeasurable
Initiative	Immeasurable
Empathy	Immeasurable
Kills	Immeasurable

The Most Powerful Being in the Shinigami Realm

The leader of the Shinigami realm. He must be very old because the Shinigami refer to him as "Old Man." He seems to be in charge of keeping track of Death Notes, but little else about him is known. Maybe he's too incredible for humans to comprehend?

Incomprehensible

☠ A Complete Analysis of the Shinigami ☠

Shinigami Observation Diary

This section will use Ryuk and Rem as examples in an attempt to reveal the abilities and behaviors of these mysterious creatures from a different world.

ABILITIES

Shinigami have many surprising abilities that set them apart from humans. These pages will present a detailed explanation of all their inhuman abilities.

← Their wings retract when not in use.

Wings

Basic Transportation Ability

Flying is a normal activity for Shinigami. When they travel about in the human world they usually do so by flying. They are capable of walking, but maybe they don't do it as much because it's more tiring?

↑ Ryuk's ability to explain things is clearly below that of Rem's.

Brains

Intelligence Varies

As with humans, intelligence levels among Shinigami vary wildly. This probably has an effect on their personality as well.

Body

↑ Physical attacks are useless against Shinigami. Being shot by a gun doesn't hurt them.

→ No need to take the long way: they can go right through walls!

Guns and Knives Have No Effect

They can materialize and dematerialize their bodies at will. However, only humans who have touched the Death Note can see them.

Eyes

↑ Shinigami are able to give "Shinigami Eyes" to the human they possess. To do this, they place their open hand above the human's head.

↑ This ability is basic to all Shinigami.

Names and Lifespans Are Instantly Visible

Along with superior vision, Shinigami Eyes grant the ability to see a person's name and lifespan when looking at them. This allows Shinigami to see people's names even remotely.

Taste

IS IT THAT GOOD?
YEAH, APPLES FROM THE HUMAN WORLD ARE... HOW DO YOU SAY IT... JUICY?
...

Similar Tastes as Humans?

Shinigami have no need for food, but they do possess a normal sense of taste. One could say that this is one of their useless abilities.

← Ryuk took the most advantage of this in the human world. Perhaps there was no food in the Shinigami realm that measured up to his tastes.

Hands

Ability to Write Is the Only Necessity

All Shinigami are able to hold a pen and write into a Death Note. This could be their most important ability, considering that it's linked to their survival.

← Of course, each Shinigami has different handwriting. Rem was supposedly bad at writing in Japanese.

Where and how do Shinigami live? Let's take a look into something that's impossible to know from the human world: the lifestyle of a Shinigami!!

Home

A Barren and Desolate Land

The Shinigami realm is apparently somewhere above the human world, but it cannot be seen by merely looking up.

Scenery

The Shinigami Realm Has Various Colonies?!

It is a very dry and desolate place. There appear to be varying landscapes, though none of them have anything that look like buildings.

↑ There are also desert areas with holes for looking down to Earth. Nothing else is necessary.

(Shinigami Realm)

↑ This area has many stones and bones. Shinigami congregate in places like this.

The Holes of the Shinigami Realm

The Place to Look Down into the Human World

These places to watch humans are very necessary to the Shinigami. Thanks to these holes, Shinigami no longer need to go down to the human world. It's unknown when they were first created.

↑ If a Shinigami knows the name and face of a human, he can learn their location by looking down from here.

KRA-KOOM

↑ The only entrance to the human world. It's rarely used.

Rules

Nothing Required Except Obedience to the Rules

Even in the wild Shinigami realm, rules exist. Depending on the offense, the punishment can be even death. But it appears that there aren't many Shinigami who know the rules well...

UMM ...
LET ME CHECK IF THERE'S A WAY TO FIND OUT...
SHINIGAMI HAVE LOTS OF RULES.

↑ The rules are important when dealing with humans. A misstep can mean death!

Strong Life Forms Who Rarely Die

Their numbers are dwarfed by that of the humans but their ability to survive is incredible. As long as they do a minimum of work, they can live forever!

Life

(Daily Activity)

Existence

Lengthening Their Lives With Human Life

Shinigami write human names into notebooks and continue living by taking people's remaining lifespans. So the question is: did they exist before humans?

IT'S BECAUSE SHINIGAMI GET EXTRA LIFE FROM HUMANS.
EXTRA LIFE?!

➜ Unless they get into some kind of trouble, Shinigami will never die.

Reproduction

Different Genders but No Reproduction

There's no specific physical difference between male and female Shinigami. Reproduction is impossible and none engage in sexual activities. How they come into being is a mystery…

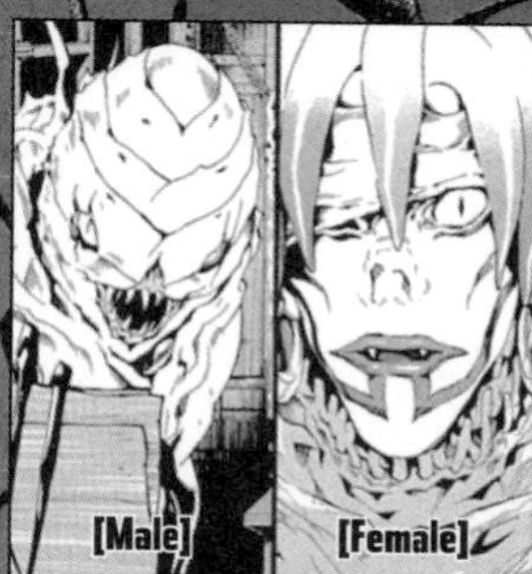

➜ It appears that Shinigami know each other's gender instinctively.

Sleep

➜ In Ryuk's case, it appears that he sleeps at the same time as Light.

Sleep Is for the Lazy

Shinigami are capable of falling asleep but they have no need for it. To them, it's just evidence of laziness.

Food

Eating Is Merely a Luxury

Food is nothing more than a luxury item to a Shinigami. Since they don't get nutrients from food, some Shinigami never bother to eat.

YOU KNOW, RYUK, THIS WILL ALL BE OVER IF YOU JUST TELL US ABOUT KIRA.
STOP BEING SO PERSISTENT. IT'S PART OF THE RULES NOT TO TELL. AND YOU'RE GETTING TOO FAMILIAR WITH ME THESE DAYS.

➜ The only things Ryuk puts in his mouth are his favorite food, apples.

Work

Working Too Much? Lame!

Though they appear incredibly lazy, Shinigami have jobs. However, they don't have a required amount of work to do, and trying too hard is seen as lame.

Searching for Victims

(Duty)

Searching for Targets to Take Life From

The main Shinigami job is to find humans they can take life from and to write their names into Death Notes. They choose humans at random!

Are they looking down into the human world like this?

Watching Over the Note Holder

Although a Shinigami sometimes will explain things about the notebook it is not required to do so.

Watching Over It 24/7

Due to the rules, a Shinigami must stay close to the human who picks up the notebook. Not that they need to do anything, though...

Protecting the Note

BUT HE DOESN'T REALIZE THAT NOBODY IS WILLING TO HELP.
"THIS IS THE GUY WHO HAS MY NOTEBOOK, PLEASE HELP ME FIND HIM..." IF HE HAD A PHOTOGRAPH INSTEAD OF A DRAWING, IT WOULD BE EASY.

When a Death Note is lost a report is given to the Shinigami King. But nobody will help search for it!

DEATH COLUMN / No Harm in Knowing: The Shinigami Ranking

Everything in the Shinigami realm seems random and chaotic, but there are class rankings. Obviously, the highest ranking belongs to the Shinigami King. However, these rankings don't seem to affect the day-to-day activities of the Shinigami very much...

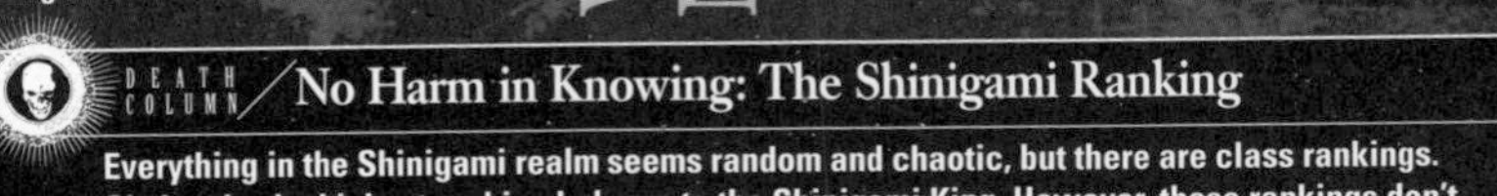

HOW TO THINK

TSUGUMI OHBA

In-Depth Interview with Tsugumi Ohba

***Death Note* Truths**

The Origins of All 108 Chapter Titles

Tsugumi Ohba is the extraordinary storyteller who created *Death Note*. In this special interview Ohba-sensei reveals the deepest secrets of the series.

⬆ Light's rival, L, is taken out in the middle of the story. This sudden twist came as a shock to many readers.

Looking Back at the Series

Congratulations on completing *Death Note*. What are your feelings now that it's over?
Thank you very much. I'm deeply grateful to the readers who supported us. I'm very thankful that I was able to complete the series almost exactly as I had planned.

I had originally planned."

Was the ending something you had envisioned since before the series even started?
Having it end with L winning and Light dying was one idea, but ultimately I decided that the story would conclude with the scene at the Yellow Box warehouse. The part where Light is punished and dies didn't change at all from the beginning, though. Also, one thing that I didn't allow to be changed was the notion that "when you die, you become nothingness." Luckily, I was able to keep this part and the series turned out almost exactly as I had originally planned.

Please tell us how the *Death Note* project began.
It all began when I brought thumbnails for two different stories into my publisher's [Shueisha] editing department. One of them was the pilot version of *Death Note*, which was received well by the editors there. Obata-sensei was brought in as the artist and the story appeared in *Weekly Jump* magazine. The fan reaction was positive and it was chosen to become a weekly series.

BEHIND THE SCENES WITH TSUGUMI OHBA

•The Vision Granted by Shinigami Eyes
A human with the Eyes will always be seeing other people's names and life spans. And, as it says in the rules, the person's eyesight increases to 3.6, so they can see very well. Yeah, that one is very close to being a stupid rule [*laughs*].

•40 Seconds and Other Numbers
They were chosen randomly. I wanted a number with four in it since the Japanese word for "four" can be pronounced like the word for "death."

•The Human Life Span Seen by Shinigami Eyes
I did create a complicated math equation for Light's life span when the numbers first appeared above his head. But now I don't even remember the formula. Every other life span number after that was added by Obata-sensei. He chose some nice numbers.

What did you concentrate on while creating the thumbnails?
Mostly the amount of dialogue and the tempo. With every chapter, I struggled with having too much text. Sometimes it can't be helped, but reading too much exposition can be tiring. As this would affect the atmosphere and air of suspense the story should have, I did my best to make it as concise as possible.

How do you create thumbnails?
I first meet with my editor to hash out and organize my ideas. Once the plot is set, I create the

Where did you get the idea of the Death Note from?
There's not really one specific source. One day I had the thought spinning in my head and started thinking about the specific rules and Shinigami. I felt like there was potential for a story.

Why did you approach *Weekly Jump* with a suspense story? That's very rare.
I didn't think I could create a normal fight-style manga, and I was thinking that it might be good to have a suspense-type fighting manga. It was so rare... That was my line of thought at the time.

"The story of *Death Note* turned out almost exactly as

panels and page flow in my head. I mostly do this while rolling around in bed, drinking tea, or taking a walk around the house. I need to be relaxed. Once my thoughts are set, I sit down and draw the panels and dialogue in a very simple manner on white paper. I usually go over my page limit, so I have to do this two or three times before I can find the right tempo and flow for the chapter. One thing I like to do is to read over the previous two to four chapters very carefully. This is for consistency, which I think is very important.

Achieving Synergy with the Art

How did you create the characters?
Information such as Light being an honors student with a methodical mind was set out in the rough draft, but the character's appearance was left to Obata-sensei. Often a character became more developed based on the art. Obata-sensei's art is so powerful. The moment I see it I think, "This is the character!" It's always better than the image in my head.

⬇ The amount of heavy dialogue and inner monologue in *Death Note* is unparalleled. Thus the choice of words was very important.

I WAS NAÏVE... I SHOULD HAVE DISPOSED OF THOSE VIDEOS AND ALL POSSIBLE EVIDENCE MYSELF. AND THAT PHONE CALL TO MISA JUST NOW ONLY WORKS AGAINST ME...
NO, IF MISA HAS BEEN CAUGHT AS THE SECOND KIRA THEN RYUGA'S SUSPICION AGAINST ME IS NO LONGER MERE SUSPICION... AND IF MISA TALKS THEN IT'S ALL OVER... I HAVE TO KILL MISA...

Tell me about your work process during the serialization.
I first created a rough draft that had the panel layout, dialogue and simple drawings. These were the thumbnails. My editor reviewed them and after that they were sent to Obata-sensei for completion. The script would be set at that point and the panel layout mostly done. But I left the expressions and camera angles to Obata-sensei.

NOT TO MENTION, HE'S USING THE CONSPICUOUSLY FAKE NAME OF HIDEKI RYUGA.
IF I WRITE HIS NAME INTO THE DEATH NOTE, EVEN IF HIS NAME REALLY *IS* HIDEKI RYUGA...

•What Nationality Is L?
I think of him as a quarter Japanese, a quarter English, a quarter Russian and...maybe a quarter French or Italian? Something like that.

•The Origin of L's Fake Name, "Ryuzaki"
It's just because "L" in Japanese is pronounced like "R"...That's really all it is [*laughs*].

•Creating the Character Names
Since most of the characters are criminals and victims, I strove hard to create names that seemed real but could not exist in the real world. This applied to the foreign names as well. Takada, however, had a normal name because I didn't originally plan on having her die. Looking back, I guess having a character with a regular name die added more unpredictability to the story.

◎ Tsugumi Ohba Interview

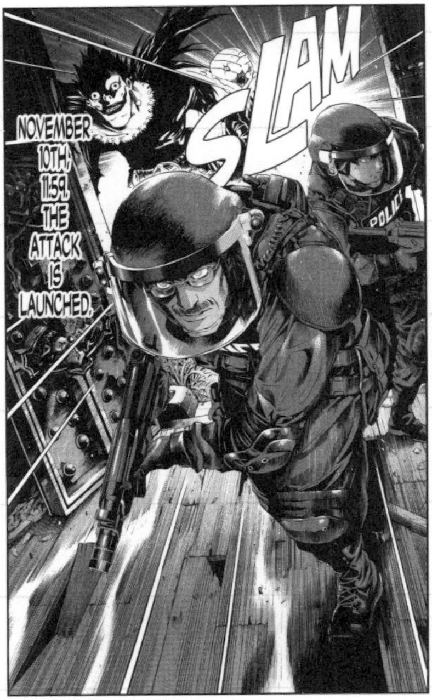

⬆ The amazing new ideas in every chapter are *Death Note*'s greatest strength!

Did Obata-sensei have any other influence besides the character designs?
I have a habit of shoving too much stuff onto every page. So my editor advised me to imagine Obata-sensei's art while creating the thumbnails. It was much more fun creating the panels with Obata-sensei's powerful artwork in mind. I'd call this "saving me" rather than "influencing me," though.

What kind of ideas did you have during the stage from pilot chapter to serialization?
It would have been easy to create episodic stories based around the concept of Shinigami and the Death Note. But since we were doing a serialization, I wanted to create a story that focused on a regular cast of characters and the incidents set in motion by the Death Note. As I thought about it, I came up with a story about Light, L and the various Shinigami.

want to use it immediately."

Once the serialization started, wasn't it hard to keep every chapter so exciting?
When writing a story, I start with the ending. I think about the story as a whole and how much I can fit into one chapter. With the end in mind, I start creating the thumbnails. However, I only work this way because I lack confidence—especially when the series first starts. I feel like I have to squeeze every single idea I have into the story or else nobody will want to read it. Plus I don't seem to be very good at extending a story. Once I think up a good idea or plot development, I want to use it immediately.

⬆ Small and detailed panels were the norm, but large panels were also used. Thanks to Obata-sensei's art, these pages were intense!

●Watari's Character
He's a guy who cultivates detectives for fun. That's kind of terrible, isn't it [*laughs*]? His appearance wasn't decided upon until his first scene in chapter 2. I left that to Obata-sensei, but I hear he struggled with it a lot. Originally the character's name was "Shadow," as in "L's Shadow," but my editor was like, "Please! Anything but that!" and convinced me to change it [*laughs*]. So we used the name "Watari," which refers to his being a "handler."

●Light's Relationships with the Opposite Sex
During college he had about five or six girlfriends, some being merely camouflage. He's likely not capable of loving a woman. This is probably because he looks down on everyone. He does possess love for his family and for humanity as a whole, however. He also had many friends.

●The Origin of Misa's Name
It was kind of random but I think it was from "*kuromisa*" [Black Mass]. It must have been based on something.

➡ As the story progresses the rules become more and more complicated. Sounds like keeping track of them was tough…

RYUK, IT'S POSSIBLE FOR YOU TO POSSESS TWO PEOPLE AT THE SAME TIME, RIGHT?
WHAT?

The Secrets of Light and L

Tell me about your characters. First, Light: what kind of a person do you think he is?
The moment he got his hands on the Death Note his life was ruined. In many ways, he was a victim. He had good intentions, but he was also very conceited. I struggled to find the right name for him. My editor suggested "Yagami." When I looked through the Japanese name registry, I found Kanji for "star" and "light." At first I wasn't too concerned about it. But the final scene in the manga gave his name deeper significance. I liked that.

I heard that you put jokes in the thumbnails.
Yes, I would put stuff like Ryuk making funny moves and Matsuda saying dumb stuff, just to make my editor laugh. My editor would usually just delete them with no reaction and pass the thumbnails on to Obata-sensei. That would make me a little sad [*laughs*].

How did you create the Death Note rules?
I created most of them early on, but some were done as the series went along. I worked hard every week to make sure things were consistent…and it was really tough [*laughs*].

What about the rules that appear in between the chapters?
Sometimes they were there as foreshadowing or to supplement past events, but basically I consider them bonus content. I even thought up some horrible ones like, "Collect all seven notebooks and your wish will…" [*laughs*]. I didn't use that one for some reason.

Did you take any trips for research?
I didn't. I don't like leaving my home, so I didn't go anywhere during the serialization. I definitely didn't go to America. But I did look stuff up on the Internet and I watched a lot of movies.

"Once I think up a good idea or plot development, I

What kind of person do you think L is?
I introduced him as the force of justice who stands in the way of Light's criminal activity and who keeps the story going. In order to go up against Light and the Death Note, you need a "super detective." Since it wouldn't have been as interesting if he were too much older than Light, I made him a young man. I didn't think up anything for his past. For him to be in such an influential position, he must have solved an amazing amount of cases, but I have no idea what kind of cases they were or how he solved them. But I would love for NISIOISIN, who wrote the *Death Note* novel, to write more stories about that [*laughs*]. The name "L" was chosen after careful consideration. I wanted a letter that felt strong by itself, but not many seemed to work as a name. I thought about "I" or "J" but they didn't feel as good as "L."

●Mogi's Character
He was a character I was saving for something really amazing. At first I introduced him simply to fill the cast. Because he's a "silent type" I planned to have him do something surprising, but…[*laughs*].

●Ide's Character
He left the team early but I needed him during the Higuchi arrest and so brought him back. The reason was simply because having him there could make for a nice solidarity scene, and I just figured having more characters there to make the arrest would be better [*laughs*].

●Aizawa's Character
He's basically a guy who yells at Matsuda for being a goof. He's also a family man who would choose his life and family over his job. But that side of him starts to change after Soichiro's death.

●Matsuda's Character
A very simple guy who's easy to use in the story. Though in some ways, he survived the greatest dangers [*laughs*]. I made him pro-Kira because I figured that in every group there would be people who would support Kira. He also helps to balance the team.

Did you ever request something from Obata-sensei in terms of character design?
For L, I left everything up to Obata-sensei, but he did ask me if it was okay if L wasn't attractive. After this, I added new ideas to the thumbnails, like the way L sits and whatnot. I did mention a few things like "he's listless" and "he's part English." Then Obata-sensei took that and worked his magic. I did add a lot of details to the thumbnails concerning L's mannerisms and his sweet tooth. But a lot of it also came from Obata-sensei; how L holds his cell phone, for example.

What went into the creation of other main character, Misa?
I just thought…it's boring if all the characters are male, so let's introduce a cute female. Misa was created before the serialization began to be the Second Kira, but I debated a lot about when to introduce her. I eventually decided that it would be good timing to do so after Naomi Misora is killed. Misa's Gothic Lolita look is simply because I'm into that fashion, and I figured it would be more interesting if she first appeared in really unique clothes. But the hardcore Gothic Lolita fashion is a bit too much, so we decided to pull it back a little.

for the Shinigami Eyes."

Is this when you decided to give her a personality that would stir everything up?
I had always intended to introduce her as a character who would have the Shinigami Eyes. To get them you need to give up half your life, so she had to be spontaneous and not too bright. Therefore her personality was determined from the start. I thought about this for Light's persona as well. Light is a character who would never decide to trade for the Shinigami Eyes. But I wanted to be able to use the Shinigami Eyes in the story, so I needed Misa to be Light's eyes.

I HAD TO TAKE THE ROLE OF KIRA AND DO IT. THIS WAS A MISSION THAT WAS ENTRUSTED TO ME.
I WAS CHOSEN TO MAKE AMENDS FOR THIS ROTTEN WORLD, AND TO CREATE A TRULY SAFE AND IDEAL WORLD.

⬆ Light takes his ideals too far and dirties his own hands. His mind becomes totally warped…

⬆ L's personality and quirks were developed by the combined work of both creators.

●The Tennis Match in Chapter 20
I thought it would be good to have a sports battle as a prelude to their battle of minds. I discussed it with my editor and he suggested tennis. He seemed to think it was the big thing in college [*laughs*]. I thought about golf, but it wasn't visual enough.

●The Reason for Ukita's Death
It's simply because he's the one who goes to Sakura TV. Any of them could have been the one, but since Matsuda is useful I didn't choose him, and I left Mogi in because I had planned to use him for something big… So then it just came down to Ukita or Aizawa…

MR. MOGI DIED OF A HEART ATTACK.
?!
I'LL HAND OVER THE BODY TO THE JAPANESE POLICE WITHIN THE NEXT FEW DAYS.

Plus, at that time the only real female character was Sayu and I wanted to introduce a cool one. Unfortunately, because Naomi uncovered too much, she had to die…

➜ The story's lone upholder of justice, his life is tragically cut short because of the case. May he rest in peace.

Tell me about Light's father, Soichiro.
I conceived of him as an honest police officer with a strong sense of justice. As the story progresses, you really feel sorry for everything he has to go through. I had a lot of hesitation over his death, even up until the final moments…but it needed to be done for future plot development. I decided that Light would never kill his own father, so I worked hard to make the death an accident.

Why did Soichiro have to die?
If he had continued to live Light's fake 13-Day Rule would be uncovered. And since he had the Shinigami Eyes, he would affect too many future plot points. Light's original plan was to use Matsuda for that purpose; it was a big miscalculation for him when his father took on that role and made the Eye Trade. Another reason Soichiro had to die was because I couldn't bring myself to kill Matsuda.

Tell me about Raye Penber and Naomi Misora.
The plot point of having the FBI tail Light was something I thought up in the very beginning. And the officer for the job just happened to be Raye. Originally, I introduced Naomi just so he'd have a character to talk to. But after Raye's death, I figured it would be natural and interesting to have his fiancée, a former FBI agent, go after Light.

"Light is a character who would never decide to trade

Did you plan to kill her from the beginning?
I actually planned to have her stick around a little longer because of how attractive a character she became once Obata-sensei drew her. But she reached the truth faster than I thought, and I needed her dead to get to the next plot point or I would be in trouble. That was the greatest difficulty I created for myself during the early part of the series.

➜ The former FBI agent who first pressured Light. Both creators were sad to see her go.

●On L Not Eating the Ham
There's no real meaning behind it. I put it in the rough draft for fun. Obata-sensei is a wonderful person who entertains my whims [*laughs*].

HEY, RYUGA. YOU EVER HEAR OF WARMING UP?
HE WHO MOVES FIRST ALWAYS WINS.
HA HA

Then right after that L is killed...
Ending the battle between Light and L here was one of the ideas I had when I first started the series. When I resolved to kill L, I was holding back a tear.

The Story Expands: The Mello and Near Arc

What informed your decision on how to introduce Mello and Near?
I decided they would be brought in together. The reason there were two characters was that L alone wasn't able to catch Kira. If I introduced them separately, it would just be a repeat of the Light vs. L battle. So I decided to have three combatants all going after each other. I left the designs totally up to Obata-sensei. The only thing I asked for was to make them both a little "L-ish." I wavered a lot on their ages. At first I even considered making them L's sons. I didn't develop their personalities much initially, intending to reveal them through their actions.

What were you trying to accomplish with the Yotsuba Kira arc?
I wanted to have Light and L investigating together and I needed to put their battle on hold for a bit. The Yotsuba members were merely stock villains intended to make the main characters look good. I always knew Light would return to being Kira.

!!
MISA AMANE HAS BEEN APPREHENDED ON SUSPICION OF BEING THE SECOND KIRA.

⬆ Misa's arrest and confinement, followed by the Yotsuba arc; the plot is always surprisingly fast-paced.

Why eight Yotsuba characters?
Right from the start I planned on eight characters, and I also wanted Mido to seem the most suspicious. After Obata-sensei drew the characters I considered various options before deciding on Higuchi. The Yotsuba storyline was intended simply to lead to Light regaining the notebook and killing L. It really didn't matter which one of them was acting as Kira; I just wanted the reader to enjoy trying to guess who it would be.

⬆ L's heirs, who compete in pursuing Kira. The story gets even more complicated.

●L's Capoeira in Chapter 38
Obata-sensei added that. In the thumbnails, it was a normal kick. Obata-sensei thought it would be more like L to kick in an unusual way. This became an important part of NISIOISIN's novel; sometimes you never know which things will leave a lasting memory.

●Profiles of the Yotsuba Members
I came up with those while eating dinner with my editor. When I look back at it now, I see that I didn't put much thought into them. Collecting glasses [*laughs*]? A lot of it was pointless information included as a red herring.

ZOOM IN OR WHATEVER AND LOOK INTO MY EYES!

●Light's Request: "Look into my eyes"
That's something the pre-Death Note Light would say. I wanted to show what Light would have been like had he never found the notebook.

●L Has No Friends?
Nope. And when he says that Light is his first friend that's a big lie. He never considers him a friend. He probably secretly thinks really negative things about him.

↑ The first incident involving Mello and Near. Even Light can't hide his emotions when his sister is involved.

God had been watching him. God had brought justice to evil because Teru never gave in.
God was on Teru's side. God was watching him, and knew him.

↑ Mikami plays a key part in the story's conclusion. He's an unusual character in that his motives for worshipping Kira are explained in detail.

When Near and Mello appear, why did you make the first incident be Sayu's kidnapping?
I discussed with my editor about what we could throw in to get things really going after L's death. So...we came up with a kidnapping by Mello. Then we struggled with who should be the victim. In the end, I decided on poor Sayu.

"The reason there were two characters was that L alone wasn't able to catch Kira."

Why not Misa?
Because if it were Misa, Light might just decide to snuff her out [*laughs*]. Light loves his family and he wants his new world to have only kind people in it. Although his desire to be godlike is warped, he's just trying to make the world a better place. He sees Misa as a bad person who had killed people. That's why he's cold to her and manipulates her.

What was behind Mikami's introduction?
I needed another character to take Misa's place. I struggled with who it should be. Actually, Mikami is the only character in *Death Note* who has a chapter about his past.

Why did you create a story about his past?
I wanted to write about why he wanted to become Kira's proxy. I needed to establish Mikami and Light as equals and show that he was special in some way. Initially, I didn't want to include any backstory in *Death Note*, so I was a bit resistant to this. One of the reasons being—and this is a personal thing—that I don't really like flashbacks.

●Misa as a Nurse in Chapter 48
I came up with it during the thumbnail stage. Fan service, perhaps [*laughs*]?

●Higuchi Telling Misa "Because I'm Kira" in Chapter 48
It's mimicking what Light said to Naomi in chapter 14. Obviously it's a coincidence, but I wanted to make Higuchi say it to show how stupid he is.

●Aiber and Wedy's Characters
I wanted to use characters with special abilities to advance the plot. Aiber did some things but I wanted to use Wedy more. Like having Light control Wedy to place cameras in the headquarters so Misa can see L's face...or something. The entire *Los Angeles BB Murder Cases* novel itself was like that [*laughs*].

Getting back to the characters, tell me about Mikami.
First, I cast him as a prosecutor. I reasoned that given his profession he would possess a hatred for societal evil… And from there I added more and more. I wanted him to be smart but also dangerous. I had no visual preferences; I let Obata-sensei handle that. The character's obsession with the word "delete" makes him more interesting, don't you think?

Is there a specific reason for that?
Lately a lot of series have been developing their characters using flashbacks, and I didn't want to repeat what others are doing. With *Death Note*, I wanted to write about the harshness of reality rather than focus on human drama.

Meaning you wanted to focus on developing the truth and moving the plot forward?
Yes. This is something I realized only recently, but the fact that I didn't focus on human drama was what made it possible for *Death Note* to have such a fast and intense pace. Had I focused on drama, things would have become heavy and the story probably would have slowed down. Plus, with human drama it's easy to get philosophical and preachy. If you go too far with that the story is no longer interesting. That's why I think it was a really good idea that I avoided all the drama.

really good idea that I avoided all the human drama."

Was there anything you were careful about when creating Mikami?
I wanted to make it clear that this is an evil guy who uses the Death Note and reveres Kira. But at the same time, I didn't want to focus on what's right and wrong. That's why I also didn't show much about people's reaction to Kira and hardly revealed what kind of people the Kira worshippers were. So because Mikami was a Kira worshipper, I paid special attention to his first appearance.

SHING
I THANK YOU FOR THESE EYES.
I CAN NOW BRING JUSTICE TO THOSE WHOSE NAMES I DO NOT KNOW, AND THOSE WITH ALIASES.

🡅 No hesitation in making the Eye Trade. His strength of conviction is similar to Light's in some ways.

Had you always planned on reintroducing Takada?
I thought about wanting to around the time of the Mello and Near introductions…but I soon forgot about her [*laughs*]. I eventually remembered while preparing for a *Jump* interview. And I really liked how she reappeared as a news anchor.

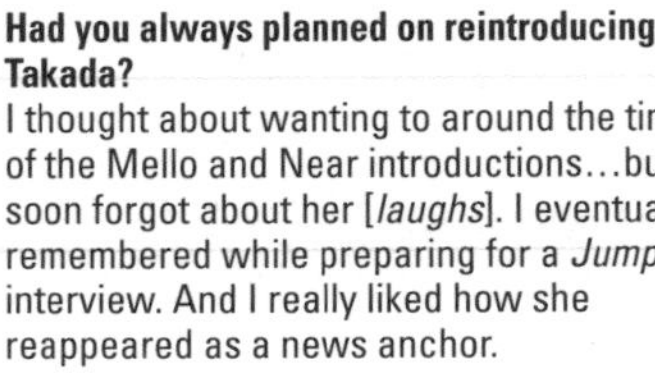

WHAT IS THIS GUY...? HE'S HUMAN, BUT HE'S SO SCARY...

●Why Did You Choose Sidoh as the New Shinigami?
I looked at all the Shinigami Obata-sensei had drawn and picked Sidoh by his looks. Daril Ghiroza was also a candidate, but I wanted this character to be pretty pathetic… I had decided to use Sidoh very early on, thus you can see him in chapter 60.

Why Does Mello Eat Only Chocolate?
Chocolate was what I came up with when I tried to choose something that represented all sweets. Plus it fits perfectly with the story's taking place in America. And it also turned out to be very useful for the plot when Mello's base is uncovered because of the boxes of chocolate [*laughs*].

➡ Once reintroduced, Takada would be one of the characters holding the keys to the conclusion of the story.

Why did she originally appear back when Light was in college?
She was camouflage for Light to hide his relationship with Misa. I figured she could be someone who would go well with Light, and that's why I made her the school idol. I probably reintroduced her because I could never forget "refined Takada" [*laughs*].

⬆ Switching the notebooks, the final trick of the series. Evidence to end the Kira case—once thought impossible to produce—is obtained by this act.

"I think it was a

The Final Trick and the Truth About Mello's Death

When did you decide on the notebook switch at the Yellow Box warehouse?
Around the end of 2005, when we decided to conclude the series. I thought up numerous ways for Light to lose and decided that switching the notebooks was best. But even after deciding that I still had to struggle with how and when to do it and also over how much Light and Near would know about each other's plans.

G-GOD... I-I DID AS YOU TOLD ME.
MIKAMI...

⬆ Mikami is an unknown element in Light and Near's advanced battle of intelligence.

What were the other ideas besides switching the notebooks?
Laminating the pages so you couldn't write on them…stuff like that. Sorry, the rest are very bad, so I can't tell you much about them [*laughs*].

●Matsuda's Good with a Gun?
It's true that he's pretty impressive at Mello's hideout and at the Yellow Box warehouse, but I never really thought about it. I used him mostly for comedy in the storming of Mello's hideout, actually. In the rough draft I originally had him celebrate with a "Yay!!" after the shot, but I figured that would remove some of the gravity of the situation [*laughs*].

●What Is Matsuda Thinking When He Volunteers for the Shinigami Eyes?
He's not thinking anything. He doesn't even realize that according to the fake rules if he killed someone he'd have to continue writing names into the notebook. He just acts on emotion. But because of that, he's very useful to a creator. That's probably why he survives [*laughs*]. By the way, I also thought about having all the task force members die in a heroic way.

●Why Is Sayu in a Wheelchair in Chapter 71?
She's still suffering from the trauma of the kidnapping.

◎ Tsugumi Ohba Interview

⬇ Mello was almost the final victor. It would have been fun to see how he would have taken Light down.

That's why his end was very plain, depicted in only one panel. I thought that if he died too dramatically, the truth behind his death would be revealed.

What was the hardest part of writing the notebook switch segment?
I didn't want Light to lose because of a total mistake on his part. So I had the mistake come from Mikami instead.

Had you always planned on Mello's heroics at the end?
I didn't decide on that until the last second. After Sidoh returned to the Shinigami realm, there was a period in which I struggled over what to do with Mello. After L's death, the idea that Mello would be the character to defeat Light was really strong in my mind. I figured that since Near was the best at Wammy's House, it would be more interesting if Mello were the final victor instead.

Why did you decide against it?
He learned too much about the notebook early on, so I had to fade him out to sustain the intensity of the story… Because of this, I wasn't able to give him a large role at the end and instead switched it to him hurting Light indirectly.

What's behind the line that appears after Light's death: "After they die, the place they go is MU (Nothingness)"?
For me, one of the premises of the series was that once a person died, they could never come back to life. I really wanted to set a rule that bringing characters back to life is cheating. That's why death equals "nothingness."

Tell me about the "nothingness" text written on the corners of the black spread when the chapter appeared in *Weekly Jump*.
Normally the editor writes those, but this time I did it. That's why in volume 12 they appear as rules of the notebook.

⬆ His cool-headed intelligence gone, Light's end is near…

●The SPK Characters
Rester was the captain of a special forces squad before joining. Halle was burning with a desire to catch Kira. A woman with a very strong core. Someone close to her was actually the victim of the Yotsuba Kira and

●The Design of the SPK
All I did for characters like Rester and Ratt was write "commander" and "spy" in the rough draft. The rest was all Obata-sensei.

●Near's Stacking Hobby
L would stack sugar cubes, so I took that portion of him and added it to Near through the device of him playing with toys and stacking things. The match and dice towers were included in the thumbnails. I was thinking how tough drawing those would be for Obata-sensei and was surprised when I saw them on the page [*laughs*].

NOBODY CAN TELL WHAT IS RIGHT AND WHAT IS WRONG, WHAT IS RIGHTEOUS AND WHAT IS EVIL.
EVEN IF THERE IS A GOD...
...AND I HAD HIS TEACHINGS BEFORE ME, I WOULD THINK IT THROUGH...
...AND DECIDE IF THAT WAS RIGHT OR WRONG MYSELF.

↑The debate over right and wrong within the series. The decision is up to the reader.

The Author's Intent with *Death Note*

Is there a theme you wished to express through the series?
Not really. If I had to choose something, I'd say, "Humans will all eventually die and never come back to life, so let's give it our all while we're alive." Given that, I don't think it's very important to debate whether Light's actions are right or wrong. Personally, I only look at it as, "Light is very evil," "L is slightly evil," and "Only Soichiro is good."

Meaning that *Death Note* is not meant to push an ideology or make a statement about good and evil?
I didn't think about that at all. Near's words toward the end about how justice is something that we all think about and decide for ourselves would probably be closest to my own beliefs. I understand that the series brings up questions of right and wrong, but because the answers to those questions always eventually become ideological I decided from the beginning that they wouldn't be a part of *Death Note*. It's dangerous, and I don't see it as being interesting in a manga.

"I decided from the beginning that right and wrong wouldn't be a part of *Death Note*."

So the series is meant to be all about enjoying the plot twists and psychological warfare?
That's why I'm very happy I was able to tell this story in *Weekly Jump*. Because it's aimed at the young, you're able to naturally push back ideology and focus on pure entertainment. If the story were aimed at an older audience, they would expect more debate over the issues and therefore it would have had to go in that direction.

●Sayu's Reappearance at Her Coming-of-Age Ceremony
I went back and forth about it but chose to show her in chapter 97. She's not necessarily recovered, although you can't be sure from this picture [*laughs*].

●Matt's Character
The third most talented member of Wammy's House and Mello's helper. Once Mello started acting on his own, it was going to be hard to advance the story unless he had someone to talk to. So that's why I created Matt. It may have seemed that all he did was play video games, but his existence itself was important [*laughs*].

that's why she volunteered. I thought of Gevanni as the young, good-looking hotshot who was asked to join because of his skills.

●Mello's Scar When He Reappears
I figured it would give him depth and added it in the thumbnails.

Tsugumi Ohba Reveals

DEATH NOTE Truths

Death Note is filled with various mysteries and secrets. Many were revealed within the series but some of them were still very complicated. Here, Ohba-sensei will explain every mystery in detail.

TRUTH 01

Vol. 01, P.162

What's the reason for Light creating the hidden message "L, do you know"?

It's simply to goad L and confuse the investigation. And because I really wanted to include it [*laughs*].

➡ The hidden message is completely meaningless. The goal is merely to distract L.

TRUTH 02

Vol. 02, P.129

What are the specifics behind the "trick to test if anyone is Kira" that L mentions when he first meets Soichiro and the others?

He'd planned on doing to them what he did to Light after the tennis match in chapter 21, but because Soichiro and the others are so simple-minded, he doesn't even bother with it…

⬅ L presumes the suspect is highly intelligent.

TRUTH 03

Vol. 02, P.181

How reliable are the percentage figures that L gives to measure how much he suspects something?

Any time L throws out a number, it basically means that he suspects that person by over 90 percent. So you can't trust it. The truth is, he's a liar [*laughs*]. I made those numbers up while trying to think as L would.

➡ At this point L is already pretty certain about Light…

TRUTH 04

Vol. 03, P.055

What's the true purpose of L attending Light's university?

He's pretty confident in his reasoning and wants to test it himself. Also, he wants to show Light that he can take the offensive. He understands that it's dangerous, but since he knows how Light thinks, he's confident that he won't be killed under the circumstances.

⬆ This seemingly rash action has a lot of thought behind it.

TRUTH 06 Is Light's comment about getting a girlfriend a foreshadowing of Misa's appearance?

Vol. 04, P.066

Light doesn't know Misa at this time so he has no reason to foreshadow such a thing [*laughs*]. It's simply an excuse for being late. I put this line in so I could have Sayu reacting to the next line about Light having eaten in a hotel [*laughs*].

↑ This line would help Light out later.

TRUTH 05 Why does L believe Misa's message about Shinigami?

Vol. 04, P.029

He immediately reasons that, taking the investigation as a whole, everything would fit if Shinigami exist. But that means he has to accept that they exist and that shocks him. While the other members are thinking stuff like, "What the heck?" L is the only one who puts it all together. Plus, I wanted to have him fall down on his butt [*laughs*].

↑ L instantly devises a new theory on the case.

↑ After returning the notebook to Rem, Light immediately asks her to hand it to Ryuk.

→ This is the moment when Light returns the notebook. But there is a period of time that passes before Rem flies away in the following panel.

TRUTH 07 Who was the original owner of the notebook that Light gives to Rem before he goes into confinement?

Vol. 07, P.032

There's actually a period of time in between the panel where Light hands the notebook to Rem and the panel where Rem flies off. This is when the shuffling of the notebooks takes place, so the Death Note that Rem takes off with is Light's original one. At this point I had already devised the trick for how L would die, so my heart was pounding with the knowledge that I could no longer change what was going to happen.

↓ The eight Yotsuba Kira suspects. Higuchi, who is later revealed as Kira, sure is acting calm here...

TRUTH 08 When the Yotsuba Eight are first introduced, is Higuchi not sweating because he's Kira?

Vol. 05, P.066

↑ But Namikawa is also acting relaxed. Their expressions are reflections of their personalities.

You mean, everyone was nervous except him because he's Kira? Not at all, it was just a coincidence that Obata-sensei drew the scene that way. The reason was probably because he wanted to make Higuchi look cold-blooded and the sweat would have interfered with that. Namikawa isn't sweating either for the same reason.

ARE YOU GUYS IDIOTS? TRY TO UNDERSTAND THAT WE'RE BEYOND THE LEVEL OF BEING "SUSPICIOUS."
...

⬆ Takahashi is called "even more foolish than Higuchi" by the others. He's also a red herring.

➡ Misa uncovers the truth first: but Light and the others wouldn't learn of it for a while.

TRUTH 09 Why was Higuchi chosen to be the Yotsuba Kira?

Vol. 06, P.095

Mido was the red herring character, so he couldn't be Kira. The same for Namikawa once he received the phone call from Light. Shimura doesn't have the right personality. The thing is, you have to be foolish to want to use the Death Note. So it had to be a foolish person, and in Yotsuba's case, a very greedy person. In the end it was a process of elimination.

➡ Since Ryuk has no feelings for humans he agrees to let Misa make the Eye Trade again.

⬅ Light's plan requires Misa to regain her memories. That's why her notebook is buried.

TRUTH 10 Why do Ryuk and Rem swap notebooks?

Vol. 07, P.031

Because it was necessary to make Ryuk the Shinigami possessing Misa. If it stayed Rem, she most likely wouldn't let Misa trade for the Shinigami Eyes again. Also, Misa would not be able to regain her memories relating to the notebook unless she dug up the Death Note that she previously used.

NOW THE OWNER OF THAT DEATH NOTE IS RYUK.
...
SO IT SEEMS.

⬅ Even the Shinigami are confused about the switch. It's all done in order to change which Shinigami possessed whom.

TRUTH 11 What is the meaning behind L's final words, "...but...I..."?

Vol. 07, P.120

My editor thought of it as, "I was right, but I lost...for now." That would also foreshadow Mello and Near's appearance. But I think it's best if everyone interprets it for themselves. Also, Matsuda's theories in chapter 108 may or may not be right. This might be unfair, but *Death Note* is about readers coming to their own conclusions. Sorry.

TRUTH 12 What did Light plan to do with the cell phone number sharing system?

Vol. 08, P.034

Actually, this is a very convenient system that allows Light to always know what everyone on his team knows. It's basically as if he were bugging everyone on the investigation [*laughs*]. I didn't plan on introducing futuristic items into the series but figured I could get away with this. Plus, since the characters were being divided among America and Japan, I needed a reason for all of them to know what was going on so I could advance the plot. I didn't want to have to always worry about explaining how a certain character learned of an event before he was able to react.

TRUTH 14 Why does Light choose Mikami as his proxy?

Vol. 10, P.028

↑ The choice was just based on intuition. Light was under that much pressure.

He must feel that Mikami would be a good choice when he sees him on TV. Also, since he's about to come under heavy scrutiny, he's forced to choose someone fast. Mikami is probably just the person who seems to be the best-suited at the time. Though Light's dialogue during this scene makes it seem as if he's still full of confidence [*laughs*].

TRUTH 13 When Sidoh drops in on Light's room, can Misa see him?

Vol. 08, P.102

No, she can't. And neither can Light. What Misa is reacting to is Ryuk, who to her appears to be mysteriously talking to himself.

→ If only Light had noticed this...

→ The amazing ability to watch multiple monitors at once and locate a suspect.

→ Mello doesn't even bother looking at the moni-tors.

TRUTH 15 Is being able to watch multiple monitors at once a special ability that Near possesses?

Vol. 11, P.064

Being able to view that many monitors at once is a particular skill of Near's, but L is able to do something similar. If you think about it, it's all about brain capacity and analytical ability. It could be said that the specialty of all the children raised at Wammy's House is the ability to absorb large amounts of information all at once. So the top students were probably able to do stuff similar to that. Though I can't imagine Mello being able to...[*laughs*].

← L watches multiple monitors while Light is under confinement.

TRUTH 16 Based on his monitoring of Mikami, does Near really believe there's no Shinigami possessing him?

Vol. 11, P.107

↓ The only rules Nears knows of are the ones told to him by Light. This disadvantage cannot be denied.

↑ After seeing Mikami's act, Near immediately thinks of switching the notebooks. But that decision is part of Light's calculations.

Near doesn't know about the rule that a Shinigami must always possess the notebook owner, and he also doesn't know that the Death Note Mikami has is a fake. So he's totally fooled by Mikami's actions and thus is lured into switching the notebooks. Because Light had predicted Near would do this, Mikami is using a fake.

TRUTH 18
Vol. 12, P.015

After being kidnapped and locked in the back of a truck, why doesn't Takada kill Mello immediately?

Because she's worried that if she kills him while he's driving, there could be an accident and she might die as well. However, if she'd known the rules well, she would know that that could not happen. So because of that, her call for help is delayed.

←Takada waits until the truck stops before killing Mello. But this would cost her her life.

TRUTH 17
Vol. 11, P.198

Why does Near request that the notebook be brought to the Yellow Box warehouse?

So he can recover and destroy all the notebooks. His line to Light about not putting his hands on it is a lie. He always planned to take it in the end. First L, now Near—those Wammy's House kids sure are a bunch of liars. They must be taught that any lie that helps the investigation is a good lie [*laughs*].

←His reason at the time was so that it wouldn't get stolen, but…

TRUTH 19
Vol. 12, P.022

Who actually carries out the "as much as you can" killings after Takada kills Mello?

Takada has Mikami send her a list and she uses the piece of the note she killed Mello with to do the rest. However, because Mikami is worried about whether she'll do it or not, he takes the real Death Note out of his bank safe, kills Takada and writes down the same names from the list he sent Takada. He's conceited to the point of thinking that what he's doing is right.

↑ Anticipating that Takada might be a target, Light had prepared her for it.

←After receiving the call from Takada, Mikami makes the same decision as Light.

←A piece Takada hides in her underwear. It has plenty of space to write down names.

TRUTH 20
Vol. 12, P.063

How is Mikami certain that Light is Kira?

↑The notebook is handed to Soichiro in order to go after Mello. After Soichiro's death, Light inherits ownership so that he doesn't have to worry about losing his memory.

↑The life span of those who have ownership of a Death Note cannot be seen even with the Shinigami Eyes.

As is shown in the chapter, Light is the only person whose life span isn't visible with Shinigami Eyes. And the reason for that is because he is the current owner of the notebook being held at the task force headquarters. The ownership of the notebook was transferred to Soichiro during the raid of Mello's hideout, but then it was switched to Light, who was the first to touch it after Soichiro's death. Light never gives it up after that.

HE... HE'S WRITING IN IT... COULD IT BE...?

⬅ Using the Death Note on the train. Mikami does this on instruction from Light.

TRUTH 21
Vol. 11, P.086

What does Light mean when he says he set Near up to doctor the notebook?

He's talking about his instructions to Mikami to use the notebook on the train or to say stuff to himself like, "There's no Shinigami possessing me." Such actions take place multiple times that are not shown in the series.

IS-IT-Y-OU-SHI-NI-GA-MI.
IT'S, "IS IT YOU, SHINIGAMI."
I SEE THAT YOU AREN'T COMMANDER FOR NOTHING.

⬅ Talking to himself to show that no Shinigami is attached to him. The purpose is to make those watching him think that he's unprotected.

TRUTH 22
Vol. 12, P.078

How does Mikami know that the notebooks have been switched?

THE NOTEBOOK MIKAMI FABRICATED WAS SIMILAR TO A NORMAL NOTEBOOK YOU CAN BUY ANYWHERE, SO IT MUST HAVE BEEN EASY FOR YOU TO REPLACE THE PAGES. BUT SINCE I KNEW THAT YOU WOULD ATTEMPT THIS, I HAD MIKAMI CHECK THE NOTEBOOK EVERY DAY.
IT'S IMPOSSIBLE TO REPLACE THE PAGES WITHOUT LEAVING ANY TRACES OF TAMPERING. AND MIKAMI'S VERY OBSERVANT, SO IT WAS EASY FOR HIM TO RECOGNIZE WHEN YOU HAD DONE IT.

⬆ Can he recognize the consistency of the paper just by touch? Or did he mark the pages in a way not visible to the naked eye?

Mikami had previously been warned by Light through Takada that Near would likely try to switch the pages. So the methodical Mikami was checking the notebook every day with a microscope. Obata-sensei drew that in during chapter 97.

TRUTH 23
Vol. 12, P.047

Could Near see Ryuk during the face-off in the Yellow Box warehouse?

Definitely. All the members had touched the notebook and thus could see Ryuk. They had been warned by Near to not betray any reaction but...that must have been tough [*laughs*]!

➡ This is the first time that Near and his team see a Shinigami.

TRUTH 24
Vol. 12, P.159

How is Light able to learn Near's true name?

Because Light instructs Mikami to kill Near first, the first name written into the notebook is "Nate River." Because Mikami overhears Near and Light's conversation he's able to determine which person Near is. By the way, speaking of Near's name, "River" symbolizes that he "flows" from L. And his first name, "Nate," comes from the word "natural." It's supposed to represent that he's a natural genius who's been blessed from above; the opposite of Mello, who works very hard for everything. Oh, and apologies to Mello, but his name doesn't really stand for anything [*laughs*].

➡ Light tries to write Near's name down as a last-gasp effort. That looks really hard to write...

NEAR... YOU'RE MAKING IT SOUND AS IF YOU'RE ACTUALLY KIRA...
YOU'RE THE ONE WHO PROPOSED THE IDEA THAT WE ALL MEET HERE, AND NOW, YOU'RE ASKING EVERYBODY TO HAVE THEIR NAMES WRITTEN DOWN IN THE NOTEBOOK... IT'S ONLY NATURAL FOR US TO THINK THAT...

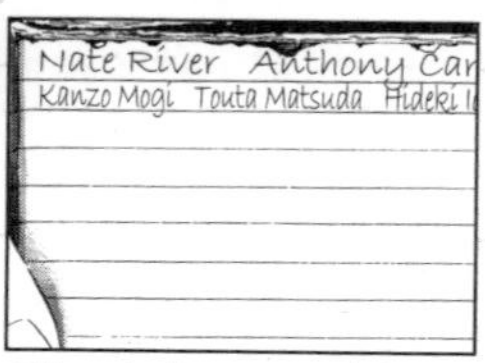

⬆ The order the names are in is important.

⬅ It's clear who Near is based on the conversations.

Tsugumi Ohba Reveals

The Origins of All 108 Chapter Titles

Most chapter titles were chosen at the thumbnail stage, but for some titles I had to come up with a few choices and bat them around with my editor. This was especially the case with the final chapters; my editor and I would often decide on a title for the next chapter as we made the final corrections to the current one. However, I had come up with the titles for chapters 107 and 108 before I even created the thumbnails. All in all, it was a lot of fun. –Ohba

CHAPTER 01 Boredom

The reasons for why Ryuk dropped the notebook and for why Light wants to become a god arise from boredom. So there was no hesitation in choosing this title for the first chapter, even though Light didn't exactly start using the notebook only out of boredom.

CHAPTER 02 L

At this point I basically wanted to present L as the main character, or at least make it clear that he was the other main character. Also, this chapter is really all about L. It's the only chapter title consisting of a single roman alphabet letter; perhaps that's out of respect to L.

CHAPTER 03 Family

I chose this title because this is the chapter in which the top Kira investigator is revealed as Light's father and Sayu is introduced as Light's sister. Also, the chapter ends with Light saying he might have to kill his own family. At this point, I decided that I'd keep all future chapter titles as one Japanese word.

CHAPTER 04 Current

Here I started to have fun and also to be careful not to spoil anything with the chapter titles. This chapter was about the hiding of the notebook, so other title candidates were "False Bottom" and "Destruction," but I thought that "Current" was the best choice.

CHAPTER 05 Eyeballs

This is the chapter about the Shinigami Eye Trade, but I didn't think "Eyes" or "Trade" alone was very interesting. I just thought "Eyeballs" sounded cooler.

CHAPTER 06 Manipulation

This one comes from Light's experimenting with how much he could control people's deaths with the notebook. Written with different Japanese characters, the word could also mean "investigation." I considered that as well, but since this chapter didn't have many scenes of the investigators I kept the one that focused on Light's actions.

CHAPTER 07 Target

Osoreda's target with his gun is Ryuk. Or, one could say that Light's target is Raye Penber's name. I created a lot of titles like this, ones that could have multiple meanings depending on how you think about them.

CHAPTER 08 Woman

Obviously this is referring to Naomi. The middle of this chapter has happy scenes with her and Raye, but it ends with her in tears. I think it's a very feminine chapter.

CHAPTER 09 Slots

The main thing is the holes in the envelopes. But it's also pointing to whether there are any "holes" in Light's plan that L can exploit.

CHAPTER 19 Humiliation

No explanation needed for this one either.

CHAPTER 20 First Move

The one who makes the first move wins. So Light wins the tennis match and invites Ryuga to tea to ask him something, but L makes the first move by saying he needs to tell Light something first.

CHAPTER 21 Duplicity

Both sides are trying to figure out what the other is really thinking.

CHAPTER 22 Misfortune

It concerns Ryuk's creepy line at the end about how humans possessed by Shinigami suffer misfortune. This statement comes up a few times throughout the series after this. The title also points to Light's belief that some people can still be fortunate while using the notebook.

CHAPTER 23 Hard Run

What else could I have used for this chapter?

CHAPTER 24 Shield

The scene of the police officers blocking off Sakura TV looks so great that I chose "Shield."

CHAPTER 25 Fool

Now that I think back on it, *Death Note* finally gets a heroine in this chapter and she's called a "fool"... How rude. But that's just *Death Note* for you.

CHAPTER 26 Reversal

This doesn't actually refer to how the story would turn upside down based on new revelations but rather to L falling out of his chair.

CHAPTER 27 Love

Technically, the way to kill Shinigami isn't to make them fall in love with humans, but I wanted to express it that way in dialogue. Also, given Gelus's feelings for Misa, the stalker's feelings for Misa, and Misa's feelings for Kira, I figured the title worked.

CHAPTER 10 Confluence

This simply represents the investigators coming together with L to risk their lives on the case.

CHAPTER 11 One

L has become one with the Japanese police and is thinking about that one extra clue. Meanwhile, Light is thinking about whether there's one flaw in his plan, and Naomi is heading to the police with her one important revelation.

CHAPTER 12 God

Things would have really turned out differently had Light and Naomi not bumped into each other here. Light talks about how lucky he is, so "Luck" was a candidate for the title. But "I was lucky" is such a boring phrase, and I thought that for *Death Note*, seeing the coincidence as proof that "the other god is on my side" is much more fitting.

CHAPTER 13 Countdown

Light is counting down to Naomi's death, and by the end of the chapter he's also counting down to when she'll reach the NPA headquarters.

CHAPTER 14 Temptation

I changed the Japanese spelling of this so that it wouldn't act as a spoiler for the chapter.

CHAPTER 15 Phone Call

I felt like I added scenes in the first three pages with Ukita answering the phone just because of the chapter title. Then there's the call from Naomi's mother to the task force. I wanted "phone" to be the important item in this chapter.

CHAPTER 16 Handstand

I think this was the title that I had the most fun coming up with. Sorry! It's one of my top three favorite chapter titles.

CHAPTER 17 Trash

I was on a roll around this time. I would often struggle with choosing titles during the run of the series, but from chapter 15 to chapter 23 I had them done really early.

CHAPTER 18 Gaze

This needs no explanation; just check out L's gaze on the last two pages.

CHAPTER 36 Father and Son

Obviously it's referring to Light and Soichiro, but...I was feeling frustrated over the titles of these chapters in contrast to the ones around chapter 17. Perhaps I didn't put enough thought into them.

CHAPTER 37 Eight

Since this chapter ran with color pages in *Weekly Jump* magazine, I worked hard to be sure I had a title that I was satisfied with. "Eight" refers to the eight Yotsuba members, of course. And I'm not saying that I only work hard when I have color pages, I promise.

CHAPTER 38 Strike

Who would have imagined this was referring to L and Light hitting each other? I like these kinds of titles.

CHAPTER 39 Separation

I felt like I was having too much fun with the previous two titles, so I went back into serious mode. This refers to the separation between the task force and the NPA.

CHAPTER 40 Allies

The ironic chapter in which the team gains Aiber and Wedy as new members while also losing Aizawa.

CHAPTER 41 Matsuda

Since this is the chapter with Matsuda running around, I named it after him. My editor laughed but gave me the okay.

CHAPTER 42 Heaven

With a title like this, people assume a character's going to die. I admit I was going for that a little bit, but it also refers to someone saying that Misa's room is like "heaven" and also to how Matsuda feels after surviving this mess.

CHAPTER 43 Black

It refers to whether the Yotsuba Eight are guilty or not, but I also got it from the black suits and ties the surviving seven are wearing on the final page.

CHAPTER 28 Judgment

This points to how the two notebook owners find each other and how Misa is able to confirm that Light is Kira.

CHAPTER 29 Weapon

In this chapter Light refers to Misa as a "weapon." It's indicative of how in their relationship Light views her only as a tool, but Misa's fine with that.

CHAPTER 30 Bomb

Keeping Misa, who knows Kira's identity, around as a weapon is like holding on to a bomb. And Rem's explosive statement that if Light kills Misa Rem will kill him makes Misa's existence even more dangerous.

CHAPTER 31 Easy

"L will die... This easily..." When I was writing this line I was thinking, "What? This easily?!" as well. The best part of this chapter is Rem saying she'll kill L right after the scene with L telling Light that he's his first friend.

CHAPTER 32 Gamble

Light's decision to kill Ryuga while still not one hundred percent sure he's L is a gamble, and so is L's decision to appear before Light at school.

CHAPTER 33 Movement

This represents Misa being arrested and moved to an unknown location just as Light is about to get L's name. And also how the ownership of Rem's notebook moves from Misa to Light.

CHAPTER 34 Imprisonment

I felt this one didn't fit that well. When I can't think of a good title I discuss it with my editor, but that doesn't necessarily mean that we'll come up with something better. I probably just figured, "Well, he's being imprisoned. Should be fine."

CHAPTER 35 Whiteout

This represents Light losing his memory, but now that I think about it, this is a bad title in terms of not wanting the story to be spoiled. It's not like it's the end of the world if the title reveals the coming plot but it kind of takes away some of the fun.

CHAPTER 52 Split-Second

This comes from Soichiro jumping in front of Wedy to take the bullet fired by Higuchi and also from Watari stopping Higuchi from killing himself. Mostly from the latter.

CHAPTER 53 Scream

Screams came from Soichiro, Mogi and, for a different reason, from Light when he regained the notebook.

CHAPTER 54 Inside

One notebook is under the ground, and inside of it is a letter. Inside the other notebook are fake rules. These are things you don't know yet from only reading this chapter. The main reason for the title is the piece of Death Note hidden inside Light's watch.

CHAPTER 55 Creation

This is in reference to Light's line, "The god of the world creates the rules."

CHAPTER 56 Embrace

Misa hugs the notebook, then Ryuk and then Light on the last two pages. Even Ryuk points out that "all this girl does is hug things…"

CHAPTER 57 Two Choices

Referencing Rem's two choices of saving Misa and dying or watching Misa be captured and put to death.

CHAPTER 58 Feelings Within

This title refers partly to Light's feelings but mostly to L's final inner monologue: "I knew it… I wasn't…wrong… But…I…" I'm often asked what L was trying to say when he died, but I dodge the question by saying that *Death Note* is about readers coming to their own conclusions. I do think some things are more exciting when you don't know everything about them.

CHAPTER 59 Zero

The timer reaching zero means that L is dead. I also wanted the readers to know that the Near and Mello arc would be starting from zero. And I wanted to remind myself of that as well.

CHAPTER 44 Successor

This comes from L's line about Light taking over as L. Although it doesn't happen until later on, L already knows at this point that if Light is Kira he'll try to kill L and take over his position.

CHAPTER 45 Crazy

Ryuzaki is being crazy and forceful in this chapter.

CHAPTER 46 Ill-Suited

Having a title that alludes to Misa and Rem's reunion was one option, but I took this one from Mogi's comment about not being suited to his new role. I thought it was funnier. Sorry.

CHAPTER 47 Impertinence

Rem knows that Light has a plan and tells Misa which of the Yotsuba guys has the Death Note. I meant this to indicate that Rem is revealing some of the secrets early.

CHAPTER 48 Give-and-Take

This one comes from a lot of things: Misa and Higuchi trading e-mail addresses, Misa trading clothes with Nori-chan at the hospital, the deal to marry Higuchi if he's Kira, and Misa using that to record his admission of guilt.

CHAPTER 49 Potted Plant

Another chapter where I used the title to mess with the fans. Now that I think about it, what's with my editor giving the okay on this? Nevertheless, I liked this title.

CHAPTER 50 Yotsuba

I chose this one because of Namikawa's smooth explanation of how a large company like Yotsuba is supposed to act.

CHAPTER 51 Misunderstanding

This comes from both L and Light seeing Higuchi write a name down in the notebook but not realizing that it's the method of killing.

CHAPTER 68 Discovery

Thanks to Misa's Shinigami Eyes, the current owner of the notebook is discovered.

CHAPTER 69 Flight

Sorry. I got the readers all excited with this title and the only things flying in the chapter are helmets.

CHAPTER 70 Tremble

This title is because of Sidoh's two instances of trembling: once when he's scared of Mello and once when he thinks about Shinigami realm punishment.

CHAPTER 71 Contact

This represents not only Kira and Ryuk's contact with the task force members but also Sayu's contact with sunlight.

CHAPTER 72 Verification

This is a chapter in which battle plans are being checked and verified, but the title refers mainly to the last two pages.

CHAPTER 73 Cornered

If there were a kanji character for "mano a mano" I would have used it. Unfortunately, there isn't, so I picked "Cornered" to express the positions both Mello and Soichiro are in.

CHAPTER 74 A Fine Performance

I won't say whether the title refers to Mello's lackey, Jose, who brilliantly plays dead, or to the tearful Light at his father's deathbed. However, if Light's tears are a performance, I don't believe it's one hundred percent acting.

CHAPTER 75 Acknowledgement

America's acceptance of Kira is probably more like "recognizing" than "accepting," but I also took the title from Light's line that Kira "knows that killing people is wrong."

CHAPTER 76 Greetings

This refers to Near's "Welcome, Mello" line. I don't remember too well, but I think the original line was "Welcome home, Mello." Anyway, I fixed it.

CHAPTER 60 Kidnapping

Refers to the kidnapping of the NPA Director and Sayu Yagami. With this being the first chapter of the Mello and Near arc, I figured I'd play it straight.

CHAPTER 61 Number Two

Mello was always number two, and the Mello and Near arc is the second story of the series.

CHAPTER 62 Decision

Chief Yagami decides to go to L.A., saying that he'll make all decisions and take all responsibility.

CHAPTER 63 Target

Near's playing darts, Mello's going after the notebook and the airplane goes off target.

CHAPTER 64 Right Angle

This is because the weird door used to trade Sayu for the notebook only turns ninety degrees. I was messing with the readers a little bit.

CHAPTER 65 Responsibility

This refers to Chief Yagami's responsibility in having the notebook taken away from him, Sidoh's lack of responsibility as a Shinigami in losing his notebook, and Ryuk's responsibility for stealing Sidoh's notebook. And also to the line at the end: "That's so irresponsible."

CHAPTER 66 Death

This chapter begins with talk of Rem's death, and soon many of the members of the SPK die. So I figured "Death" was fitting.

CHAPTER 67 Button

The word "button" has many meanings here. Like the button on his cell phone that Soichiro presses early on in the chapter. Or the keyboard keys Matsuda suddenly hits. But the scariest thing in this chapter is the "nuclear button." Oh, I never even knew there was a Japanese kanji character for "button."

CHAPTER 85 Election

This refers to the election of Takada as Demegawa's replacement in being Kira's representative. If you want to force another meaning onto it, perhaps it also refers to Mogi passing the test as Misa's cook?

CHAPTER 86 Japan

This is all about the fact that the characters are returning to Japan to end the battle there. Thinking about it now, it seems like I stopped messing around with the title choices at this point and just went with the obvious.

CHAPTER 87 Tomorrow

No deep meaning; I just took it from the final page where Light asks if he can see Takada the next day.

CHAPTER 88 Conversation

This is a manga that's full of conversation, but here the title is referring to the first conversation between Light and Mikami. I just thought it was great how they're able to get in touch with each other during the secret meeting with Takada even though it's being monitored by the task force.

CHAPTER 89 Kindred Spirits

This represents how both Light and Near want to battle it out to see who's on top and to settle things for good.

CHAPTER 90 Preview

This refers to Near explaining that he won't just kill L-Kira and X-Kira and see if the killings stop, but rather will force Kira to write into the notebook and arrest him on the spot.

CHAPTER 91 Standstill

Mogi stops Misa from saying something that could get her killed and Lidner stops Misa from attacking Takada. Also, Near pauses the footage of Mikami on all his screens.

CHAPTER 92 Night

I debated whether this title should refer to Mikami on the train or to Misa and Takada's dinner, but thought that the Misa and Takada scenes were more interesting. For that I came up with "Rivals in Love," "Cat Fight," "Battle" and "Easy Win," but since these all seemed too obvious I just went with when the dinner took place: at night.

CHAPTER 77 Use

Is Near using Mello? Or is Light using the investigation team as bait for Near and Mello? Is he using the president? Is Demegawa using Sakura TV to shift public opinion towards Kira? Or all of the above?

CHAPTER 78 Prediction

In this chapter Near makes several predictions, like the 13-Day rule being fake and the task force members meeting the original L. Also, Light predicts that Mello will try to contact one of the task force members. By the way, the reason so many of these predictions are right is to keep the story moving forward. I figured it wouldn't work as well if they were wrong.

CHAPTER 79 Lies

In all of Light and Near's conversations both sides are trying to uncover the truth, but I think this is the first time it's acknowledged verbally that Light is lying.

CHAPTER 80 Clean-Up

This refers to the clean-up of the group of Kira worshippers who gather around the SPK members and to the clean-up of the money scattered about.

CHAPTER 81 Warning

This alludes to the contact between the different parties: from Aizawa to Near, from Light to Misa, from Misa to Mikami, etc.

CHAPTER 82 Himself

"Himself" refers to the fact that Near learns of Soichiro's plans to kill Kira and himself, and also to the fact that Aizawa is now acting on his own will.

CHAPTER 83 Delete

"Delete" is a line that reveals what kind of a character Mikami is. He uses this word a lot.

CHAPTER 84 Coincidence

This is the chapter about Mikami's past. So many coincidences happened to him that he refused to believe they were mere coincidences. To put it coldly, he misunderstands everything.

CHAPTER 101 Inducement

Both sides create a situation in which Mikami will be induced to appear, and both sides construct things to induce the other to fall for their plan.

CHAPTER 102 Patience

There's the part where Matsuda and the others are asked to not move, but this is all about Light holding in his laughter and waiting until the 35-second mark to declare his victory.

CHAPTER 103 Declaration

The chapter starts with Light declaring victory and ends with Near's declaration that Light is Kira. "I owe this to Mello" could be considered a declaration as well.

CHAPTER 104 Answer

I know Near's explanation is very long and I'm sure many readers struggled through it. Plus, since Light—who previously had said he'd never confess—answers it with a, "Yeah, I'm Kira. Got a problem with it?" attitude, I figured the chapter title was fitting.

CHAPTER 105 Impossible

It would be impossible for Light to change Near's and the others' feelings with such a speech. He's attempting to buy time with a plan he knows is impossible.

CHAPTER 106 Intent to Kill

The chapter starts off with Light trying to kill Near, and then Matsuda tries to shoot Light to death, and at the end Light is demanding that someone kill Near... Talk about a lot of killing intent!

CHAPTER 107 Curtain

This is what I was trying to represent with the final two pages being all black. I figured "Nothingness" as a title would reveal too much, and I had already used "Black" for chapter 43. Since this is for all intents and purposes the final chapter, I went with "Curtain." I also considered "Black Curtain," but in Japanese that term can refer to a person hiding behind the scenes controlling things and I thought it would be bad to make the readers think a new character was going to be introduced.

CHAPTER 108 Finis

No explanation needed: the end.

CHAPTER 93 Decision

This is a reference to Near's team being sure that Mikami is X-Kira after seeing him use the notebook and overhearing him talk about the Shinigami. And also to their deciding that Light Yagami must be popular with the ladies.

CHAPTER 94 Outside

This comes from Near's remarks to Aizawa that he's not part of the battle but is rather on the outside looking in. And this information is relayed on a public phone, which is outside.

CHAPTER 95 Convinced

This word appears on the first page, when both sides are advancing their plans while convinced they are doing the right thing.

CHAPTER 96 Meanwhile

This is basically supposed to mean, "Meanwhile, Gevanni was..."

CHAPTER 97 Miscellaneous

For the two weeks between January 7th and January 22nd, I did something very rare in *Death Note*. I'm sure many readers were grateful that there were eight pages with absolutely no dialogue. Still, all the characters are very busy during these eight pages.

CHAPTER 98 Everybody

One of the conditions of the two sides meeting is that all the members have to show up. And Mello finally reappears, so the title is also saying, "All the actors are now assembled."

CHAPTER 99 Two

"Two" refers to the deaths of Mello and Takada, and to something you don't find out until later, which is that both Light and Mikami write Takada's name down at around the same time.

CHAPTER 100 Face to Face

I wanted to use "Mask" instead, but I didn't want to reveal the fact that Near would be wearing a mask. At this point I was seriously wondering just how many wonderfully passionate fans were trying to guess the next chapter's plot based on the chapter titles given in the *Weekly Jump* magazine previews.

HOW TO READ

STORY

Story Commentary 11.28.2003—11.05.2004

Intermission 11.06.2004—10.07.2009

Story Commentary 10.08.2009—01.28.2010

Epilogue 01.29.2010—

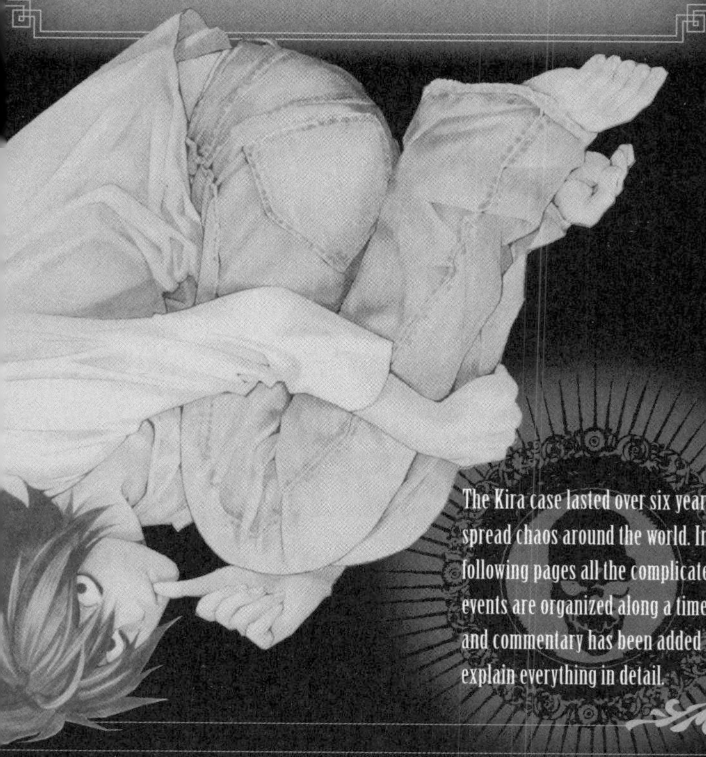

The Kira case lasted over six year
spread chaos around the world. In
following pages all the complicate
events are organized along a time
and commentary has been added
explain everything in detail.

◎ Story Commentary

12.20.2003

KIRA'S ACTIONS

Light Yagami Picks Up the Death Note in School Yard

11.28.2003

Light Yagami picks up a notebook that can kill "the human whose name is written" in it. After the subject he tests it on dies and the Shinigami Ryuk appears, he confirms that it is real. He decides to use the power of the notebook to eliminate evil people and become the god of a new world.

L'S ACTIONS

OIPC ICPO
L HAS BEEN INVESTI-GATING THIS CASE FOR SOME DAYS NOW.
WATARI...

12.4.2003

L Announces Commencement of the Kira Investigation at ICPO Meeting

The subject of the meeting is the mysterious phenomenon of criminals dying of heart attacks all over the world. L, considered the greatest detective in the world, concludes that this is a serial murder case. He announces that he has already begun investigating it and seeks the aid of the ICPO.

CHRONOLOGY

11 . 28 . 2003	Light Yagami picks up the notebook.
	Kurou Otoharada is killed by the power of the Death Note.
	Takuo Shibuimaru is killed by the power of the Death Note.
12 . 03 . 2003	Light Yagami meets the Shinigami Ryuk and announces that he'll become the god of a new world.
12 . 04 . 2003	At an ICPO meeting on how to deal with the Kira incidents, L announces his investigation.
12 . 05 . 2003	Lind L. Tailor is killed by the power of the Death Note.
	L proves that Kira is in the Kanto region of Japan.
12 . 09 . 2003	Light Yagami helps Sayu with her homework.
12 . 10 . 2003	Twenty-three criminals held in prison are killed one by one, on the hour, by the Death Note.
12 . 11 . 2003	Twenty-three more criminals are killed by the Death Note.
12 . 12 . 2003	L confirms that Kira can control the victim's time of death.
	L confirms police information is being leaked to Kira.
	Light Yagami creates false bottom in desk drawer to hide Death Note.
12 . 14 . 2003	Twelve FBI agents enter Japan to investigate Kira case.
12 . 18 . 2003	Raye Penber begins probing Light Yagami.
12 . 19 . 2003	Light Yagami uses the Death Note to perform tests on imprisoned criminals.
12 . 20 . 2003	Matsushiro Nakaokaji is killed by the power of the Death Note.

record of 11.28.2003

DEATH COLUMN / L and Naomi Misora's Meeting

JOINED FBI IN SEPTEMBER 2001 AND ATTAINED RANK OF SPECIAL AGENT WITH UNUSUAL SPEED FOR A WOMAN. ARRESTED PERPETRATOR OF THE "LOS ANGELES BB SERIAL MURDER CASE" ON AUGUST 22, 2002.

↑ Factoid: Beyond died on January 21st, 2004, from a heart attack. It was assumed to be the work of Kira.

In the summer of 2002, Los Angeles and the rest of the country were riveted by the "Los Angeles BB Serial Murder Cases." A man named "Beyond Birthday" set up a challenge to L, the man he revered. L and Naomi Misora had contact during the investigation, and the case would not have been solved without Naomi's help. Afterward, L assumed the alias "Ryuzaki" for the first time.

** Another Note: The Los Angeles BB Murder Cases,* by NISIOISIN

CHRONOLOGY

09 . 01 . 2001	Naomi Misora enters the FBI.
07 . 31 . 2002	The first victim in the L.A. BB Serial Murder Cases is found.
08 . 14 . 2002	Naomi Misora and L first have contact.
08 . 22 . 2002	Naomi Misora arrests suspect in the L.A. BB murders.
09 . 01 . 2002	L learns capoeira from Naomi Misora.
07 . 04 . 2003	Raye Penber proposes to Naomi Misora.
09 . 30 . 2003	Naomi Misora quits FBI in anticipation of marriage.

KIRA'S ACTIONS — Death Note Experimentation Begins

12.10.2

Accepting L's challenge, Light prepares to bury him on the way to the creation of a new world. In order to break the cooperation between the police and L, and also to send L a message, Light tests the notebook by killing criminals in a variety of ways.

AND JUST LIKE THE DAY BEFORE, THEY WERE ALL PRISON INMATES... SO WE'D KNOW IMMEDIATELY THEY DIED... AND ALL 23 OF THEM...
DIED EXACTLY ONE HOUR APART FROM EACH OTHER...

L'S ACTIONS — Twelve FBI Agents Enter Japan

2003

THIS GUY'S BEEN FOLLOWING EVERY STEP YOU TAKE.

L begins to think that Kira has connections to the Japanese police force. In order to investigate the police and their families, he brings FBI agents into Japan. Light is included in those being investigated.

◎ Story Commentary

01.21.2004

KIRA'S ACTIONS

The Murder of the 12 FBI Agents

2.27.2003

Light learns from Ryuk that he's being followed. By staging a bus-jacking, he discovers that his shadow is FBI agent Raye Penber. In order to isolate L and prevent himself from being investigated further, Light murders all 12 FBI agents who had come to Japan.

L'S ACTIONS

The Kira Investigation Team Shrinks

12.31.20

The Japanese Police learn that L has been investigating police personnel. Upset with L's tactics, many officers leave the case. However, after deciding that he can trust the remaining members, L shows himself.

ONLY THOSE WHO ARE READY AND WILLING TO SACRIFICE EVERYTHING AND FIGHT, WHO ARE TRULY COMMITTED TO STOPPING THIS PSYCHOPATH...
...ARE ASKED TO REMAIN. I'LL FIND OUT WHO YOU ARE WHEN I RETURN AT FIVE O'CLOCK FROM MY MEETING UPSTAIRS.
...

CHRONOLOGY

12 . 27 . 2003	Yonegoro Nusumi dies near Raye Penber from the power of the Death Note.
	All twelve FBI agents are killed by the power of the Death Note.
12 . 31 . 2003	The Kira task force under L shrinks.
	Soichiro Yagami and his men meet L.
01 . 01 . 2004	Naomi Misora goes missing.
01 . 02 . 2004	Naomi Misora is killed by the power of the Death Note.
01 . 05 . 2004	L views security tapes of FBI agents dying.
01 . 08 . 2004	The Yagami family is put under surveillance by L.
	A fake news bulletin announces 1,500 Kira investigators are coming to Japan.
	Embezzler, purse-snatcher are killed by the power of the Death Note.
01 . 10 . 2004	Three small-time thieves are killed by the power of the Death Note.
01 . 12 . 2004	L decides to end surveillance at the Yagami home.
01 . 17 . 2004	Light Yagami and L see each other at university exam hall.
01 . 21 . 2004	Beyond Birthday is killed by the power of the Death Note.

record of 12.21.2003

Naomi Misora Goes Missing After Contact with Light Yagami

OTHERS' ACTIONS

1.2004

KIRA CAN KILL PEOPLE USING MEANS OTHER THAN HEART ATTACKS.
WHO IS THIS WOMAN ...?

The woman Light runs into at NPA headquarters was the fiancée of the FBI agent he killed. Light fears Naomi will go to L and kills her with the notebook.

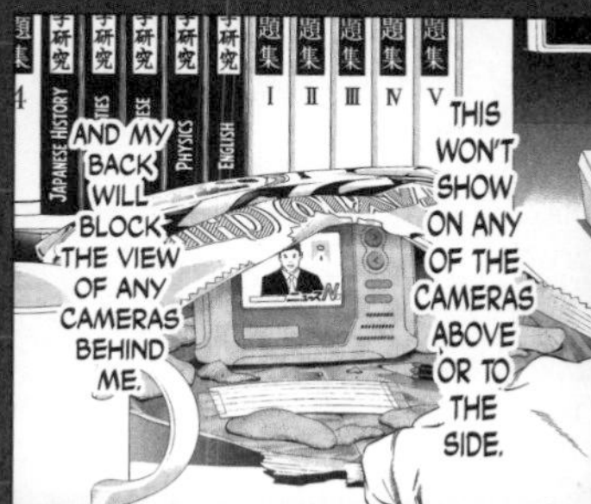

THIS WON'T SHOW ON ANY OF THE CAMERAS ABOVE OR TO THE SIDE.
AND MY BACK WILL BLOCK THE VIEW OF ANY CAMERAS BEHIND ME.

KIRA'S ACTIONS

Aware of the Hidden Cameras, Light Uses Them to His Advantage

1.8.2004

. determines that there could be a Kira suspect among the Yagami nd Kitamura families, whom Raye was investigating. L sets up idden cameras in both homes, but Light quickly notices and uses hem to deect suspicion.

DEATH COLUMN

The Women in Light Yagami's Life

True to his comment about being popular with girls, Light never has trouble attracting women. The girls he's been close to are: Yuri, Mayu, Shiho, Emi, Kiyomi Takada and Misa Amane. Yuri is the girl he uses to help uncover Raye Penber's identity, and Shiho and Emi are girls he kisses (with Ryuk watching). He meets Takada and Misa while he's in college. The only remaining girl is Mayu but...nothing about her is known. It is assumed that, as with Yuri, he met her in high school.

GOSH, I HAVEN'T BEEN TO SPACELAND SINCE JUNIOR HIGH. THIS IS GONNA BE FUN!
PLUS, I GET YOU ALL TO MYSELF TODAY, LIGHT...
UH, YEAH ...

I'M GOING TO BE THE GOD OF THAT NEW WORLD, AND YOU'LL BE THE GODDESS.
YAGAMI...

↑ It is assumed that Light was on close terms with Yuri even before he gained the Death Note.

→ His relationship with Takada is full of adult issues.

◎ Story Commentary

04.23.2004

L'S ACTIONS

First Contact with Light at To-Oh University

4.3.2004

Though Light has an alibi, L senses that something about him is too perfect and decides to investigate Light himself. He enters the same university as Light under a fake name and reveals himself as L during the middle of the entrance ceremony. He succeeds in dealing a humiliating blow to Light.

MISA'S ACTIONS

Videotapes Said to Be Messages from Kira Arrive at Sakura TV

4.13.2004

Misa, who supports Kira, sends four videotapes to Sakura TV in the hope that doing so will lead to a meeting with Kira. A producer there named Demegawa believes the tapes are from the real Kira and pushes to have them broadcast.

"IF YOU DO NOT BROADCAST THESE TAPES AS INSTRUCTED, I WILL KILL YOUR COMPANY'S BOARD OF DIRECTORS ONE BY ONE, STARTING WITH THE PRESIDENT"...
IF I DON'T... BROADCAST THESE TAPES...? ARE YOU KIDDING ME...? *SHEESH*, IF THESE ARE REAL, THIS IS GOING TO BE INSANE...
WOOH, MAN. I'M SO STOKED. I THINK I'M HAVING A HEART ATTACK...
Panasonic
2

CHRONOLOGY

04 . 05 . 2004	Light Yagami starts school at To-Oh University.
04 . 07 . 2004	Light Yagami and L play a game of tennis.
	Soichiro Yagami collapses due to stress.
04 . 13 . 2004	The Second Kira's videos are received at Sakura TV.
04 . 17 . 2004	The Second Kira begins planned action.
	Seiichi and Seiji Machiba are killed by the power of the Second Kira's Death Note.
04 . 18 . 2004	The Second Kira's video is broadcast by Sakura TV; Kazuhiko Hibima and others are killed.
	Investigator Ukita is killed by the power of the Second Kira's Death Note.
	Soichiro Yagami crashes armored truck into Sakura TV.
04 . 22 . 2004	The police release video stating refusal to aid the Second Kira.
	Heads of state demand L appear on television.
04 . 23 . 2004	L announces possibility of a Second Kira.
	Light Yagami passes L's test and joins team of investigators.
	L broadcasts fake Kira message aimed at the Second Kira.

record of 01.22.2004

DEATH COLUMN / The Meeting Between Misa and Rem

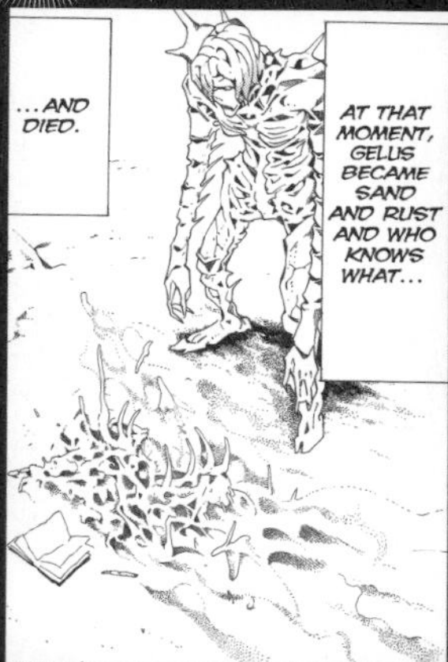

...AND DIED.
AT THAT MOMENT, GELUS BECAME SAND AND RUST AND WHO KNOWS WHAT...

⬆ Does Rem become attached to Misa because she's female? Or because she shares Gelus's feelings...?

Gelus, a Shinigami that had fallen in love with Misa Amane, writes the name of the man fated to kill her into his Death Note. For thus breaking the Shinigami rules, Gelus is destroyed. Rem, who witnesses this, decides that Gelus's Death Note should now belong to Misa, the one who received his life. Whether that was a wise choice, nobody knows.

CHRONOLOGY

05 . 19 . 2003	Misa Amane's parents are murdered by a burglar.
01 . 28 . 2004	Misa Amane's modeling career begins in the March issue of *Eighteen*.
02 .02 . 2004	The killer of Misa Amane's parents is killed by the power of the Death Note.
03 . 12 . 2004	Misa Amane is attacked by a stalker. The Shinigami Gelus falls in love with her and dies.
03 . 20 . 2004	Misa Amane gains the Death Note and meets Rem.
04 . 02 . 2004	Misa Amane comes to Tokyo.

OTHERS' ACTIONS — Soichiro Yagami Recovers Tapes from Sakura TV

4.18.2004

The tapes broadcast on Sakura TV contain a bold message from Kira. Soichiro Yagami had been hospitalized with fatigue but, unable to stay in bed, he rams a truck into the TV station and succeeds in recovering the tapes.

HAND IT OVER!
YOU DO THAT, AT LEAST YOU WON'T BE KILLED THIS VERY MINUTE!
WHAT THE... HECK DO YOU THINK YOU'RE DOING?! HEY!! ARE YOU CRAZY?!
Chak

THANK YOU, YAGAMI-KUN.
NOT AT ALL, RYUGA. I WANT TO CATCH KIRA AS MUCH AS YOU DO.

KIRA'S ACTIONS — Joins L and the Task Force

4.23.2004

Due to his being a suspect and to his impressive reasoning ability, Light is asked by L to join the investigation. By coming to the same conclusion as L that the person who sent the videotapes to Sakura TV was a Second Kira, Light gains the trust of the team. Nonetheless, L makes Light create a fake message from the real Kira to send to the Second Kira.

◎ Story Commentary

06.07.2004

FIRST I'LL LOOK FOR SOMEONE HOLDING A NOTBOOK. THEN IF I CAN TOUCH IT WITHOUT HIM NOTICING...

KIRA'S ACTIONS

Attempted Contact with the Second Kira

22.2004

While Light is deciding how to uncover the Second Kira before L does, a diary from the Second Kira arrives. It contains a message, written in a way that only the two Kiras could understand, suggesting that both sides show each other their notebooks. Light heads to Aoyama on the scheduled day but finds nothing.

MISA'S ACTIONS

Into Light Yagami's Home

5.25.2004

After seeing the police announcement urging the Second Kira to surrender, Misa heads to the Yagami residence so that Light will not worry. There she gives her notebook to Light and asks him to make her his girlfriend. Light reluctantly agrees, but...

CHRONOLOGY

04 . 25 . 2004	Video #2 from the Second Kira arrives. Hearing the word "Shinigami," L falls out of his chair.
05 . 12 . 2004	A mysterious diary arrives from the Second Kira.
05 . 22 . 2004	Misa Amane locates Light Yagami in Aoyama.
05 . 23 . 2004	Misa Amane mails video to Sakura TV.
05 . 25 . 2004	Misa Amane's message about finding Kira is broadcast. L broadcasts a message urging the Second Kira to work with the police. Misa Amane goes to Light Yagami's house and reveals her identity.
05 . 26 . 2004	Sayu Yagami gets ¥5,000 from Light for not telling anyone about Misa Amane.
05 . 27 . 2004	Light begins seeing Miss To-Oh, Kiyomi Takada. They take classes together. L tells Light Yagami that he is his first friend. Misa Amane comes over to see Light Yagami for a second time.
05 . 28 . 2004	L arrests Misa Amane at the university. Misa Amane's manager is arrested on drug charges.
05 . 31 . 2004	Misa Amane gives up ownership of the Death Note.
06 . 01 . 2004	Light Yagami gives up ownership of Rem's Death Note. Light Yagami announces he may be Kira and begins confinement. Soichiro Yagami also begins confinement.
06 . 03 . 2004	Third day of confinement.
06 . 05 . 2004	Fifth day of confinement.
06 . 07 . 2004	Seventh day of confinement. Light Yagami gives up ownership of Ryuk's Death Note and loses his memories of being Kira. Ryuk leaves the human world.

record of 04.24.2004

L'S ACTIONS

Misa Amane Arrested as the Second Kira

6.23.2004

soon thinks that Kira and the Second Kira have joined forces. Suspecting Misa, who has recently started hanging around ight, L has Watari search her home. A large amount of evidence mplicating Misa as the Second Kira is soon recovered.

KIRA'S ACTIONS

Gives Up the Death Note While Imprisoned

6.7.2004

Light adds a fake rule in the notebook stating that a person who doesn't write down a name within 13 days will die. This is the most important trick he devises to protect himself, and once he sets everything in place he has L put him into confinement. Seven days later, he gives up ownership of the Death Note and loses his memories of being Kira.

DEATH COLUMN / Memory Loss After Giving Up the Death Note

YOUR MEMORIES OF KILLING WITH THE NOTEBOOK, AND OF LIGHT YAGAMI AS KIRA, WILL VANISH. YOU WON'T BE ABLE TO BETRAY ANY SECRETS...
AND WHILE YOU WILL BE NO LONGER BE ABLE TO SEE ME OR RYUK...
...YOUR LOVE FOR LIGHT YAGAMI, THAT EMOTION WILL REMAIN. I TOLD THIS TO MISA...

↑ After losing her memories connected to the notebook, Misa doesn't remember that she found Light in Aoyama using the Shinigami Eyes. Her memory has been altered so that she only remembers seeing Light and falling in love with him at first sight.

The reason Light induces L to put him in confinement is to take advantage of the rule that those who give up ownership of the Death Note lose all memory related to it. Thus he has no fear of saying anything incriminating, and if the confinement lasts long enough the others will think the fake 13-Day Rule will come into effect. Also, Light's memories relating to Naomi and Raye are altered to make sense to him. Had Light honestly told L about those memories, a different ending may have awaited the two...

◎ Story Commentary

10.08.2004

YOTSUBA'S ACTIONS

The Yotsuba Kira Gains the Death Note and Begins His Scheme

6.11.2004

On July 16th, 2004, Rem follows Light's instructions and gives the notebook to a human with status who will use it for his own gain. Higuchi, who would later be revealed as the Yotsuba Kira, begins acting as Kira from this day.

L & LIGHT'S ACTIONS

Light Yagami Rejoins the Task Force and Begins Investigating Kira

7.2.2004

After fty days in confinement, Aizawa's pleas and Soichiro's test, Light and Misa are finally proven innocent. Light starts helping with the Kira investigation but is also chained to L...

CHRONOLOGY

06 . 14 . 2004	Rem gives Death Note to high-ranking Yotsuba employee Kyosuke Higuchi. The Yotsuba Kira begins operating.
06 . 15 . 2004	fifthteenth day of Light Yagami and Misa Amane's confinement.
07 . 20 . 2004	fiftieth day of confinement. L tells Soichiro Yagami his conclusions.
07 . 23 . 2004	Light Yagami and Misa Amane are released. Light Yagami and L begin to investigate as a team.
08 . 01 . 2004	The investigation headquarters are moved to a special facility built by L.
08 . 02 . 2004	The first big fight between Light Yagami and L. Misa Amane garners first place in *Eighteen* magazine fan voting.
08 . 03 . 2004	Misa Amane is announced as starring in director Nishinaka's newest movie.
10 . 01 . 2004	Confirmation of Yotsuba group's stock rise.
10 . 02 . 2004	Soichiro Yagami is told by his superiors to quit the investigation. Soichiro, Mogi, Matsuda quit the NPA.
10 . 04 . 2004	Aiber and Wedy are contacted.
10 . 07 . 2004	Aiber and Wedy join the team on L's request.
10 . 08 . 2004	Matsuda presents Misa Amane to high-ranking Yotsuba employees. Matsuda falls off the balcony of Misa Amane's apartment (the investigation headquarters).

record of 06.08.2004

DEATH COLUMN / Those Killed by the Yotsuba Kira

Aside from the criminals broadcast on TV, whom he promised Rem he would kill, Kyosuke Higuchi mostly kills people connected to competitors of the Yotsuba Group. The targets are chosen by eight young, high-ranking Yotsuba employees who hold weekly meetings. However, so that the killings won't stand out too much, they also kill some employees within their own company. Light soon uncovers all this, but it also could be the case that the Death Note was just too much for a guy like Higuchi to handle.

GINZO KANEBOSHI, BIG TIME LOAN SHARK. HE'S FAMOUS FOR COMMITTING VILE ACTS IN ORDER TO COLLECT HIS MONEY.

↑ Ginzo Kaneboshi is killed by Rem while Misa is investigating Higuchi. In some ways, he's also a victim of the Yotsuba Kira.

CHRONOLOGY

06 . 19 . 2004	Koutarou Ashimoto is killed by the power of the Yotsuba Kira's Death Note.
06 . 26 . 2004	Kenji Tanimi is killed by the power of the Yotsuba Kira's Death Note.
06 . 27 . 2004	Roppei Tamiya is killed by the power of the Yotsuba Kira's Death Note.
07 . 02 . 2004	Kouji Aoi is killed by the power of the Yotsuba Kira's Death Note.
07 . 04 . 2004	Tatsuya Kawajima is killed by the power of the Yotsuba Kira's Death Note.
07 . 30 . 2004	Takeyoshi Moriya is killed by the power of the Yotsuba Kira's Death Note.
09 . 10 . 2004	Junichi Yaibe is killed by the power of the Yotsuba Kira's Death Note.
10 . 01 . 2004	Tokio Yokoda, controlled by the Yotsuba Kira's Death Note, commits embezzlement and then dies.
10 . 28 . 2004	Yukito Shiraba is killed by the power of the Yotsuba Kira's Death Note.

I'M AIBER, PROFESSIONAL CON ARTIST. NICE TO MEET YOU.
WEDY, I'M A THIEF.

L'S ACTIONS — Aiber and Wedy Join the Task Force

10.7.2004

Light and the others surmise that the Third Kira is connected to the Yotsuba Group. However, with pressure being put on them by the government, they are no longer allowed to continue the investigation. Soichiro, Mogi and Matsuda decide to quit their jobs as government employees to continue working with L, but Aizawa returns to the NPA. Seeing that they need help, L recruits Aiber and Wedy.

OTHERS' ACTIONS — Matsuda Fakes His Own Death to Avoid the Yotsuba Kira

10.8.2004

he team plots a strategy with the new members, but it's all uined when Matsuda breaks into the Yotsuba headquarters on is own. He uncovers the connection of the eight high-ranking members to Kira, but to avoid being killed he is forced to fake is own death.

HEY, YOU'RE DRUNK. BE CAREFUL!
WHOA...

◎ Story Commentary

10.25.2004

HELLO
I BELIEVE YOU HIRED ME FOR A JOB.

OTHERS' ACTIONS

Aiber Contacts Yotsuba as Eraldo Coil

10.12.2004

In order to rid themselves of the troublesome L, Yotsuba hires Eraldo Coil, a detective famous for his ability to track people down. However, "Eraldo Coil" is one of L's aliases, and Aiber uses this to get in contact with Yotsuba. Not knowing that they are being tricked, Yostuba hands over five million dollars.

I'M L.
L?! IMPOSSIBLE!.. IT CAN'T BE!..

L & LIGHT'S ACTIONS

The Call and the Deal with Namikawa During the Meetings of Death

10.15.2004

The team succeeds in bugging the Yotsuba meetings. Wanting to end the murders, Light contacts Namikawa, who they do not believe is Kira, and posing as L has him delay the planned killings. Even L is impressed with this move by Light.

CHRONOLOGY

10 . 12 . 2004	Aiber, acting as detective Eraldo Coil, contacts Yostuba employee Masahiko Kida.
	Yostuba Kira meeting is held.
	The Yotsuba Kira members agree to pay Coil.
10 . 13 . 2004	Arayoshi Hatori is killed by the power of the Yotsuba Kira's Death Note.
10 . 15 .2004	Yotsuba Kira meeting is held.
	Posing as L, Light Yagami contacts Yotsuba employee Reiji Namikawa and offers him a deal.
10 . 21 . 2004	At a Yotsuba Kira meeting the group demands that Coil join them.
10 . 22 . 2004	Mogi takes over for Matsuda as Misa Amane's manager.
10 . 24 . 2004	Misa Amane is reunited with Rem inside the Yotsuba building.
10 .25 . 2004	Misa Amane goes for a drive with Kyosuke Higuchi while wearing a nurse's outfit.
	At the request of Misa Amane, Rem kills Ginzo Kaneboshi with the Death Note.
	Thanks to Misa Amane's recordings, the team determines that Kyosuke Higuchi is the Yotsuba Kira.

record of 10.09.2004

I AM ON YOUR SIDE.
ON MY SIDE...? THIS THING...? EWW...

MISA'S ACTIONS

Reunion with Rem

10.24.2004

L's plan is to use Misa as bait for Kira. With Aiber, he succeeds in getting the high-ranking Yotsuba employees to become interested in hiring Misa as a model. Misa then is reunited with Rem, who is attached to the Yotsuba Kira, but...

L & LIGHT'S ACTIONS

Yotsuba Kira Confirmed as Higuchi

10.25.2004

YAY!
THAT WOULD BE TRUE.
...HIGUCHI HAS THE POWER OF KIRA. THAT IS CLEAR.

isa is told by Rem that she and Light used to both be Kira. earning that handing over the notebook to the Yotsuba Kira was ll part of Light's plan, Misa acts on her own and contacts Higuchi. he records him admitting that he is Kira and passes this on to the nvestigation team. L confirms that Higuchi is Kira and comes up vith a plan to arrest him.

DEATH COLUMN / What Is the Yotsuba Group?

YOTSUBA GROUP'S MAIN TOKYO OFFICE...
THEN HOW ARE WE GOING TO MAKE THE MOVIE?
WE'LL JUST ACT LIKE WE'RE KISSING.

With over 300,000 employees involved in everything from heavy industry to resort development, Yotsuba is a massive corporate conglomerate. Powerful enough even to buy military weapons, Yotsuba increases its influence further with the "Meetings of Death." But after April 10th, 2005, when six high-ranking members are killed, rumors begin to swirl. This causes Yotsuba's stock to plummet and greatly reduces its status as a first-class company.

BUT IF I CAN JUST GET BY THIS SECURITY GUARD...
RETURN VISITOR BADGES
SOME-ONE HERE TOO...

←↑ The giant Yotsuba main office building. However, according to Wedy, their security is very lax.

◎ Story Commentary

11.05.2004

The Plan to Catch the Yotsuba Kira Begins

10.2.2004

L & LIGHT'S ACTIONS

IS HE GOING TO GO?

The plan relies on Matsuda appearing on a television program and saying that he will reveal Kira's identity, thus forcing Higuchi to try and stop him. Higuchi falls for it and is apprehended with Aizawa's help.

KIRA'S ACTIONS

EXACTLY AS PLANNED!
DEATH NOTE

Light Yagami Regains His Memories as Kira

10.29.2004

Light gets his hands on the Death Note that Higuchi had and regains his memories. Some unexpected things happen but he succeeds in killing Higuchi with the piece of the notebook he has hidden in his watch. Light regains ownership of his notebook.

CHRONOLOGY

10 . 28 . 2004	The plan to arrest Kyosuke Higuchi begins at Sakura TV.
	L confirms the existence of Shinigami and the Death Note.
	Kyosuke Higuchi is killed by the power of Light Yagami's Death Note.
10 . 30 . 2004	Misa Amane is released from the investigation headquarters.
11 . 04 . 2004	Misa Amane finds the Death Note Light had buried.
	Ryuk returns to the human world in order to possess Misa Amane.
	Misa Amane regains the Shinigami Eyes by making another trade with Ryuk.
	The Kira murders resume, with Misa taking over.
11 . 05 . 2004	Watari and L are killed by the power of Rem's Death Note.
	Light Yagami gains Rem's Death Note.

record of 10.26.2004

DEATH COLUMN / Rem, the Shinigami Manipulated by Light Yagami

Taking advantage of Misa's devotion to him, Light has her continue the killing of criminals after the Yotsuba Kira dies. Rem soon realizes that at this rate Misa will be captured by L and that the only way to prevent this is to kill L. Rem figures out this was all part of Light's plan, but with Misa's happiness on her mind she kills both L and Watari. Thus Rem, who had feelings for Misa, dies by her own hand.

THIS IS MISA'S HAPPINESS, TO BE WITH LIGHT YAGAMI...
BUT LIGHT YAGAMI... TO KILL EVEN A SHINIGAMI... HE'S SURPASSED THE SHINIGAMI...

↑ Rem dies right after killing Watari and L. Light later picks up her Death Note and gains ownership of it.

↓ The most important thing to Rem is for Misa to live happily. She's always prepared to give up her life to make that happen.

IF YOU DON'T SAVE MISA, I'LL KILL YOU.

MISA'S ACTIONS — Regaining Her Memory as the Second Kira

11.4.2004

On Light's orders, Misa digs up the buried Death Note and regains her lost memories. In order to be useful to Light, she trades for the Shinigami Eyes with Ryuk and takes on the role of Kira once again.

L'S ACTIONS — Dies Along with Watari by Rem's Hand

11.5.

HEY, RYU-ZAKI!!

lthough he believes that Light and Misa are Kira, L can't prove t because of the fake 13-Day Rule. His name is written into the Death Note by Rem and he dies a sad death, as does Watari. This is the moment of L's defeat.

◎ Intermission Commentary

The World Quietly Accepts Kira

State of the World

New Rules Against Broadcasting the Identities of Criminals, but the Killings Do Not Stop

L demands that the police and media stop revealing criminals' names and faces. The whole world agrees to this, but the dissemination of information on criminals switches to the Internet, which is hard to regulate. And so Kira's judgment continues uninterrupted...

Summer, 2009. Kira's judgment starts gaining momentum.
The world's reaction to Kira is divided among those who scream in fear and those who cheer him on. More and more, the latter are emerging.

↑ Despite Kira's attempt to eradicate evil, many criminals still exist. Countries that support Kira begin to emerge, and Kira becomes more and more accepted.

11.06.2004–10.07.2009

CHRONOLOGY

11 . 15 . 2004	Soichiro Yagami convinces superiors to continue the Kira investigation.
	Light Yagami takes over as "L" at the request of the investigation team.
	Light Yagami begins living with Misa Amane.
12 . 05 . 2004	Roger, the director of Wammy's House, confirms L's and Watari's deaths.
	Mello and Near are told of L's death by Roger.
	Mello leaves Wammy's House.
01 . 10 . 2005	Wedy (real name: Mary Kenwood) is killed by the power of the Death Note.
04 . 07 . 2005	Aiber (real name: Thierry Morello) is killed by the power of the Death Note.
04 . 10 . 2005	Six high-ranking Yotsuba employees are killed by the power of the Death Note.
05 . 01 . 2005	L creates new rules for police and media forbidding the release of criminals' identities.
05 . 15 . 2005	Confidential information on criminals begins flooding the Internet.
03 . 05 . 2009	Near relays the results of his Kira investigation to the U.S. president.
	Near reveals L's death and the existence of the Death Note.
03 . 12 . 2009	The SPK (Special Provision for Kira) is created.
04 . 01 . 2009	Light Yagami enters the NPA as an agent in the Intelligence and Information Bureau.

Light Yagami's Actions

Moving the World as Both L and Kira

At the request of the Japanese task force, Light takes over its leadership as the Second L. Suggesting that the original L's defeat was caused by his reckless challenging of Kira, Light fights Kira without taking any bold action. In 2009, Light enters the NPA and gains direct access to information on criminals, becoming even more aggressive in his actions as Kira. Everything goes exactly as he planned.

April, 2009. Light Yagami, age 23, enters the National Police Agency and is assigned to the Intelligence and Information Bureau.

←Light becomes an officer in the Intelligence and Information Bureau. This enables him to gather information on criminals and release it onto the Internet.

INTERMISSION

Others' Actions

The SPK Is Created to Go After Kira

Near, who knows of L's death, investigated the Kira case himself, and together with the Director of the FBI makes his report to the president of the United States. The SPK is created and a new part of the story begins.

LET'S JUST SAY... HE'S L'S TRUE SUCCESSOR.

←The newly created anti-Kira task force, the SPK, is filled with members of the CIA and FBI, and has no connection to the Second L.

And then…

© Story Commentary

10.13.2009

NPA Director Takimura's Kidnapping

MELLO'S ACTIONS

SO THE JAPANESE POLICE ARE SO AFRAID OF KIRA THAT THE ONLY ONES ACTUALLY WORKING WITH L ARE SOICHIRO YAGAMI, KANZO MOGI, AND TOTA MATSUDA...
...THAT RIGHT?
YEAH... THERE WAS ANOTHER GUY NAMED UKITA, BUT HE DIED...

Director Takimura is abducted by mafia members working under Mello. Meanwhile, the FBI requests that the Death Note be handed over to the American government

Sayu Yagami's Kidnapping

MELLO'S ACTIONS

After Director Takimura commits suicide, Mello goes after the families of the task force members and targets Sayu Yagami. With this act, the team is forced to accept a trade for the Death Note.

CHRONOLOGY

10 . 08 . 2009	NPA Director Kanichi Takimura is abducted by mafia members working under Mello.
10 . 11 . 2009	FBI agent John McEnroe demands the Death Note be handed over to the U.S.
	Kanichi Takimura commits suicide (controlled by the Death Note?).
	Sayu Yagami is kidnapped by the mafia.
10 . 12 . 2009	The kidnappers instruct the task force to bring the Death Note to L.A.
	Light Yagami talks to Near by phone for the first time.
10 . 13 . 2009	Light Yagami and Misa Amane arrive in L.A. The other members join them later.
	Flight SE333 out of Narita is hijacked by the mafia.
	Soichiro Yagami exchanges the Death Note for Sayu.
	The mafia get their hands on the Death Note.
	Zakk Irius and the other hijackers are all killed to keep them from talking.
	Most SPK members are killed by the power of the Death Note.
	Light Yagami and Near exchange information.

record of 10.08.2009

The Japanese Task Force Sets Up in L.A.

OTHERS' ACTIONS

10.13.2

ANYWAY, WE SHOULD CONTACT THE FBI AND ASK FOR THEIR HELP. IT'S HAPPENING IN L.A. AND THEY'VE ALREADY COME FORWARD SAYING THAT THEY'RE WILLING TO COOPERATE WITH US.
RIGHT.
YEAH, THE AMERICANS WILL BE ABLE TO USE THEIR SATELLITES TO WATCH AROUND THE HOTEL.

n order to exchange the Death Note for Sayu Yagami, oichiro is asked to come to Los Angeles. Complying vith that request, the task force prepares to head to merica.

KIRA HAS THE ABILITY TO KILL OTHERS JUST BY SEEING THEIR FACES.
BUT WE CAN'T KILL PEOPLE THE SAME WAY KIRA DOES.

Mello Gains the Death Note

MELLO'S ACTIONS

0.13.2009

The task force members travel to Los Angeles separately. However, Mello foresaw this and the mafia nabs Soichiro with an elaborate plan. In the end, Mello gets his hands on the Death Note.

DEATH COLUMN / Mello's Plan to Get the Death Note

In order to get the Death Note from the Japanese police, Mello plots extensively. He stations his men at the airport to force Soichiro onto flight SE333, after having bought off the pilot. Then he has the plane land in the remote desert and makes the trade underground, where satellite cameras can't reach. And finally, he loads the Death Note onto an untraceable missile. All that's left is to recover the remains after it hits the ocean. Also, he has all the men involved directly in the trade killed.

↑ The missile that carries the Death Note. Its remains are found in New York harbor.

↓ Entrance to an underground passage that was used in trades by another organization.

THAT'S THE ENTRANCE, YAGAMI. GO IN.

◎ Story Commentary

10.27.2009

KIRA'S ACTIONS

Confirms That Mello and Near Are L's Heirs

After beginning communication with "N" of the SPK, Light learns that the kidnapper is Mello and that "N" is Near, and that they're two young men who were raised at the same orphanage as the original L. While their actions differ from L's, their aim is to succeed him. Light quickly realizes that he must kill them both.

MELLO'S ACTIONS

Threatening the President

Confident now that he has the Death Note, Mello confronts the U.S. president directly and demands the information that the SPK has. The president has no choice but to comply.

S-STOP JOKING AROUND! IF YOU DO THAT, YOU'LL START WORLD WAR THREE!
THAT'S RIGHT.
SO YOU'VE GOT NO CHOICE BUT TO LISTEN TO US.

CHRONOLOGY

10 . 14 . 2009	Aizawa and Matsuda learn about Wammy's House from Roger.
10 . 15 . 2009	Light Yagami confirms that Mello and Near are L's successors.
10 . 18 . 2009	Mello calls Soichiro and demands the identity of the current L.
	Near admits his identity to the Japanese task force.
	Mello demands cooperation of U.S. president.
	Light Yagami determines that the current Death Note owner is Kal Snydar.
	Kal Snydar trades for the Shinigami Eyes with Sidoh.
10 . 19 . 2009	Special forces captain "Joe" arrives at White House.
	Light Yagami shares his plan with the president and the special forces captain.
10 . 23 . 2009	Kal Snydar is compelled by the Death Note to reveal the location of Mello's base to Light Yagami.
10 . 27 . 2009	The special forces squad storms the L.A. mafia base.
	The squad is wiped out by the power of the Death Note.
	Misa Amane retires from the entertainment industry at Light Yagami's request.
	U.S. president David Hoope kills himself by the power of the Death Note.

record of 10.14.2009

DEATH COLUMN / Sidoh, the Third Shinigami, and His Effects on the Human World

Sidoh comes down to the human world to retrieve his Death Note but is overwhelmed by Mello and becomes the mafia's servant. Because of the unexpected existence of Sidoh, the attack by the president's special forces squad ends in failure. Not that it would have been possible for him to have anticipated Sidoh's existence, but this was a rare opportunity to see Light lose his cool in front of others.

🡅 Many incidents would not have happened had Sidoh not lost his Death Note.

CHRONOLOGY

10 . 13 . 2009	The Shinigami Sidoh comes down to the human world to search for Ryuk and his own Death Note.
10 . 18 . 2009	Sidoh locates the mafia hideout.
10 . 27 . 2009	Sidoh removes the helmets of the attacking special forces squad so that Kal Snydar can see the soldiers' names.
11 . 10 . 2009	On Ryuk's advice, Sidoh stays quiet as the Japanese task force storms Mello's new hideout.
11 . 11 . 2009	Sidoh regains his Death Note and returns to the Shinigami realm.

KIRA'S ACTIONS

Ordering the President and His Special Forces

10.19.200

Having been threatened by Mello, the U.S. president contacts the Second L. Light figures out the situation instantly and wins the trust of the president while coming up with a plan to eliminate Mello. With the support of the president, Light prepares his plan.

The President's Task Force Storms the Mafia Base but Fails

OTHERS' ACTIONS

.27.2009

Light completes his preparations by getting the owner of the notebook to reveal the location of Mello's base. But when the attack commences, the plan fails due to the Shinigami Sidoh assisting Mello. The entire squad is wiped out...

◎ Story Commentary

11.23.2009

Sending the Death Note to the Japanese Task Force

KIRA'S ACTIONS

11.11.2009

Light's next plan for regaining the notebook is to team up with the Japanese task force. In order to do so, he hands his notebook over to the team members.

OTHERS' ACTIONS

The Japanese Task Force Storms the Mafia Base

11.10.2009

Having borrowed Kira's notebook, Soichiro trades for the Shinigami Eyes, and the team attacks the mafia base to get back the notebook and kill Mello. Soichiro faces off with Mello but is unable to kill him. He is then shot by one of Mello's men and dies later in the hospital.

CHRONOLOGY

10 . 28 . 2009	Light Yagami keeps Misa Amane's Death Note, hiding it under his clothes.
	Light Yagami returns his Death Note to Ryuk and gives up ownership.
	Light Yagami explains his plan to Misa Amane and Ryuk.
10 . 30 . 2009	Soichiro Yagami receives a call from Kira on his cell phone requesting the retrieval of the Death Note.
11 . 01 . 2009	The Death Note from Kira arrives at the Japanese task force headquarters.
11 . 07 . 2009	The Japanese task force locates Mello's whereabouts.
11 . 10 . 2009	The task force surrounds Mello's base.
	Soichiro Yagami makes the Eye Trade with Ryuk.
	Most of the mafia members are killed by the power of the Death Note.
	The task force storms Mello's base.
11 . 11 . 2009	The task force retrieves the Death Note.
	Mello's real name is revealed.
	Mello blows up his base and escapes.
	Soichiro Yagami dies from gunshot wounds.
11 . 18 . 2009	Near suspects the Second L of being Kira.
	The American vice-president announces the country's acceptance of Kira.
11 . 19 . 2009	With America's announcement, the Japanese government and those of other countries fall into chaos.
	The American vice-president announces the disbandment of the SPK.
	Mello comes to SPK headquarters and shares information with Near.
11 . 22 . 2009	Hitoshi Demegawa stars in Sakura TV program "Kira's Kingdom."
11 . 23 . 2009	Near uncovers the fake 13-Day Rule in the Death Note and questions the Second L.
	Mello requests that Mogi come to New York.
	Mogi is guided by Mello to the SPK headquarters.

record of 10.28.2009

NEAR'S ACTIONS

Concludes That the Second L Is Kira

11.18

...THE NEW L IS KIRA.

Based on the interactions between Kira and the task force, Near concludes that the second L is in fact Kira. But the vice-president announces that the U.S. government will no longer pursue Kira and closes the SPK down.

AND IF THE MAJORITY OF THE PUBLIC OPINION HAPPENS TO BE AGAINST KIRA, THEN KIRA WILL JUST FADE AWAY AND BECOME A THING OF THE PAST.
...AND I SEE NO REASON NOT TO. AS A MATTER OF FACT, WE SHOULD ARGUE OVER IT.

KIRA'S ACTIONS

Demegawa Chosen as Kira's Spokesperson

.22.2009

With America's acceptance of Kira, Light decides it's time for the public to hear Kira's ideals. Demegawa, having gained a reputation as a Kira supporter, is chosen to be Kira's mouthpiece. Demegawa tells the world that those who try to capture Kira are evil and will be punished.

DEATH COLUMN / How Near Figures Out That Light Is Kira

From the beginning, based on their lack of results in the Kira investigation, Near has his doubts about the Japanese task force and the Second L. After the assault on Mello's base, Near becomes confident that the second L is Kira. Believing, as the original L had, that the way to defeat Kira is to put him in a position where he can make no excuses, Near carries on L's legacy and plans his moves.

...SEVEN PERCENT SERIOUS.

↑ Near uses the same methods of deduction as the original L to arrive at his suspect's identity, even if he has no evidence.

The Reasons Why Near Thinks Light Yagami (the Second L) Is Kira

◎ The Kira investigation had gone nowhere since the Second L took over.
◎ Even when the Japanese task force gains a Death Note, Kira does nothing to them.
◎ After the Japanese task force retrieves the Death Note from Mello, Kira does not ask them to return the one he had sent them.
◎ After learning of the fake 13-Day Rule, Near concludes that someone in the task force used it to clear himself of suspicion.
◎ There's a Shinigami at the Japanese task force headquarters (where the Second L is).
◎ In the past, the Second L and a suspect as the Second Kira were placed under confinement by the original L. Plus, the Second L had suggested putting himself under confinement.
◎ Based on information from Shuichi Aizawa that Soichiro Yagami had threatened to kill Kira and then himself, Near theorizes that the Second L is a member of the Yagami family.
◎ Thus, the Second L is Soichiro's son, Light Yagami, and Light Yagami is Kira.
*More evidence is provided by Rester, who investigates Light Yagami's past. It's revealed that Light Yagami was close with someone resembling L and that they both disappeared after Misa Amane appeared at their university.

◎ Story Commentary

12.07.2009

OTHERS' ACTIONS

Demegawa and his Kira Worshippers Surround SPK Headquarters

11.25.2009

Near speaks to the Japanese task force in an effort to make them suspect that Light is Kira. In response, Light has a large group of Kira worshippers attack the SPK base, but the attack fails and Near escapes.

KIRA'S ACTIONS

He too had
God not only accepted him, but even granted him godly powers.

Teru Mikami Chosen as Kira's Proxy

Because of Near's prompting, Aizawa, Mogi and Ide begin to have doubts about Light. Sensing this, Light realizes that it will be risky to have Misa continue killing criminals and sends the Death Note to Teru Mikami.

11.26.2009

CHRONOLOGY

11 . 25 . 2009	Demegawa and his men surround the SPK base.
	A large amount of dollar bills are released from the sky in lower Manhattan.
	The SPK and Mogi escape the Kira worshipper mob.
11 . 26 . 2009	Light Yagami chooses Teru Mikami as his proxy.
	Near gives the task force fake news of Mogi's death by heart attack.
	Misa Amane sends her Death Note to Teru Mikami and gives up ownership. She loses all memories of Kira.
11 . 27 . 2009	Aizawa goes to the SPK to assist Near.
	Based on Aizawa's statements, Near figures out the Second L is Light Yagami.
	Teru Mikami receives the Death Note and begins activity as Kira.
	Matt is contacted by Mello and agrees to help him.
	Anthony Rester heads to Japan to investigate Light Yagami.
	Aizawa and Mogi return from the SPK.
	Mello and Matt begin following Aizawa, Mogi and Misa.
	Teru Mikami does the Eye Trade with Ryuk.
	Demegawa and his "Kira's Kingdom" executives are killed by the power of Teru Mikami's Death Note.
12 . 01 . 2009	Rester tells Near the results of his investigation into Light Yagami.
	Teru Mikami appeals to Kira on the "Kira's Kingdom" show.
12 . 05 . 2009	NHN reporter Kiyomi Takada is chosen as Kira's spokesperson.
	Light Yagami suggests the task force should head back to Japan in order to investigate Kiyomi Takada.
12 . 06 . 2009	Light Yagami has a secret meeting with Kiyomi Takada at the Imperial Hotel.
12 . 07 . 2009	Kiyomi Takada airs her own opinions as Kira's representative, on the suggestion of Light Yagami.
	Light Yagami and Teru Mikami talk by phone for the first time and discuss how future judgments will be handed down.
	Light Yagami reveals to Kiyomi Takada that he is Kira.

record of 11.24.2009

DEATH COLUMN / Misa Amane vs. Kiyomi Takada: The Battle of Women

OH, LITTLE KIYOMI, I HAPPEN TO BE OLDER THAN YOU.
I SHOULD HAVE WAITED TO INVITE YOU TO DINNER UNTIL AFTER YOU GREW UP AND LEARNED SOME MANNERS, AMANE.

↑ Takada's dislike of Misa. Several times during her meetings with Light, she suggests killing Misa. Scary!

→ Misa grinning over potential trouble for Takada. Small-minded…

Light's only reason for meeting with Kiyomi Takada is to be able to contact Mikami. Takada reveres Light, who happens to be behind the movement she supports. Because of this, Light becomes even colder towards Misa. Realizing that she has a rival, Misa prepares to strike back. Does the fact that Takada died first mean that she lost this battle?

...
OH WELL... I GUESS KIYOMI'S ANGRY AT ME AGAIN, BUT THIS'LL TEACH HER A LESSON. SHE'S LOST FACE NOW AS THE HOST OF THE SHOW!

X-KIRA'S ACTIONS: Makes Kiyomi Takada Kira's Spokesperson

12.5.2009

After receiving the Death Note from Light, Mikami kills Demegawa, who had gotten out of hand. Mikami realizes that Kira is in a position where he cannot act, but he decides that it's important to keep spreading Kira's ideals. After seeking Kira's advice on TV, he chooses NHN announcer Kiyomi Takada as the new Kira representative.

...PEOPLE WITH AN ABILITY WHO DO NOT USE THAT ABILITY FOR THE GOOD OF SOCIETY WILL ALSO NOT BE TOLERATED.
REAL?
WHAT...?

ARE YOU GOD?
GOOD!!
GOD!! KIRA...!

KIRA'S ACTIONS: Contact with Teru Mikami and Correction of Ideals

Wanting to correct Mikami, who has been veering away from Kira's ideals, Light contacts Kiyomi Takada while making it appear that he's investigating the Kira case. During the second meeting with Takada, he succeeds in talking to Mikami on the phone.

◎ Story Commentary

01.25.2010

I AM IN JAPAN RIGHT NOW IN ORDER TO CAPTURE KIRA.

NEAR'S ACTIONS

Moves Headquarters to Japan

12.9.2009

Near is confident that Light Yagami is Kira but lacks evidence to prove it. Thinking that one of the few paths to Kira is through Takada, Near brings his team to Japan to begin the battle with Kira.

KIRA'S ACTIONS

DON'T WORRY, THERE'S NOTHING TO BE AFRAID OF.

Asks Kiyomi Takada to Carry Out Judgments

Light has Takada take over the killing of criminals from Mikami. He has Mikami send Takada pages from the Death Note in the form of fan mail yet continue to act as if he were killing criminals, using a fake notebook. This is one of Light's plans to dispose of Near.

12.9.2009

CHRONOLOGY

12 . 09 . 2009	Misa Amane announces her comeback with a scheduled appearance on a New Year's Eve celebrity singing show.
	Near arrives in Japan and sets up new SPK base.
	Light Yagami and Near exchange confrontational words.
	Near explains to the SPK members his theories on Kira's current situation and the team's future plans.
	Light Yagami reveals the existence of the Death Note to Takada and has her kill criminals.
12 . 14 . 2009	Halle Lidner chosen as Kiyomi Takada's bodyguard.
	Misa Amane runs into Kiyomi Takada at NHN studios.
	Near uncovers Teru Mikami.
12 . 21 . 2009	Kiyomi Takada and Misa Amane have dinner together.
	Gevanni witnesses Teru Mikami use the Death Note on a train.
	Near is convinced that Teru Mikami is the X-Kira.
12 . 22 . 2009	Light Yagami is questioned by Kiyomi Takada about Misa Amane.
	Light Yagami has Kiyomi Takada mention wanting to arrest Kira.
12 . 25 . 2009	Near focuses on whether or not Teru Mikami has a Shinigami.
	Gevanni notices Teru Mikami talking to himself.
	Aizawa checks the memo pads used by Light Yagami and Kiyomi Takada.
	Aizawa contacts Near and agrees to continue watching over L.
12 . 31 . 2009	Misa Amane and Mogi are placed in confinement by the SPK.
	Gevanni touches Teru Mikami's Death Note at the gym.
01 . 01 . 2010	After hearing from Gevanni and Mogi, Near formulates plan that will unfold over the next 24 days.
01 . 03 . 2010	Light Yagami instructs Kiyomi Takada on what to do when she receives Teru Mikami's "confirmed" message.
01 . 06 . 2010	Near orders Gevanni to take photos of Teru Mikami's Death Note.
01 . 08 . 2010	Near views photos taken by Gevanni.
01 . 21 . 2010	Near has Gevanni tamper with Teru Mikami's Death Note.
01 .22 . 2010	Near receives word from Gevanni and begins plans for direct confrontation.
01 . 23 . 2010	Light Yagami receives "confirmed" message from Teru Mikami.
01 . 24 . 2010	Gevanni checks Teru Mikami's Death Note again at the gym.
01 . 25 . 2010	Near receives report from Gevanni on Teru Mikami's use of the Death Note.
	Light Yagami is confident of victory after figuring out Near's plan.
	Near and Light Yagami decide to meet at 1 p.m. on the 28th.
	Light Yagami has Kiyomi Takada tell Teru Mikami the location of the meeting.

record of 12.08.2009

NEAR'S ACTIONS

Recognition of Teru Mikami as X-Kira

12.21.2009

On the train, Mikami takes a picture of a man harassing a woman and e-mails the man's name and photo to Takada. Soon after he writes the man's name down in the fake notebook and gets off the train before the man dies. To Gevanni, who's following him, it simply appears that Mikami killed the man with the fake Death Note.

I KNOW WHAT YOUR PLAN IS...
...AND I'M GOING TO WIN.

KIRA'S ACTIONS

Agreement on Direct Confrontation with Near

22.2010

Confirming that Mikami is X-Kira from Gevanni's report, Near initiates the plan to tamper with Mikami's notebook. Near believes that Mikami hasn't realized the alterations made to the Death Note and chooses the day of the confrontation with Kira. Light agrees to the date.

DEATH COLUMN / Those Who Touched the Death Note

?
B-BOSS... IS THIS UGLY-LOOKING GUY IN THE COSTUME A NEW RECRUIT OR SOME-THING?

During the Kira case three notebooks were brought down into the human world. To the right is a list detailing which character touched which Death Note. Interestingly, Aizawa touched all three Death Notes, and way too many mafia members touched Sidoh's notebook.

Sidoh's Notebook	Gelus's Notebook	Rem's Notebook
Light Yagami	Misa Amane	--
Kiichiro Osoreda	Light Yagami	--
Misa Amane	--	--
After Light Yagami and Misa Amane are confined		
Kyosuke Higuchi	--	Light Yagami
Soichiro Yagami	--	--
Kanzo Mogi	--	--
L	--	--
Touta Matsuda	--	--
Shuichi Aizawa	--	--
In 2009		
Y462	Teru Mikami	Soichiro Yagami
Kal Snydar	Kiyomi Takada	Shuichi Aizawa
Mello	Stephen Gevanni	Touta Matsuda
Rod Ross	Near	Kanzo Mogi
Glen Humphreys	Anthony Rester	Hideki Ide
Rashual Bidd	Halle Lidner	Near
Roy	Shuichi Aizawa	--
Skyer	--	--
Jose	--	--
Other mafia members	--	--

◎ Story Commentary

01.28.2010

OTHERS' ACTIONS

Kiyomi Takada and Mello Die by Death Note

01.26.2010

Near's plan relies on his own name being written into the Death Note by Kira during their confrontation. After hearing this from Halle, Mello abducts Takada but is killed by the piece of the notebook Takada has hidden on herself. She is killed soon after by Light.

NEAR'S ACTIONS

Successfully Switches Teru Mikami's Death Note with a Fake

01.27.2010

IT WASN'T DIFFICULT FOR US TO SNEAK INTO THE SAFE DEPOSIT ROOM TO CRACK IT. IT WAS AN OLD-FASHIONED SAFE AT A LOCAL BANK.
ALSO, SINCE YOU ALLOWED US TO LOOK THROUGH MIKAMI'S BAG WHEN HE WAS AT THE GYM, WE ALREADY HAD MADE COPIES OF ALL HIS KEYS AND CARDS.
THAT'S RIGHT, IT WAS AN EASY TASK TO OPEN THAT SAFE.

Deciding that he should eliminate Takada in Kira's place, Mikami heads to the bank for the second day in a row and writes down Takada's name in the Death Note being stored in the bank's vault. Based on this action, Near realizes that the Death Note Mikami had been carrying around is a fake and prepares to replace the real notebook in the bank.

CHRONOLOGY

01 . 26 . 2010	Kiyomi Takada is abducted by Mello. Matt is killed by Kiyomi Takada's guards. Mello is killed by the power of Kiyomi Takada's Death Note. Kiyomi Takada is killed by the power of Light Yagami's Death Note. Teru Mikami writes down Kiyomi Takada's name in the Death Note (but without effect). Media frenzy over coverage of Kira spokesperson abduction.
01 . 27 . 2010	Gevanni creates copy of Teru Mikami's Death Note and switches it with the real one. Near releases Misa Amane and sends her to the Imperial Hotel.
01 . 28 . 2010	Light Yagami and the Japanese task force come face to face with Near and the SPK at the Yellow Box warehouse on Daikoku wharf. Near takes off the L mask. Teru Mikami writes the names of the SPK members into the (fake) Death Note. Light Yagami admits he is Kira. Touta Matsuda shoots Light Yagami. Light Yagami is killed by the power of Ryuk's Death Note. Near burns both Death Notes. Ryuk returns to the Shinigami realm.

record of 01.26.2010

DEATH COLUMN / Light Yagami's Final Stage: The Yellow Box Warehouse

↑ Aerial view of the warehouse. There's nothing in the vicinity.

The confrontation finally takes place on January 28th. In order for Near to achieve his plan of forcing Kira to admit defeat by having names written into the Death Note without any effect, he needs a place with no windows and only one entrance. The Yellow Box warehouse is perfect. Having figured out Near's plans and devised a way to defeat them, Light calmly agrees to the location. The truth is that when the location was chosen on the 22nd Near had fallen into Light's trap, but he's saved by Mello's actions and Mikami's mistake.

↓ The important feature is that there's only one entrance. Both Near's and Light's plans rely on Mikami looking in from there and writing names down in the notebook.

I ASSURE YOU THAT THIS PERSON WILL COME. SO WE MUST WAIT.
THIS BUILDING IS COMPLETELY SEALED. THE ONLY WAY TO LOOK INSIDE IS TO OPEN THAT DOOR RIGHT THERE.
THEREFORE, THIS VERY IMPORTANT PERSON WILL COME THROUGH THAT DOOR, OR AT LEAST TRY TO PEEK THROUGH IT.

KIRA & NEAR's ACTIONS — Kira and Near Face Off Inside the Yellow Box Warehouse

01.28.201

nside the warehouse, Light and Near see each other for the first ime. Light believes that Near hasn't realized that the notebook he eplaced is a fake and announces his victory after Mikami writes everyone's names down in the notebook. But the investigators do ot die. This is the moment of Light's defeat...

KIRA'S ACTIONS — Death Arrives When Ryuk Writes Name Down into Death Note

28.2010

Light's face betrays myriad expressions as Near explains how he defeated Kira. Even Light's final weapon, a hidden piece of the Death Note, is taken by Aizawa. Sensing Light's defeat, Ryuk writes his name down into his Death Note and kills him. The case finally comes to an end.

Kira, the Eliminator of Evil, Vanishes and the World Returns to "Normal"

State of the World

Returns to What It Was Before Kira Appeared

It's been a year since Kira's killings have ended. The public continues life without much change while pathetic criminals once again stir in the darkness. Kira is now a thing of the past and the world has returned to exactly how it was seven years ago.

HA
HA
HA
HA
THERE ARE STILL THOSE WHO BELIEVE THAT KIRA IS ONLY TAKING A REST.
BUT THE WORLD IS BACK TO THE WAY IT USED TO BE BEFORE KIRA APPEARED, ISN'T IT?

↑ Youngsters taking over the streets in the city. Those who contribute nothing to society continue to increase in number.

01.29.2010 –

A future filled with hope?

CHRONOLOGY

02 . 07 . 2010	Teru Mikami loses his mind and dies while imprisoned.
01 . 28 . 2011	As the Third L, Near discusses new cases with Aizawa and the others.
02 . 14 . 2011	Misa Amane dies.

Near's Actions

Takes Over as Third L

SPK, the anti-Kira task force, is disbanded for good and the members return to their old jobs. Now free, Near takes over the role of top detective in the world as the Third L. Roger, the caretaker at Wammy's House, becomes the new Watari and continues supporting Near.

MR. AIZAWA, I'M SORRY FOR THIS UNEXPECTED CALL, BUT A CRIME SYNDICATE, WHICH I HAVE BEEN PERSONALLY FOLLOWING FOR THE PAST SIX MONTHS, WILL HOLD A DRUG DEAL IN JAPAN.
COULD YOU HELP ME CATCH THEM IN THE ACT?
CRUNCH

➔Near's obsession with toys escalates and he's even seen eating chocolate, in homage to Mello.

epilogue

Others' Actions

Task Force Members Return to the Police Force

The Japanese task force succeeds in stopping Kira, and the members return to the NPA as high-ranking officials. With Aizawa as the leader, the team of Mogi, Ide and Matsuda stays the same. Perhaps it's because they solved the Kira case together, but Near asks the team for help from time to time.

And then…

WELCOME BACK.
WELCOME BACK.
HEY, YAMAMOTO. YOU CAN ATTEND THESE MEETINGS NOW? I GUESS YOU'RE MOVING UP.

🡅 Looks like they have a new member named Yamamoto. But scenes of Aizawa yelling at Matsuda will never change.

What Was "Kira"?

Why Did the Public Not Change?

Human evil is always sudden and without logic. Kira's killings suppressed it for a time, but once it becomes known that such power no longer exists, humanity falls back on old habits. This is something seen again and again throughout history; it is a constant, unlikely ever to change.

Did Kira Become God?

There are those who worship Kira as a god. These are people who were saved in one way or another by Kira's judgments. Kira will never return, but if these people really believe that they were saved by Kira, then there's something real about their futile prayers. This shows the power of faith.

What If a Shinigami Had Never Appeared...?

When Light lost his memories of the Death Note, he became a young man who could understand the pain of others. Had Ryuk never become interested in the human world Light may have become one of the greatest police leaders in the world and fought against criminals alongside L.

Was the Death Note a Murder Weapon?

Near called the Death Note the worst murder weapon ever created, but to the Shinigami, it is merely a tool that allows them to live. Even if it is a weapon, in the end it all depends on the person who has it and how it's used.

HOW TO DRAW

TAKESHI OBATA

In-Depth Interview with Takeshi Obata

Character Design Secrets

keshi Obata is the master behind the utiful art in *Death Note*. Let's take ok at the techniques that went into rything from the character designs he final pages.

The First Challenge in Creating *Death Note*'s Dark World

Congratulations on finishing the series. To get right into it, tell me what led to your working on *Death Note*.
It was just after I had finished *Hikaru no Go*. I got a call from my editor and then read over the rough draft of the *Death Note* pilot chapter. Because it presented an opportunity to draw things I hadn't before—like Shinigami and grotesque creatures, basically really dark stuff—I was very interested.

It does seem to be quite different from anything you've drawn in the past. Did you think about changing your art style?
I never considered drastically changing my style. With each work I create, I first think about the atmosphere that the work requires. Then, once I understand that, I design the characters accordingly. For *Death Note*, it was more of a gothic air, with

happen next resulted in a better work."

the crosses and skulls. Comparing it to *Hikaru no Go*, I basically just replaced the sakura blossoms and the Heian period setting with skulls and the Shinigami realm. But perhaps those details give the impression of a different style.

Concerning the main characters, like Light and L, did Ohba-sensei give you any direction or suggestions to work with?
Sometimes I'd receive comments through my editor but most of the time I wasn't told anything and made the decisions myself. I would look at the dialogue and think about what kind of character would say those lines. I was usually able to naturally create the character designs just based on that.

So you were spot-on with all your character designs, then?
I thought I was but...thanks to Ohba-sensei's unpredictable story sometimes I found that the characters would become totally different from how I'd initially imagined them. So I became totally clueless sometimes...[*laughs*]. However, Ryuk was an easy character to understand, as were Rem and Gelus. Perhaps Shinigami are better at expressing their feelings?

↑ Most color illustrations were based on character-specific rules.

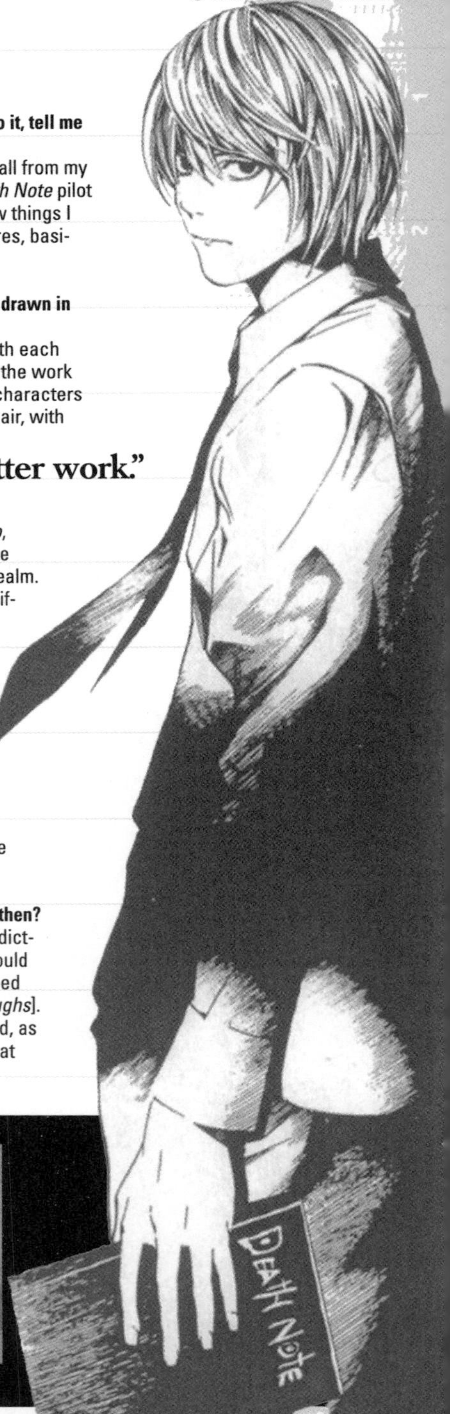

🠅 Basing the character design on the character's dialogue: that's the Obata style!

At one point, Light loses his memory and his personality changes. During the serialization, were you not aware of future plot developments?
Yes, that's right. I would receive the thumbnails but only about four to five chapters ahead. So I didn't know anything further out than that. But I also never bothered to ask my editor for more of the plot, because I wanted to keep the surprise and inspiration I'd derive from reading each new rough-draft chapter. I believe that not knowing too much about what would happen next resulted in a better work. Though of course when new characters like L were appearing for the first time or other important scenes were coming up, I would receive calls from my editor warning me. Personally, I feel that reading the thumbnails each week and being totally surprised was very fun.

"I believe that not knowing too much about what would

🠅 Obata-sensei's idea to show Light's facial expression made Raye Penber's death scene even more powerful.

Making It Easier to Read with Panel Diversity

Was there anything particular you focused on when you began?
This story takes place in our world but also includes fictitious things like Shinigami and the Death Note. So I made sure those two aspects were balanced well. The art is drawn realistically, but from time to time I tried to add something bizarre that would muddy the realistic feel of the art.

Were you in charge of the layout?
I did work on getting the right camera angle for each panel, but I mostly used the layout provided by Ohba-sensei in the thumbnails to create my own version. Though sometimes I would make changes. For example, I had some ideas for the Raye Penber death scene and altered that a bit. In Ohba-sensei's thumbnails, Raye collapses in one panel; I wanted to add more intensity, so I stretched it out a bit. And the part where Light says, "Goodbye, Raye Penber," was something I added in so I could show Light's facial expression. I went beyond my place with that one [*laughs*]. Since this is a series with a lot of dialogue I did my best to use panel layouts and camera angles to make it as easy to read as possible.

🠅 The controversial restraint equipment.

•A Controversial Scene in a Kids' Magazine: Misa in Restraints
When chapter 33 was going into the magazine, my editor said the drawing was on morally dangerous ground for a children's magazine, so they placed the title logo over the middle of the page. I was surprised by the reaction, since I'd held back when I was drawing the panel.

•Each Main Character Has an Image Color
Each main character has a color assigned to them. For example, Light is a lack of color or clear, L is gold, Misa is pink or black. With this decided, it makes it much easier to get the atmosphere right when drawing color images.

© Takeshi Obata Interview

The Sports Battle Between Light and L that Almost Became Fencing

Are there any scenes from the series that really stick with you?
Specifically, the tennis scene between Light and L. Because it was so much work… When I received the thumbnails, my editor said that the chapter would have tennis in it. My surprised response was, "Huh? Tennis in this series?" I was worried also because I don't know anything about the rules of tennis. So I worked carefully while getting tennis explanations from an assistant who knew the rules [*laughs*]. But since I doubt I will ever do a tennis manga on my own, I was very happy that I got to experience drawing a tennis scene.

"After Ohba-sensei's comment, I soon realized how important apples were."

🡅 Obata-sensei was also captivated by the constant appearances of L's sweets.

Did you receive any instructions from Ohba-sensei concerning the story art?
Not really. I was given tremendous freedom when it came to the art. However, early on I neglected to draw an apple that appeared in the thumbnails. I then received a comment from Ohba-sensei through my editor saying how the apple needed to be in there. At the time I didn't think they were an important part of the story, but after Ohba-sensei's comment I soon realized how important apples were. So there were a few things like that that Ohba-sensei wanted to make sure were included. Otherwise, I could do as I wished.

What were some other things that Ohba-sensei made sure were included?
In terms of minor things, one was L's many sweets. If Ohba-sensei wanted pudding in a certain scene, the word "pudding" would be written in the thumbnails. When the melon with ham came up I got all worried for some reason that we were switching to fruit. And L's manner of sitting was also something Ohba-sensei made sure was included, though the way that L holds things was something that I came up with. At first I drew him holding things regularly, but I felt that was lacking artistically. So I kept redrawing and had him use the "as if holding something dirty" technique, and instantly felt that it was perfect. I personally see L as a clean-freak, so it just seemed to fit really well.

Was it the same for Ryuk's funny, twisted-up pose in chapter 18?
Ohba-sensei mentioned that he was "twisted up" in the thumbnails so I went with that. Ryuk started becoming comic relief around that point, didn't he?

🡆 Light and L fighting. The fighting scenes in the series are pretty original!

●L's Capoeira-Style Fighting
I'm often told that L's fighting style is similar to capoeira, the Brazilian fight-dance created by African slaves during the 16th century, but I didn't consider that at all when I was drawing it. I was merely thinking about the best way to kick someone while handcuffed. But if it looks like capoeira, that adds another element to it and that makes me happy.

↑ The important tennis scene that Obata-sensei took extra care to draw. He didn't know the rules, but it sure doesn't look like it here.

↑ Obata-sensei enjoys drawing humans who are losing control. A lot of effort was put into this scene.

I heard that the tennis scene was almost something else.

That's true. What I first heard was that it was supposed to be either fencing or golf. When I asked, Ohba-sensei mentioned wanting to have Light and L in some kind of competition at the college, so we were considering what to use. I felt more strongly about the "why?" of the competition than the "what?", but the visuals of Light and L battling it out in white fencing tights would probably have been very fun [*laughs*]. However, fencing requires the characters to cover their faces with masks, and we couldn't have a crowd appearing with golf, so in the end we went with tennis.

Did anything else surprise you about the plot?

When it was revealed that Higuchi was Kira in the Yotsuba arc. At that point I was drawing it not knowing which character was Kira, so I was very surprised to hear that it was Higuchi. I was guessing it would be Mido or Namikawa, so I kind of dislike that it ended up being Higuchi [*laughs*]. To me, Higuchi was too pathetic to be a villain, so I wasn't even considering him. But drawing Higuchi falling apart was a lot of fun. It's enjoyable to draw characters deteriorating.

Showing the Future with Cell Phones and Accessories

With the Mello and Near arc, the story jumps to the future and also to America, doesn't it?

Yes, I was very surprised when I heard this. But as the Mello and Near arc advanced, I prepared myself for anything. I think that had I been told, "Next week we start the outer-space arc," I could have drawn it [*laughs*].

↑ The more Near appears, the more toys he has.

●L's and Near's Peculiar Tastes

The notion that Near was "immature" got stronger and stronger as I kept drawing him. So at first, he pretty much only had darts as a toy. But, and I can say this regarding L as well, I think it works best when things like this are revealed gradually. Had L been eating mountains of sweets before his face was revealed I think people would've been wondering if he was crazy, and he wouldn't have much credibility as a super detective [*laughs*].

© Takeshi Obata Interview

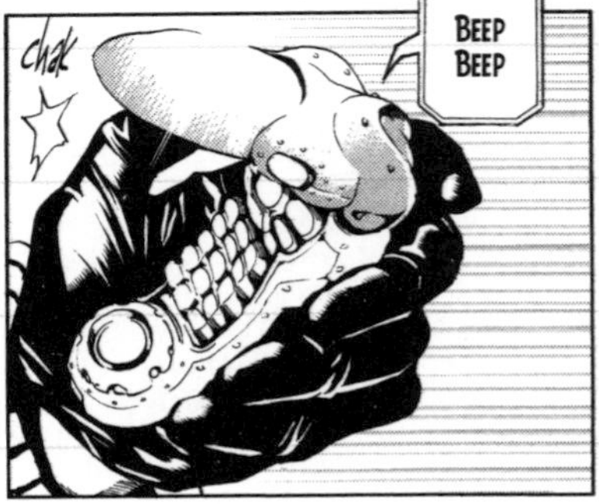

↑ Mello's futuristic cell phone. Will we see this design some day…?

That's pretty amazing [*laughs*]. Was there anything you concentrated on when drawing a story that takes place in the near-future?
I drew while thinking about what 2009 would be like. There are a lot of parts where I did poorly in drawing the future. But what I really tried to do was to make the reader feel like it was the future from the cell phones and other small devices that the characters used.

Mello's cell phone has an interesting design.
I thought doing something that looked "retro-future" would work well, so that's why it looks that way. I used the same concept for Mello's helmet as well. But the truth is, conveying the sense that the story jumps ahead to 2009 may not have been very important.

Was there any change in how you worked between the L arc and the Mello and Near arc?
Not really. But everything was scaled up for the second arc, so I worked really hard on the small details like the tower of matchsticks.

That's one of the things Near stacks, right? Were these also included in Ohba-sensei's thumbnails?
Yes, it was in Ohba-sensei's drawings. It was a super-simple match tower with only three matchsticks [*laughs*]. But because the story had expanded so much, I had my assistants draw a really large match tower.

Then later a really detailed dice tower appeared.
Yeah! I asked my assistants to draw a dice tower even greater than the match tower [*laughs*]! It gets to the point of ridiculousness when you spend so long drawing something so detailed…

That must have been tough on your assistants.
They must have hated it, but it was like they did it while thinking, "We came this far, might as well finish it."

WHEN I SAID I WOULD COOPERATE, I WAS TALKING ABOUT THE KIDNAPPING INVESTIGATION. AND I CLEARLY STATED THAT WE'D TALK ABOUT THE NOTEBOOK AND KIRA AFTER THAT. BUT YOU PRACTICALLY LET THE KIDNAPPERS HAVE THE NOTEBOOK...

↑ A very detailed dice tower. This was completed thanks to some hard-working assistants!

↑ These panels were created after a trip to a trucking company. No expense was spared when it came to research.

• The Takada Kidnapping Scene
In order to draw the scene where Mello kidnaps Takada, I took my digital camera to a local shipping company and took a lot of pictures. I usually buy books for reference, but I also sometimes go out on my own and do some research. I think about the panel layout and page construction while taking the photos.

The Desire to Show Something Fresh

Did you have a hand in the creation of any of Near's toys?
I made some changes to the duck in the pool seen in chapter 86.

↑ While talking to Light, Near is always playing with something. This fills the important function of adding movement to the scene.

In Ohba-sensei's thumbnails, the duck was just floating in the water. But these scenes with people talking indoors really lack movement, so I tried to give it a sense of speed by making it a radio-controlled duck. If you use too many panels at sharp angles for the dialogue scenes, the eyes don't stay focused and it gets really hard to read. But if you keep the camera angle set, it's not a very dynamic page. That's why I tried to use props to make it feel like the story was really flowing.

Do the block figures and finger puppets serve the same function?
Yes. But the block figures were extremely hard to draw, so I stuck with the finger puppets. Drawing the block figures was stressful because they're so simple: that's what makes them difficult. And there were small differences depending on which assistant drew them. So I thought up the handmade finger puppets that Near uses. I have forgotten why I went with finger puppets…but now that I think about it, I should have just used the finger puppets the whole time.

Do you have an assistant who specializes in drawing small, detailed objects?
Yes, I do. We have specialized artists: those who can draw detailed things, those who are good with cars, those who are good with natural things, etc. One is really good at drawing food; he drew that ham and melon L was eating and made it look delicious. Also, for the sweets, we actually went out and bought the real things to help us draw them accurately. So during the L arc, the office was full of sweet things [*laughs*]. But I have a sweet tooth, so I was happy about it.

"I think that had I been told, 'Next week we start the outer-space arc,' I could have drawn it."

➜ A lot of research went into keeping up with all the fast-paced action.

Also, for the scenes in America, I relied on photo books and movie scenes that feature abandoned buildings. And I used models and photos for drawing the cars and motorcycles.

◎ Takeshi Obata Interview

The Masterfully Drawn Scene of Light's Final Speech

The scene of Light's final speech at the warehouse is really powerful.
For that, I pretty much knew that Light was about to crumble, so I put a lot of effort into making it perfect. Because Light had hidden his true expressions throughout the series, I really wanted them to burst free here. I just knew that would make the scene really good. Plus, this was the only place in the series where we could really have Light reveal his emotions. However, since this is a scene that is read slowly because of the dialogue, I struggled a lot with the panel layout and many other things. Light's facial expressions were especially important; I would discuss them with my editor while drawing them. In the rough pencil stage Light had a much more evil face, but I realized that he's still calm at the beginning of his speech, so I changed various parts.

Why did you change his expressions?
Since he's saying stuff that could possibly convince someone like Matsuda, I figured he should still have a normal expression on his face. This was in order to keep the reader thinking that perhaps Light's plan still had a chance. Also, I was really happy with the art of Light flailing pathetically after being shot by Matsuda. I think it captured well how a desperate person would act.

⬆ A lot of work went into keeping even the long dialogue scenes interesting.

In the background of chapter 96 is a set for making the finger puppets. Was that done to point out how they're handmade by Near?
No. That's there just because we try to throw in something fresh for each chapter. For every chapter with lots of dialogue, we think hard about what new prop we can include. So we decided to draw in the puppet set.

⬆ Light's confession scene. To read more about Obata-sensei's struggle with Light's facial expressions, check out the next page.

●Mikami's Notebook Full of Names
For the shots of Mikami's notebook in chapters 103 and 104, we filled every space on each page with names because Mikami is so methodical. It had to be really detailed; one of my assistants worked his butt off to complete it [*laughs*]. Anyway, I felt really bad for causing my assistants to suffer with jobs like this.

⬅ Obata-sensei requested that every little space on the pages be filled with names...

A-AM I GOING TO DIE?!
I'M GOING TO DIE!

↑ Light's death scene, which made Obata-sensei actually feel sick. His powerful art blew away most readers.

With *Death Note* Over...

So how is it now thinking back on the experience?
Right when it ended, I was really pumped up and felt like I wanted to keep drawing it. But after about a month, the strain really caught up to me... Serialization is a very stressful experience.

Was there anything that you really wanted to draw in this work?
Not really. I saw my job as supporting Ohba-sensei's creation as best I could. Though I was really thankful that I was given the challenge of drawing things like Shinigami, which I love, and also people dying, which is something I usually don't draw.

Finally, is there a theme you hope to draw in the future?
I've always wanted to work on something sci-fi. Or, conversely, maybe something that's very realistic. Also, and this isn't a theme, but I'd like to draw realistic human muscles. Recently, when I've read fighting manga, I've realized that drawing realistic muscles and drawing muscles that give the reader a sense of speed are totally different things. So if I were to draw a fighting manga I know I'd have to study how it's done. I plan on working really hard on my next project, so thank you for your support.

There were times when you changed characters' expressions for the book release, correct?
That's true. The thing with preparing pages for a magazine is that you often do the pages out of order based on what will get things finished the fastest. That's why I'll sometimes go back and fix things I missed before the series is released in the graphic novel format. For example, sometimes I won't like the angle of a character's face. Basically, if there's something that I have a problem with, I'll try and correct it as best I can.

What about Light's death scene?
That was more than just difficult: it made me sick to draw it. But the two black pages indicating "nothingness" were something I really wanted to do, so I was happy about that. By the way, I'm personally very scared about what happens to us after we die. Ever since I was young, I would think about going to hell and get really scared, but at some point I started thinking about how "nothingness" is even scarier than hell. Drawing this chapter reminded me of that.

"I really wanted Light's emotions to burst free."

NO MATTER HOW I LOOK AT IT, YOU'VE LOST, LIGHT.
ONCE A NAME IS WRITTEN DOWN IN THE DEATH NOTE, YOU CAN'T DO ANYTHING ABOUT IT. YOU MORE THAN ANYBODY ELSE HERE SHOULD KNOW THAT.
GOODBYE, LIGHT YAGAMI.
...

•The Evil-Looking Shinigami Ryuk in Chapter 107
I didn't really have any instructions from Ohba-sensei for drawing Ryuk in this chapter. And I also wasn't consciously trying to make Ryuk look more like a Shinigami. It just naturally turned into a white-eyed Ryuk. Though I am very happy with how it turned out.

← An unexpectedly cruel Ryuk. This reminded readers that he in fact is a Shinigami.

In-Depth Interview with Takeshi Obata: Special Project

Light's Speech Scene at the Yellow Box Warehouse

A Behind-the-Scenes Look

Light's scene at the Yellow Box warehouse just before his death was Obata-sensei's greatest challenge. Some of the work that went into it is now revealed!

SCENE 01

Chapter 103 "Declaration"

Here are the corrections made to the page where Light screams that he is being framed. Because showing a close-up of Light here would add too much emphasis, his whole body was shown instead.

◎FINAL

◎PRE-CORRECTIONS

Obata-Sensei Reveals HOW TO DRAW in Black and White

① Creating Thumbnails, Obata-Style

Once I receive Ohba-sensei's thumbnails, I create my own version while concentrating on the camera angles within the panels and the panel size.

② Penciling on Manga Paper

After the thumbnails are done, I immediately use them for reference as I pencil the whole chapter. Doing them in the correct order is the ideal situation, but if I cannot finish them before the day my assistants come, I do the pages with complicated backgrounds first.

SCENE 02

Chapter 105 "Impossible"

Admitting to being Kira, Light explains the world as he sees it. His initial expression was begging for adoration but it was corrected to a saner version for the final.

◎FINAL

◎PRE-CORRECTIONS

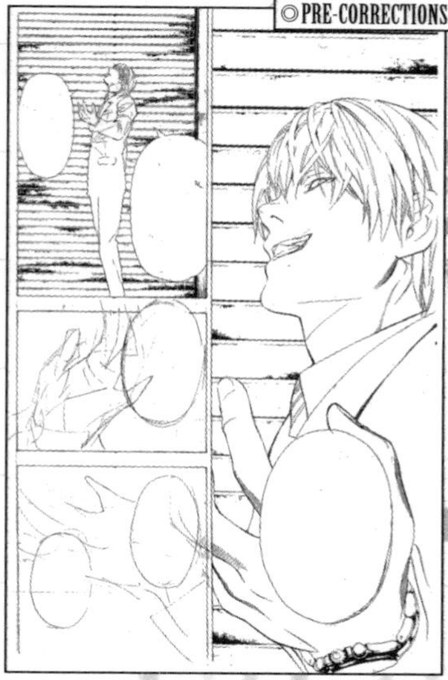

◎PRE-CORRECTIONS

◎FINAL

SCENE 03

Chapter 107 "Curtain"

The moment of Light's heart attack! In the final page, the width of his mouth was fixed to be less than it was before the correction, where his mouth is open very wide. Also, his hands were added in to express his struggle.

What Is Left to the Assistants?

I almost never give an assistant something completely blank. Even for drawing a prop, I like to give them a sketch so that the size of the object is clear. I then check over their pencils and give guidance or suggestions for how to change it. For something like Near's match tower, I will at least draw the outline.

③ Inking and Assistant Help

I do all the inking of the characters, even ones without names. Before my assistants come, I try to have as many pages inked as possible so that they can add the backgrounds. Once they arrive, I give them the pages with the most backgrounds first. So their first day of work each week is the toughest… After that we try to go in page order.

④ Completion

At the end I add the final touches by myself or with one assistant. At this stage, I will often go without sleep until the pages are complete.

Takeshi Obata
Production Note

Character Design Secrets

Through delicate and brilliant lines, the original characters of *Death Note* come to life. Obata-sensei now gives us a behind-the-scenes look at how the characters were designed.

Characters

DESIGN CONCEPT

"A brilliant honors student who's a little out there," was the character description and concept. Because the character description I was given was so clear and detailed, I had no trouble with Light's look and I completed him very quickly. He didn't change during the Mello and Near arc, which took place four years later.

I'M A SERIOUS, STRAIGHT-A STUDENT... A MODEL TEENAGER.

◎ INITIAL DESIGN

VISUAL

Because of the demands of a weekly serialization, you start unconsciously removing unnecessary lines as you draw the characters over and over. Because of that, I believe I got better at drawing Light as the series progressed. However, I really freaked out while preparing for chapter 35, when my editor told me that Light loses his memories and that I needed to return to how I drew him in chapter 1. It was like I had to forget everything I had learned...

Light Yagami

↑ A rough sketch of Light drawn before the Mello and Near arc. Four years have passed since L's death, and Light has become a grown member of society.

WHAT AM I DOING HERE ...?
...

◎ AFTER LOSING MEMORY

CLOTHES

I spent a lot of effort on his clothes. I couldn't even imagine what kind of clothes a brilliant person would wear, so this part was very difficult. I used a lot of fashion magazines for reference when I was coming up with ideas. I thought of him as a slim and smart guy who wears a formal shirt. I tried to avoid casual clothes like jeans; most of what he wears is fitted.

L

↓→ The picture on the right is a rough sketch for chapter 11. The one below is a picture from Obata-sensei's thumbnails.

DESIGN CONCEPT

The truth is that until he appeared in chapter 11, I was drawing him as if he were an attractive young man. But once it was time to show him, I figured it might be better if his appearance contrasted with Light's. My idea just happened to match Ohba-sensei's, so I switched the concept to a more odd-looking character. Though during L's early appearances, I was worried for no reason about how he looked so suspicious that Light would know instantly it was L if they ever met.

VISUAL

My editor mentioned that I should make his face capable of looking cool based on the angle. That's when I added the black bags under his eyes. To me, bags under the eyes can be cool… For example, the main character in *Devil Man*, Akira Fudou, has bags, and I thought they really looked cool. Also, one concept was that he had "dead eyes," so I gave him mostly no eyebrows and all-black eyes. Black eyes usually make a character look goofier, but the bags help sharpen the character's gaze. You get a feeling of mystery, or that you can't tell what the character is thinking, and I really liked that. Also, the bags under his eyes bring out a lot of speculation about his lifestyle and his past; I later realized just how useful they are. In Ohba-sensei's thumbnails, L didn't have the bags: he had a very plain face with no expression [*laughs*]. It was great and I wish I could have used it as is.

◎ WHEN L'S FACE WAS HIDDEN

HMM... SO INTERPOL'S FINALLY STARTING TO MOVE ON THIS.
WELL, THIS IS ONE CASE WHERE I'M GOING TO NEED SOME HELP FROM THE POLICE.

CLOTHES

I wanted to convey the impression that L doesn't put much thought into his clothes, so I chose a simple T-shirt and jeans outfit. His clothing basically never changes, but he probably has a whole closet full of that outfit [*laughs*]. It's never shown, but Watari probably has to take care of his clothing needs.

Initial Rough

This is the L prototype I drew on a blank part of the thumbnail. With a cool expression and no bags, he looks like a totally different person.

DESIGN CONCEPT

Ohba-sensei and I both naturally wanted to go with a "Gothic Lolita" look. I think it really fits in with the gothic imagery of the Shinigami and that world. For Misa, I imagined a mix of an energetic Japanese artist and a foreign rock and roll singer. I was pretty much set on the design the first time I drew her.

I BET THAT GOT HIS ATTEN-TION.
TABASCO
COUNTRY STORE

◎FIRST APPEARANCE

VISUAL

At first I did have some apprehension over the length of her hair. I personally wanted her bangs to be straight across but I figured it would be too much if she was completely in the Gothic Lolita style. So I made her look a little more natural. I wanted her to look cute to people who weren't into the Gothic Lolita style as well.

And by the time of the Mello and Near arc, she had become a top idol, so I had her graduate from the Gothic Lolita look and focused on making her look like a popular actress.

AHA!

◎DURING L ARC

Misa Amane

LETS GO HOME NOW, REM.
HUH? BUT YOU FINALLY FOUND HIM.

◎IN DISGUISE

➡ Misa when she's a top idol. She looks much more mature here than during the L arc.

CLOTHES

I was really psyched about having a female main character. I remember having a lot of fun drawing her while looking through Gothic Lolita magazines.

◎ INITIAL DESIGN

Soichiro Yagami

DESIGN CONCEPT

I wanted him to look like a stereotypical detective. Since he already had the mustache and glasses in the thumbnails, I created him while maintaining those elements. He's the character who changes the most visually during the series. Early on he has a double chin and good physique, but as time goes on he loses a lot of weight [*pained laugh*]. But even in Ohba-sensei's thumbnails he started to age poorly.

◎ MELLO AND NEAR ARC

↑ Soichiro in the Mello and Near arc. He would age a lot more as the series went on…

◎ INITIAL DESIGN

Touta Matsuda

DESIGN CONCEPT

In the beginning I was drawing the NPA characters with no knowledge of who would end up remaining. But Matsuda actually appears a lot early on, doesn't he [*laughs*]? Matsuda is a guy who is hard to predict and thus hard to draw. His character concept was an "average young detective," but there was nothing unique about his features and his actions weren't consistent, so I didn't really like him [*laughs*]. The truth is that I'm kind of a Matsuda-type of person, so I must not have liked the feeling of seeing my own inconsistency reflected in him.

◎ L ARC

↑ The only character who actually looks younger during the second arc. Is it because of his worry-free personality?

◎ INITIAL DESIGN

Shuichi Aizawa

DESIGN CONCEPT

I never planned on him being a character I would draw for long, so I started to worry when he kept appearing more and more. I didn't think his face was good for a main character, so I worked hard to gradually make him more presentable [*laughs*]. I even kept increasing the volume of his hair…Aizawa was really easy to draw, though. It's easier for me to draw a character who acts consistently. I would draw him while thinking that it would be nice if there were lots of people like him in Japan.

↑ Aizawa was redesigned to look older and really make it feel like four years had passed since L's death.

◎ L ARC

Kanzo Mogi

→ For better or worse, Mogi is a character who didn't really have much change in his design.

DESIGN CONCEPT

I didn't even draw him as a main character and then he lasts the whole series [*laughs*]. That's why I think his design wasn't very coherent.

Hideki Ide

DESIGN CONCEPT

I actually liked Ide. I guess it was because I could really understand his mental process in leaving the team and then rejoining them later. Characters who reveal the motivations for their actions are easier to draw for me.

Hirokazu Ukita

DESIGN CONCEPT

As an emotional and easy-to-understand character, he was easy to draw. Though when I designed him, I didn't know he was going to be killed off. So I was really surprised when I saw him dead in the thumbnails.

Sayu and Sachiko Yagami

→ Sayu as a college student. Obata-sensei says he struggles with drawing women, but that's hard to imagine here.

DESIGN CONCEPT

Sayu and the other female characters have no real concept behind them. It might be a mental thing, but I have trouble coming up with a variety of female designs. They all end up looking the same except for their hairstyles [*laughs*]. For females, unless she's one of the main characters, I don't have many opportunities to spend time going over what kind of character she's going to be, so it's very difficult for me.

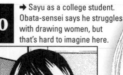

Raye Penber

DESIGN CONCEPT

Since he's Japanese-American, I struggled over his design, but I tried to make him look like a foreigner. I wish I could have drawn him to look a little better.

Naomi Misora

DESIGN CONCEPT

This is a character I really looked forward to drawing after hearing about the plot. Because she's a type I've never drawn before, I think I became really invested in her. Her design color is black because it fits with her mourning over Raye. And as a battle uniform to go against Kira, I gave her a black leather jacket. I then designed her face and hair to fit the clothes. She's really a character born from her clothes.

Watari

DESIGN CONCEPT

Because his face doesn't appear early on I didn't even put any thought into it. In Ohba-sensei's rough draft, he was an old man with just one single hair on his head. I wanted to keep him as an elderly man and did so in chapter 13, when his face is finally revealed. The elderly are just fun to draw. With young characters, the only options seem to be to make them attractive, normal or ugly. But old characters have wrinkles and their faces can have weird angles, so they're more fun. And I like leather coats, so I chose to have Watari wear one.

◎ IN DISGUISE

LOOKS LIKE WE'RE ALL HERE. LET'S BEGIN OUR MEETING.

Yotsuba Members

DESIGN CONCEPT

When I had to create the eight Yotsuba members, I remember hearing how there would be eight new Kira characters and being really excited. I tried to create them in the mold of *The Seven Samurai*, giving each of them an individualized look: one's a skinhead, others look privileged, etc. I remember making Mido and Namikawa look more attractive to try and make the reader think they might be Kira.

◎ OBATA-SENSEI'S KIRA CANDIDATES, NAMIKAWA AND MIDO

Aiber and Wedy

DESIGN CONCEPT

When Aiber was to appear, I was told by my editor that he was a sarcastic, comic relief character. So I wish I could have drawn him to be a little more comedic. For Wedy, I wasn't sure what kind of character she was going to be, so I just made her look like a female model. She's got the stereotypical female spy look. Had I drawn them to be a little bit more original, Ohba-sensei may have liked them enough to have made them a bigger part of the story… That's something I think about now that it's over.

◎ AIBER

OH NO!!
I HEARD A LOUD SOUND SO I CAME OUT TO LOOK... I BETTER CALL 911!

◎ AIBER DISGUISED AS MATSUDA

◎ WEDY

Teru Mikami

DESIGN CONCEPT

I was told that he's supposed to be a stoic character similar to Light, so I kept that in mind when designing him. Because at the time I wasn't aware that he was a prosecutor or a Kira worshipper, I based him on the main character in the pilot story, Taro Kagami. Later on, I drew him as an insane fanatic.

Also, glasses are in these days, so I had Mikami be a glasses wearer. Things were a little haphazard at that point…

◎ AFTER SEEING LIGHT

◎ CHILDHOOD

◎ IN COLLEGE

Kiyomi Takada

DESIGN CONCEPT

I'm not very good with female characters, so the Takada in college didn't have much thought put into her [*laughs*]. For the Mello and Near arc, I pretty much just aged her, but it was very difficult. I was thinking, "This doesn't look like her," while I was drawing her [*laughs*]. In some ways, I tried to make her clothes contrast with Misa's. I think I chose the more formal clothes she wears because of her job as a news announcer.

◎ WORKING

Mello

DESIGN CONCEPT

Because Mello and Near are L's successors, my order from Ohba-sensei was to include a little L in them. I tried to keep the weirdness and the dead eyes, but because L was such an important character to me I think I made them look too much like him… Their designs were a major struggle. Also, I was assuming that they would team up and work together, so I imagined them as twins when creating them.

◎MELLO

↑ Mello drawn before he was revealed in the story. Perhaps it's because of his clothes, but he looks much happier here.

VISUAL

I tried to give Mello more energy than Near. At first his hair is cut straight across, but later on it becomes a mess, which I like much more. Also, I was able to draw him looking cooler with the scar on his face, and I was so grateful that Ohba-sensei added that. That's why I was really sad he died soon after.

CLOTHES

Mello's clothes are based on what I like. I really love drawing shiny leather. They aren't clothes that I love wearing, just ones that I love drawing.

◎INITIAL DESIGN

◎REAPPEARANCE

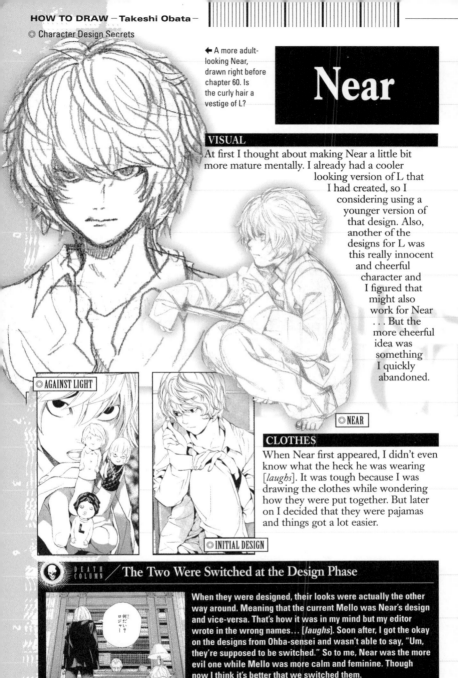

⬅ A more adult-looking Near, drawn right before chapter 60. Is the curly hair a vestige of L?

Near

VISUAL

At first I thought about making Near a little bit more mature mentally. I already had a cooler looking version of L that I had created, so I considering using a younger version of that design. Also, another of the designs for L was this really innocent and cheerful character and I figured that might also work for Near . . . But the more cheerful idea was something I quickly abandoned.

◎ NEAR

◎ AGAINST LIGHT

◎ INITIAL DESIGN

CLOTHES

When Near first appeared, I didn't even know what the heck he was wearing [*laughs*]. It was tough because I was drawing the clothes while wondering how they were put together. But later on I decided that they were pajamas and things got a lot easier.

DEATH COLUMN / The Two Were Switched at the Design Phase

When they were designed, their looks were actually the other way around. Meaning that the current Mello was Near's design and vice-versa. That's how it was in my mind but my editor wrote in the wrong names… [*laughs*]. Soon after, I got the okay on the designs from Ohba-sensei and wasn't able to say, "Um, they're supposed to be switched." So to me, Near was the more evil one while Mello was more calm and feminine. Though now I think it's better that we switched them.

BUT IT'S SO BORING WATCHING SOMETHING THAT NEVER CHANGES.
BEEP BOOP

Matt

DESIGN CONCEPT

His character concept was a young man who loves gaming and doesn't really care much about the world. I was told nothing about Matt ahead of time; I remember seeing the thumbnails and asking my editor, "Who's this character?!"[*laughs*]. In the thumbnails he had a bowl haircut and round glasses, but in the end I just went with what I liked. During the Mello and Near arc I had a "he probably won't do much" mentality regarding the new characters, so I was able to create Matt naturally [*laughs*].

SPK

DESIGN CONCEPT

When they first appeared in chapter 60, I just drew them without thinking too much. I had heard that there was a spy sent by Mello, so I wanted to make him suspicious looking. And since I didn't know which SPK characters would survive, I had to work hard on every one. Generally I'm poor at drawing foreign characters… I imagine them being from so far away…and then I forget how to draw them.

DEATH COLUMN / Creating Characters, Obata-Style

I never create a group of possible characters. For some reason, it doesn't seem like I'm capable of stocking character designs [*laughs*]. So each time a new character appears, I have to design him then. And I don't really bat ideas around in my head; I just receive some inspiration and do it. That's probably why my character drawings can be so inconsistent [*laughs*]. I almost always dislike my art when I look at it later.

➔ Minor characters like Lind L. Tailor are created based on what Obata-sensei is feeling at the time.

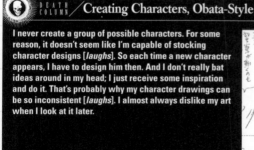

Shinigami

Ryuk

THEY DIED FROM HEART ATTACKS BECAUSE YOU DIDN'T WRITE THE

◎ PILOT

DESIGN CONCEPT

My original idea for the pilot chapter was for Ryuk to look like a young man similar to Light, but with black hair and wings. I had the notion that Shinigami should look like attractive rock stars. But if he were more attractive than Light, Ryuk would appear to be the main character and things wouldn't work as well. So then my editor told me that he didn't have to look human…and I erased what I had and created the current version. I like how he looks like a monster, and with that mask-like face you can never really tell what he's thinking. Now that I think about it, there could have been a twist that his face is a mask and when he removes it he's really attractive underneath [*laughs*]. For the pilot chapter, it was really hard to draw him because I didn't have a good handle on the bone structure of his face. But during the serialization I got so used to it that it was like I could see the bones. That's why his face looks very different in the pilot and in the series.

Rem

DESIGN CONCEPT

When I was told she's female I tried to come up with something that would really contrast with Ryuk, so I gave her a white body with rounder lines. I took her motif from some fashion collections. It's like she's wearing a really bizarre suit. Also, her head is inspired by Medusa.

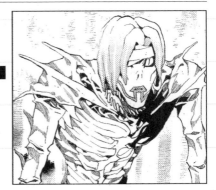

Sidoh

DESIGN CONCEPT

I'd heard that a new Shinigami would be coming to Earth, so I went through the designs and nominated Sidoh and Daril Ghiroza. I personally thought it would be Ghiroza and was preparing for it, but Ohba-sensei chose Sidoh. The reason was that Ghiroza seemed to have a high Shinigami rank and thus wouldn't suit the role of being pushed around by a human. And actually, thank goodness Sidoh was chosen: Ghiroza has so many details in her design that I would've been in real trouble if I'd had to draw her every chapter [*laughs*]. Sidoh is based on a bird and his mouth on a canary's beak. But his foldable arms are more insect-like. As with most of Ohba-sensei's characters, Sidoh is very funny, especially when he becomes the first Shinigami to ever hand out flyers. I really liked him and wished we could have seen more of him.

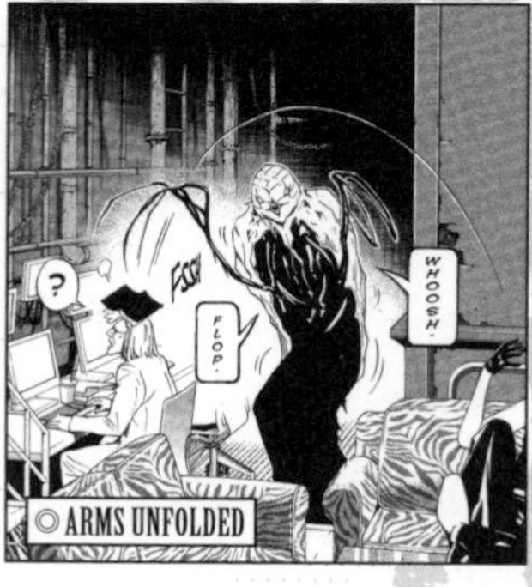

◎ ARMS UNFOLDED

Gelus

DESIGN CONCEPT

He seemed to be a really beautiful Shinigami in the thumbnails but I went with my idea instead, which was in the other direction. Story-wise he was a really pitiful character, so I thought the patchwork body would fit well. I even made it so he has trouble writing names into his Death Note. I figured the readers could relate more to him and feel sorry for him if he looked pathetic rather than beautiful.

Deridovely

DESIGN CONCEPT

He's based on a gross-looking transparent insect. The bandages help with that effect.

Gukku

DESIGN CONCEPT

He's a Shinigami who appears in the first chapter, so I had him look like a monster to keep it simple. Since a regular skull would be boring I used a cow skull.

Kinddara Guivelostain

DESIGN CONCEPT

She appears on the spine of volume 12. Since it's the final volume, I wanted to create a new Shinigami for it. She never actually appears within the story.

Midora

DESIGN CONCEPT

I like her because she looks more like a salamander and is vastly different from the other designs. Since her skin is moist like an amphibian's, I worry if she can survive in the heat of the Shinigami realm [*laughs*].

Zellogi

DESIGN CONCEPT

As you can tell from the feathered headdress, the motif is American Indian. I started off by covering his eyes and adding the feathers; the rest just came naturally [*laughs*].

Calikarcha

DESIGN CONCEPT

I based him on bird masks from Bali. He appears around the time Sidoh is looking for his Death Note.

Shinigami King

DESIGN CONCEPT

I was too scared to think of designing him… A few times I considered putting him on the spine of a book, but that probably wouldn't be enough space to contain him.

Nu

DESIGN CONCEPT

Like a giant rock covered in eyes that sticks out of the ground. There are Shinigami like this, but they are rare.

Daril Ghiroza

DESIGN CONCEPT

More of an orthodox-looking Shinigami. I created her at the same time as Sidoh for possible use as a new character, so in some ways she is a contrast to him. I based her on Ryuk's design but tried to make her look higher-ranked.

Armonia Justin Beyondormason

DESIGN CONCEPT

I created him as a conceited Shinigami who sits on a throne. For his body, I referenced Tibetan art that features skulls. Also, I've seen Italian antique accessories that have a face covered in jewels, so I used that idea too.

DEATH COLUMN / Creating Shinigami, Obata-Style

Designing the Shinigami was a lot of fun for me. However, since I had to start with nothing, it was also very difficult. I know I struggled a lot until finally completing Ryuk. Early on I created Shinigami that looked like beasts, but later, with Sidoh and others, I based them more on crustaceans and insects. That was because it was easier. Basing characters on different animals yet still keeping the same feeling of the series was very difficult. Before basing them on beasts, I even considered having them look more like wizards, but I killed that idea. The reason some Shinigami are wearing rags is a remnant of that idea. Also, there's no physical difference that separates the males and females. I knew their gender when drawing them, but the only differences are details I added subconsciously.

...?!
I HEARD RYUK'S BEEN TURNED INTO SOME HUMAN'S PET OR SOMETHING.

↑ Even Shinigami who barely appear in the story have concepts behind them!

Other Details

The Death Note

DESIGN CONCEPT

There were no real suggestions from Ohba-sensei about the Death Notes, so I drew them as I pleased. At first I thought of them as bible-like, something you would automatically think was a Death Note, but they seemed difficult to use that way… So I switched it to a basic college notebook that would be easy to use. Also, and this was something I thought up later, their appearance could change based on the era. Like in old Japan they could look like scrolls, or in medieval Europe like the Old Testament.

The Text on the Death Note

©RYUK'S

RYUK'S NOTE

I designed it while thinking about what Ryuk's writing would look like. The text on the cover was written directly by Ryuk. The reason the same thing is written on Sidoh's notebook is because Ryuk added that after he picked it up.

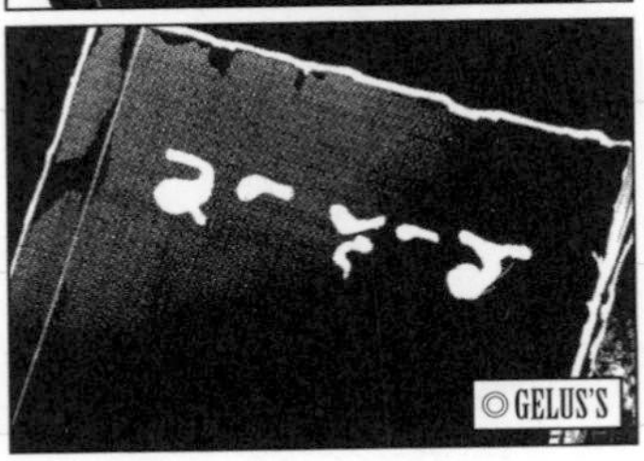

©GELUS'S

GELUS'S NOTE

At first I had detailed patterns on his notebook but I felt like they were too pretty for Gelus and covered them with black. So the white on it is all that's left from that. The text is in the Shinigami language and each Shinigami has their own written language. Some use letters while some use pictures. Though I'm assuming that all Shinigami can read each other's languages.

The Shinigami Realm

DESIGN CONCEPT

There's no real design motif, but I like to imagine it as an abandoned building with chunks of steel just sitting around… I think of it being inside something and really having a claustrophobic feeling. But since I never settled on anything concrete, it would change every time it appeared. Sometimes it was a dry field, sometimes it was a room full of bones… If it were ever to be used as the setting for a story, I would really like to develop it further.

HOW TO READ

RULES & TRICKS

The rules for using the notebook and the tricks the characters devised are two of the hallmarks of *Death Note*. Let's look at how they shaped the story.

Death Note Investigation File

1 Death Note Basic Knowledge

There are so many rules for using the Death Note that not even the Shinigami know all of them. This section will explain the many features of the mysterious notebook and how it is used.

I The Death Note's Outer Appearance

It looks and feels like a normal college notebook. However, it is made out of material not found on Earth and said to be impossible to analyze with human science.

◎ Color
Most notebooks are black, but there are some in other colors. The color and shape do not affect the notebook's function.

◎ Material
They are created from an unknown material. However, the pages look and feel like regular paper and it is possible to tear and burn them.

COVER

Usually, nothing is written on the cover of a Death Note. However, Shinigami sometimes write their name or the notebook's title as a joke.

◎ Shape
Although they may currently look like notebooks, other forms have existed in the past—scrolls, for example. It could be that the notebook's form changes based on the human era.

INTERIOR

The interior looks exactly the same as that of a school notebook, with ruled white pages. The notebook is activated when someone's name is written in it.

← A mysterious feature: No matter how many names you write down, the notebook never runs out of pages.

INSIDE COVER

The inside cover of Ryuk's notebook has a list of rules in English. This is something Ryuk added for the benefit of humans picking up the notebook.

"HOW TO USE IT..."
GEEZ, IT'S ALL IN ENGLISH. WHAT A PAIN...

← The reason the rules are in English is because it's the most commonly understood language.

II

A human will die 40 seconds after his name is entered into the notebook. It's also possible to specify the cause and conditions of the victim's death.

ause and Conditions of Death

f you write in a name and cause of death, you are iven an additional six minutes and 40 seconds to write he conditions of the death. If an impossible condition s specified, the person will die of a heart attack.

➔ You an first vrite the ause and onditions of death and hen add in he name.

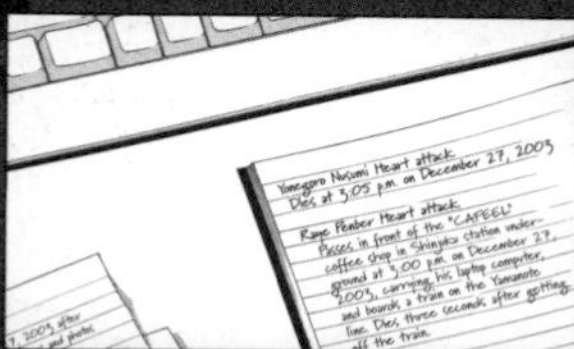

Jsing Pieces of the Notebook

Vriting names on pieces of the notebook will have he same effect. The benefits are that you don't ave to worry about carrying the notebook around nd you can quickly dispose of the evidence.

➔ Using pieces of the otebook enables you to ill people in numerous nd unobserved ways.

WHILE I REACH INTO THE BAG WITH MY LEFT...
WRITE OUT ONE LETTER OF THE GUY'S NAME...

Name and Cause of Death

When a name is written down, it is necessary to have the person's face in mind. This is to prevent every human who has the same name as the one you have written into the notebook from being killed. If you neglect to write down a cause of death, the person will die of a heart attack.

↑ You can first write the cause and conditions of death and then add in the name.

III Ownership of the Death Note and Shinigami

Those who become owners of a Death Note will be possessed by its previous owner, a Shinigami. The Shinigami is attached to the person until the Death Note is returned or ownership changes.

ONCE A NAME IS WRITTEN DOWN IN THE DEATH NOTE, YOU CAN'T DO ANYTHING ABOUT IT. YOU MORE THAN ANYBODY ELSE HERE SHOULD KNOW THAT.
GOODBYE, LIGHT YAGAMI.

↑ Ryuk writes down Light's name because he's bored of watching im. According to the rules, this allows him to go home.

Shinigami Possess Those with a Death Note

Those who touch a Death Note will be able to see and hear the Shinigami it belongs to. The Shinigami will not interfere with the human, but it also has no obligation to help, either. It will most likely just sit back and observe.

↑ The owner is able to talk to the Shinigami. To people nearby, it will seem like he's talking to himself.

Death Note Investigation File

2 Change of Ownership

The Kira case revolved around three notebooks, not counting Ryuk's personal one. Here their ownership will be tracked chronologically and their impact on the case examined.

➡ After visiting Light's house, Misa lends him her Death Note. In this case, she keeps ownership.

⬇ When the notebook is forfeited, all memories relating to it are lost. Thus the evidence is eliminated.

I FORFEIT OWNERSHIP OF THIS DEATH NOTE.

IF YOU CAN'T TRUST ME NO MATTER WHAT, THEN TAKE MY DEATH NOTE.

Following the Complicated Web Left by the Notebooks

Light transferred ownership of the notebook while continuing to kill criminals. This was a ploy to avoid suspicion from L and his investigators. By following the movements of his notebook, you should be able to understand Light's plans. When examining the path the notebooks took, please pay special attention to the following two rules: "When ownership is forfeited, memories relating to the notebook are erased and cannot be regained unless the previous owner touches the notebook again," and "lending the notebook to someone does not cause loss of ownership."

THE FOUR NOTEBOOKS SEEN IN THE HUMAN WORLD

Gelus's Notebook

This is the notebook that caused Gelus to die when he saved Misa. It would pass from Rem to Misa and eventually to Mikami. This was the notebook that played the key role in the battle with Near.

Ryuk's Notebook

AND ...

This is the notebook that Ryuk owns and keeps on his hip. It wasn't used in the Kira case until Light's name was written into it.

Rem's Notebook

This is the notebook that was left behind when Rem died. Light then picked it up and gained ownership. During the battle with Mello, this notebook was given to the task force in order to attack the mafia members.

Sidoh's Notebook

DEATH NOTE

This is the notebook that Ryuk picked up in the Shinigami realm. He wrote rules into it and dropped it into the human world. It passed through Light, Higuchi and Mello until finally being returned to its original owner.

'he Tracks of the Death Notes n the Human World

take a look at how Light managed the notebooks in his battles with L, Higuchi, Mello, and Near.

The Battle with L

When pressured by L, Light shuffled the two notebooks. The aim was to have Rem search for someone to take over as Kira and to recover Misa's memory and her knowledge of Ryuzaki's name.

idoh's Notebook

11.28.2003

er: Light, Shinigami: Ryuk
picks up the Death Note at his school campus. He d soon begin killing criminals with it.

↓ Light had the notebooks passed back and forth a total of five times. It was all part of his plan.

6.1.2004

er: None, Shinigami: Ryuk
shuffles the notebooks a fourth time. He forfeits rship and returns it to Ryuk.

6.1.2004

er: None, Shinigami: Rem
shuffles notebooks a fifth time. It is passed from o Rem.

rder to save Misa, Rem takes Sidoh's notebook and es for a new Kira, but...

● Gelus's Notebook

3.20.2004

Owner: Misa, Shinigami: Rem
Misa receives Gelus's notebook from Rem.

5.25.2004

Owner: Misa, Shinigami: Rem
Misa comes to the Yagami home and gives her Death Note to Light. Ownership does not change.

5.31.2004

Owner: Light, Shinigami: Rem
Misa is captured by L and forfeits ownership. At this point, it transfers to Light.

6.1.2004

Owner: None, Shinigami: Rem
Light shuffles the notebooks. He then forfeits ownership and returns the notebook to Rem.

6.1.2004

Owner: None, Shinigami: Ryuk
Light shuffles the notebooks again. Rem hands the notebook to Ryuk.

6.1.2004

Owner: Light, Shinigami: Ryuk
Light shuffles the notebooks a third time. Ryuk drops the notebook for Light to retrieve, and Light once again gains ownership. He then hides the notebook in the ground.

6.7.2004

Owner: None, Shinigami: Ryuk
While confined by L, Light forfeits ownership. Ryuk returns to the Shinigami realm.

The Battle with the Yotsuba Kira

After Higuchi is arrested, Sidoh's notebook is confiscated by the Japanese task force. But Light acquires Rem's notebook and continues his killing spree.

● Sidoh's Notebook

▪▪▪ 6.14.2004

Owner: Higuchi, Shinigami: Rem
Rem gives the notebook to Higuchi. This notebook is then used to restart the killing of criminals.

▼

▪▪▪ 10.28.2004

Owner: Light, Shinigami: Rem
Light touches this notebook and regains his memories. By killing Higuchi he gains ownership of it as well. After that, it is held at the task force headquarters.

▼

▪▪▪ 11.15.2004

Owner: Light, Shinigami: None
After L's death, the surviving members choose to have Soichiro watch over the notebook; the ownership switches to Soichiro.

● Rem's Notebook

➔ After Rem's death, Light picks up her notebook. Until he hands it to Ryuk, this notebook has no Shinigami attached to it.

▪▪▪ 11.5.2004

Owner: Light, Shinigami: None
Rem kills L and Watari, bringing about her own death. Light recovers her notebook and becomes the owner.

● Gelus's Notebook

➔ Misa's notebook is returned to her. She regains her memories but cannot remember Ryuzaki's name.

▪▪▪ 11.4.2004

Owner: Misa, Shinigami: Ryuk
On Light's orders, Misa digs up the notebook and regains ownership of it. She keeps enough pages to kill criminals and then reburies it.

The Battle with Mello

Mello and his gang go after Sidoh's notebook, held at the task force headquarters. In order to dispose of Mello, Light gives up Rem's notebook temporarily and hands it to Soichiro.

● Gelus's Notebook

▪▪▪ 10.28.2009

Owner: Misa, Shinigami: Ryuk
Misa gives her notebook to Light but doesn't surrender ownership. Incidentally, it's never revealed exactly when Misa dug up this notebook.

🠉 In order not to lose his memories, Light makes sure a notebook is touching him at all times.

● Sidoh's Notebook

🠉 Sidoh comes to Earth to retrieve his notebook.

▪▪▪ 10.13.2009

Owner: Snydar, Shinigami: Sidoh
Mello and the mafia take the notebook that was being held at the task force headquarters. Sidoh appears and attaches himself to Snydar.

▪▪▪ 11.11.2009

Owner: None, Shinigami: Sidoh
Snydar dies the moment the task force storms the mafia base. Ownership eventually transfers to Light, and the notebook is returned to Sidoh, who then leaves the human world.

● Rem's Notebook

▪▪▪ 10.28.2009

Owner: None, Shinigami: Ryuk
Light gives the notebook to Ryuk and forfeits ownership. But because he has Misa's notebook he does not lose his memories.

▼

▪▪▪ 11.1.2009

Owner: Soichiro, Shinigami: Ryuk
Ryuk hands the notebook to Soichiro. Ownership transfers to Soichiro, and Ryuk becomes attached to this notebook from here on.

▼

▪▪▪ 11.11.2009

Owner: Light, Shinigami: Ryuk
After Soichiro dies the notebook is kept in a safe at the task force headquarters; the first person to touch it and gain ownership is Light. He then gives the notebook he borrowed from Misa back to her.

The Battle with Near

At this point, the two notebooks remaining on earth are Gelus's and Rem's. Light sends Gelus's notebook to a Kira worshipper named Mikami and plans to eliminate Near.

Gelus's Notebook

▪ 11.27.2009

wner: Mikami, Shinigami: Ryuk
Light's orders, Misa sends the notebook to Mikami and
en forfeits ownership. Kira's killings continue with this
tebook. Initially, Ryuk is attached to this notebook, but
ly for a short while.

▪ 12.11.2009

wner: Mikami, Shinigami: Ryuk
ikami sends pages of the notebook to Takada. After that,
e notebook is placed in a bank safety deposit box.

▪ 1.27.2010

wner: Mikami, Shinigami: Ryuk
ivanni steals it from the bank and hands it to Near.
ecause Mikami did not deliberately make the transfer,
ere is no change in ownership.

▪ 1.28.2010

wner: Mikami, Shinigami: Ryuk
e notebook is burned by Near and disappears from the
man world.

● Rem's Notebook

← After Soichiro's death, the ownership transfers to Light.

↓ Near burns Gelus's and Rem's notebooks; none remain in the human world.

THE MOMENT NEAR FOUND OUT THAT THE 13-DAY RULE AND THE RULE ABOUT EVERYBODY DYING IF THE NOTEBOOK IS BURNT WEREN'T TRUE, HE BURNED BOTH NOTEBOOKS ON THE SPOT.
HE WAS DESTROYING THE EVIDENCE THAT HE WROTE MIKAMI'S NAME. I'D BE TOO SCARED TO EVEN TRY TO BURN THAT THING...

▪▪▪ 1.28.2010

Owner: Light, Shinigami: Ryuk
Aizawa brings the notebook to the Yellow Box warehouse. It is later burned by Near and disappears from the human world.

Ryuk's Notebook

Light Yagami

Sidoh's Notebook

Kuro Otoharada, Takuo Shibuimaru, Lind L. Tailor, Kiichiro Osoreda, Raye Penber, Naomi Misora, Arayoshi Hatori, Yukito Shiraba, FBI agents, SPK members

Gelus's Notebook

Kazuhiko Hibima, Hirokazu Ukita, Rod Ross, Hitoshi Demegawa, Mello, mafia members

Rem's Notebook

Ginzo Kaneboshi, L, Watari

The Important Names Written into Each Notebook

When you take a look at the Kira case, you'll see that the following characters' names are written into the notebooks. The main Death Notes that Light uses are Sidoh's and Rem's.

↑ Ryuk's notebook plays no part in the case until Light's name is written in it.

Death Note Investigation File

3 How to Use It: The Complete Rules

This section reveals the rules governing the use of the Death Note. They have been divided into four parts: How to Use It, Ownership, the Shinigami Eyes, and the Shinigami Rules. Here the rules will be explained by highlighting specific scenes from the series.

I. How to Use It

1.1 ENTERING NAMES

The human whose name is written in this note shall die. This note will not take effect unless the writer has the subject's face in mind when writing his/her name. This is to prevent people who share the same name from being affected.

The Death Note will not ever affect a victim whose name has been misspelled four times.

When the same name is written in two or more Death Notes, the Note which was used first will take effect, regardless of the time of death.

If the same name is written in two or more Death Notes within 0.06 seconds, the entry is regarded as simultaneous; the Death Notes will not take effect and the individual will not die.

If a Death Note owner accidentally misspells a person's name four times, that person will be free from being killed by the Death Note. However, if the Death Note owner intentionally misspells the name four times, the owner will die.

The Death Note will not take effect if a victim's name is written on several different pages. However, the front and back of a page is considered to be one page. For example, the Death Note will still take effect if the victim's last name is written on the front page and first name on the back.

IF I WRITE HIS NAME INTO THE DEATH NOTE, EVEN IF HIS NAME REALLY IS HIDEKI RYUGA...
NOT TO MENTION, HE'S USING THE CONSPICUOUSLY FAKE NAME OF HIDEKI RYUGA.

Realizing that people sharing the same name cannot all be killed at once, L uses the name of an idol singer named Hideki Ryuga and approaches Light.

KYOSUKE
HIGUCHI

This rule isn't applied in the series but it could be useful if an owner only has a small piece of the notebook available to use.

1.2 ENTERING THE CAUSES AND CONDITIONS OF DEATH

If the cause of death is written within 40 seconds of the subject's name, it will happen.

If the cause of death is not specified, the subject will die of a heart attack.

After writing the cause of death, the details of the death should be entered within the next six minutes and 40 seconds.

URGH!

If a cause of death isn't specified, the victim dies of a heart attack in 40 seconds. However, this rule can be delayed for twenty-three days, meaning you can write down "dies by heart attack in [XX] days."

How to Use It

Although it is possible to control a person's actions, if an impossible situation is written down the person will die of a heart attack.

Light was able to wipe out all the FBI agents by writing their conditions of death ahead of time and having Raye write in the names.

"Accident" is a condition of death, so six minutes and 40 seconds are provided to write down additional details. The conditions do not take effect until this time has passed.

As with an accident, when "death by disease" is written, the time cannot be specified unless you use a heart attack. It takes more time than an "accident," but you can kill a person in a much more natural way.

If the time of death is specified within 40 seconds after writing the cause of death as a heart attack, the time of death can be manipulated and can go into effect within 40 seconds after writing the name.

The conditions of death will not be realized unless they are physically possible for that human or could be reasonably assumed to be carried out by that human.

Since the limitations applying to the conditions of a death are unknown to the Shinigami, Death Note owners must find out on their own.

You may write the cause and/or details of death prior to filling in the name of the individual. Be sure to insert the name in front of the cause of death. You have about 19 days (according to the human calendar) to fill in a name.

Suicide is a universally valid cause of death as all humans are thought to possess the potential to commit suicide. It is, therefore, something that may be reasonably assumed of an individual.

Whether the cause of the individual's death is either suicide or an accident, if it would lead to the death of more than the intended victim, the person will simply die of a heart attack. This is to ensure that other lives are not impacted.

After an individual's name, time of death, and conditions of death are entered in the notebook, the time and conditions of death may be altered as many times as desired as long as they are changed within six minutes and 40 seconds from the time they are filled in. But, of course, this is only possible before the victim dies.

If you write "dies of accident" for the cause of death, the victim will die from a natural accident six minutes and 40 seconds after the time of entry.

Even if only one name is written in the Death Note, if the victim's death causes other humans that are not written in it to die, the cause of death will default to a heart attack.

If you write "dies from disease" and specify which disease and the time of death, there must be a sufficient amount of time for the disease to progress. If the set time is too tight, the victim will die of a heart attack six minutes and 40 seconds after the entry in the Death Note.

If you write, "dies from disease" as the cause of death but specify only a time of death and not the actual disease, the victim will die from a plausible disease.

The Death Note can only operate within a 23-day window (in the human calendar). This is called the 23-Day rule.

If you write "dies from disease" and specify which disease but not a time of death, if the progression of the disease takes more than 24 days, the 23-Day rule will not take effect and the human will die at an appropriate time depending on the disease. However, rewriting the cause and/or details of death must be done within six minutes and 40 seconds: you cannot change the victim's time of death, however soon it may be.

In order for the Death Note to take effect the victim's name must be written on one page; however, the cause and conditions of death may be entered on other pages. This will work as long as the person who writes in the Death Note keeps the specific victim's name in mind when writing the cause and conditions of death.

If the cause and conditions of death are written in before the victim's name is, multiple names can be written as long as they are entered within 40 seconds and the cause and conditions of death are not impossible. In the event that the cause of death is possible but the conditions are not, only the cause of death will take effect for that victim. If both the cause and the conditions are impossible, that victim will die of a heart attack.

When you write multiple names in the Death Note and then write down one cause of death within 40 seconds of writing the first victim's name, the cause will take effect for all the written names. Also, after writing the cause of death, even if the conditions of death are written within six minutes and 40 seconds in the human world, the conditions will apply only to the victims for whom they are possible. Those for whom the conditions are not possible will simply die from the specified cause.

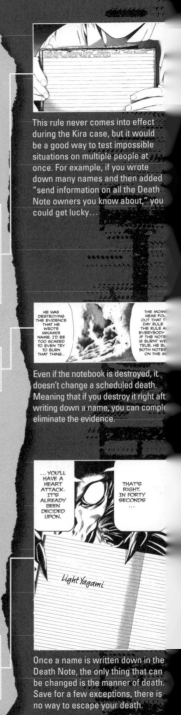

This rule never comes into effect during the Kira case, but it would be a good way to test impossible situations on multiple people at once. For example, if you wrote down many names and then added "send information on all the Death Note owners you know about," you could get lucky...

A human death caused by the Death Note can indirectly lengthen another human's original life span in the human world even without the owner's specific intention to do so.

Once the victim's name, cause of death, and conditions of death have been written down in the Death Note, the death will take place even if that Death Note, or the part of the note used, is destroyed before the stated time of death.

HE WAS DESTROYING THE EVIDENCE THAT HE WROTE MIKAMI'S NAME. I'D BE TOO SCARED TO EVEN TRY TO BURN THAT THING...

Even if the notebook is destroyed, it doesn't change a scheduled death. Meaning that if you destroy it right aft writing down a name, you can comple eliminate the evidence.

If the victim's name has been entered and the Death Note is destroyed while the cause of death is being written, the victim will be killed by a heart attack 40 seconds after the name was entered. If the victim's name and cause of death have already been written, then the victim will be killed within six minutes and 40 seconds via the stated cause of death if it is possible within that period of time. Otherwise, the victim will die by heart attack.

1.3 ALTERATIONS

If you wish to change anything written in the Death Note within six minutes and 40 seconds after you wrote it, you must first rule out the characters you want to erase with two straight lines. The time and conditions of death can be changed, but once the victim's name has been written, that individual's death can never be averted.

It is useless to try to erase names written in the Death Note with erasers or to white them out.

Even if a new victim's name, cause of death, or conditions of death are written on top of the original victim's name, cause of death, or conditions of death, there will be no effect on the original victim's death. The same thing will also apply to erasing what was written with a pencil, or whiting out what was written with a pen.

THAT'S RIGHT. IN FORTY SECONDS ...
...YOU'LL HAVE A HEART ATTACK. IT'S ALREADY BEEN DECIDED UPON.
Light Yagami

Once a name is written down in the Death Note, the only thing that can be changed is the manner of death. Save for a few exceptions, there is no way to escape your death.

1.4 LIMITATIONS

The Death Note will not affect those less than 780 days old.

You cannot kill humans who are more than 124 years of age with the Death Note.

You cannot kill humans with less than 12 minutes of life left (in human calculations).

You cannot set a death date longer than the victim's original life span. Even if the victim's death is entered in the Death Note, if it is beyond his or her original life span, the victim will die before the set time.

1.5 OTHER THINGS TO CONSIDER

The human who uses this note can go neither to Heaven nor to Hell.

One page taken from the Death Note, or even a fragment of the page, possesses the full power of the note.

Any writing instrument or medium (cosmetics, blood, etc.) may be used, as long as it can write directly onto the note and create legible text.

The pages of the Death Note will never run out.

Some limited number of Death Notes have white or red front covers, but this makes no difference in their effectiveness as compared with the black Death Notes.

II Ownership

2.1 THE BEGINNING OF OWNERSHIP

This note shall become the property of the human world once it touches ground in the human world.

The owner of a Death Note can recognize the image and voice of the original owner—a Shinigami, for example.

The human who touches the Death Note can recognize the image and voice of its original Shinigami owner, even if the human is not the owner of the note.

Whenever a Shinigami in the human world dies and leaves behind its Death Note, the note's finder automatically becomes the owner. However, in this case, only a human who can see and hear that Shinigami is able to see and touch the Death Note. It is very unlikely, but if by any chance another Shinigami picks up the Death Note, that Shinigami becomes the owner.

ight had realized that the notebook vould work even if the name were vritten in blood. He kills Higuchi by vriting with his own blood and tries o do the same against Near when ie's pushed to the brink.

f a notebook has been dropped, wnership is gained the moment it s picked up. However, a Shinigami nust only appear within 39 days, so here's no guarantee that you will neet a Shinigami immediately.

3y touching the notebook, you are ıble to see its former Shinigami wner. You are able to see and hear hat Shinigami but not any others.

2.2 SITUATIONS SURROUNDING OWNERSHIP

If you lose the Death Note or have it stolen, you will lose its ownership unless you retrieve it within 490 days.

When the owner of the Death Note dies while the note is on loan, its ownership will be transferred to the person who is holding it at that time. If the Death Note is stolen and the owner is killed by the thief, its ownership will automatically be transferred to the thief.

The individuals who lose ownership of a Death Note will also lose their memories of it. However, this does not mean that they will lose all memories from the period of ownership: they will only lose the memories involving the Death Note.

When an individual with ownership of more than two Death Notes loses possession of one of them, he will no longer be able to recognize or hear that Death Note's Shinigami anymore. The Shinigami will leave, but all the memories involving that Death Note will remain to the owner as long as he maintains ownership of at least one other Death Note.

If a person loses possession of a Death Note he will not recognize its Shinigami by sight or voice anymore. However, if the owner lets someone else touch that Death Note, from that time on that person will recognize the Shinigami. Accordingly, that person will continue to recognize the Shinigami's appearance and voice until he or she actually becomes the owner of the Death Note and subsequently loses possession of it.

When regaining ownership of a Death Note, the memories associated with it will also return. In cases where the owner was involved with other Death Notes as well, memories of all the Death Notes involved will return. The memories will return just by touching the Death Note, even without obtaining ownership of it.

Memories related to a Death Note are lost when its ownership is lost. But they may regained by either obtaining the ownership once again or by touching the Death Note. This can be done up to six times per Death Note. Any times more than that, the person's memory of the Death Note will not return and they will have to use it without any previous memory of it.

Even if you do not actually possess the Death Note, you may still use it to full effect.

You may lend the Death Note to another person while maintaining its ownership. The borrower may lend it to yet another person as well.

The person who borrows the Death Note will not be followed by a Shinigami. The Shinigami always remains with the owner of the Death Note. Also, the borrower cannot trade for the Shinigami Eyes.

When Light touches Higuchi's notebook, he's merely borrowi By killing Higuchi, he's able to ownership.

When held as a suspect by L, L forfeits his ownership of the D Note.

Misa regains her memories by touching the buried notebook. she never owned that notebo memories would not have retu

In order to transfer ownership to another person, you must consciously intend to do so. Ju handing it to someone will not accomplish this.

A SHINI-GAMI!!

By touching Misa's notebook, Light can finally see Rem. The same situation happens later with Sidoh's appearance.

Only by touching each other's Death Notes can owners recognize the appearance or voice of each other's Shinigami.

Losing memory of the Death Note by passing the ownership to another or by abandoning ownership will only occur when someone is actually killed using that Death Note. You will not lose memory of the Death Note if, for example, you merely owned it and did not write down anyone's name. In this case, you will not be able to hear or see the Shinigami anymore. You will also lose the power of the Shinigami Eyes if you made the trade.

2.3 MULTIPLE NOTEBOOKS

Someone possessing more than one Death Note may write down a victim's name in one of the Death Notes and the cause of death in the other, and the death will still occur. The order of writing, however, is unimportant: if you write down the cause of death in one Death Note and afterward write the name in the other, the death will occur. This can also be accomplished by two Death Note owners working together. In this case, it's necessary that the two touch each other's Death Notes.

HOAP! SHINI-GAMI.

Three Shinigami—Ryuk, Rem, and Sidoh—visit the human world. Since the number of Death Notes in the human world is three (not counting those owned by a Shinigami), this rule never comes into effect.

Only six Death Notes are allowed to exist at a time in the human world. Of course, the Death Notes that the Shinigami own do not count. This means only six Shinigami that have passed on their Death Notes to humans can be in the human world at once.

One Shinigami is allowed to pass on Death Notes to only three humans at a time. However, it is possible for a single Shinigami to hand out up to six Death Notes—by handing three humans two Death Notes each, for example. In other words, one human could potentially own all six Death Notes.

If a seventh Death Note is given to a human when six already exist in the human world, nothing will happen when it is used.

In the event that there are more than six Death Notes in the human world, only the first six Death Notes that have been delivered to humans will have effect. The seventh Death Note will not become active until one of the other six Death Notes is destroyed or a Shinigami takes one of them back to the Shinigami realm.

III The Shinigami Eyes

3.1 THE EYE TRADE

A human who becomes the owner of a Death Note can, in exchange for half of his or her remaining life, acquire the power of the Shinigami Eyes, which will enable him or her to see a human's name and remaining life span when looking at them.

HE GOT ME! NO WAY...
MISA... HER REMAINING LIFESPAN HAS DECREASED AGAIN...
SHE MADE THE EYE TRADE WITH RYUK...

Misa trades for the Shinigami Eyes on two occasions. Had Misa's remaining life span been 60 years, the first trade would have cut it down to 30 years and the second trade down to 15 years.

If you have traded for the Shinigami Eyes, you will lose that power as well as the memories of the Death Note once you lose ownership of the note. Moreover, the half of your life you traded away will not be restored.

An individual with Shinigami Eyes can see the name and life span of another human by looking at that person's face. By gaining ownership of a Death Note, an individual not only gains the ability to kill but also cannot be killed by a Death Note. From this point on, a person with a Death Note cannot see the life span of other Death Note owners, including him- or herself.

In order to see the names and life spans of humans using the power of Shinigami Eyes, the owner must be able to see more than half of that person's face. When looking from top to bottom, he must be able to see at least from the head to the nose. If he looks at only the eyes and under, he will not be able to see the person's name and life span. Also, even though some parts of the face—for example the eyes, nose or mouth—are hidden, if he can basically see the whole face he will be able to see the person's name and life span.

It is still not clear how much exposure is needed to see a name and life span (more research needs to be done). If the above conditions are met, names and life spans can be seen using photos and digital images, no matter how old they are. But this is sometimes affected by the resolution and size of the image. Also, names and life spans cannot be seen using drawings, however realistic they may be.

Those with Shinigami Eyes will have eyesight of over 3.6 in the human measurement, regardless of their original eyesight.

If you have traded for the Shinigami Eyes, you will see a person's primary life span in the human world.

The names you will see with the Shinigami Eyes are the names needed to kill that person. You will be able to see a name even if it isn't officially registered anywhere.

Humans who have traded for Shinigami Eyes cannot see the names or life spans of humans who have already passed away (by looking at photos of them, for example).

The use of the Death Note in the human world sometimes affects other humans' lives or shortens their original life spans, even if their names are not actually written in the notebook itself. In these cases, no matter the cause, the Shinigami sees only the original life span and not the shortened life span.

No matter what medical or scientific method is employed, it is impossible for humans to distinguish whether or not a human has Shinigami Eyes. Even Shinigami cannot distinguish this fact, except for the very Shinigami that traded his or her eye power with that human.

IV The Shinigami Rules

4.1 RELATIONSHIP WITH THE OWNER

The human owner of a Death Note is possessed by its original Shinigami owner until he or she dies.

Those who have the Shinigami Eyes cannot see the life spans of those who own a Death Note, including their own. Meaning that if someone with the Shinigami Eyes sees another owner, they will know instantly that that person possesse a Death Note.

OH, HERE'S ANOTHER PERSON WITHOUT A NAME OR A LIFE SPAN...
IF YOU CAN'T SEE EITHER, THE PERSON'S ALREADY DEAD.
I GUESS IF YOU'RE IN THE MAFIA, YOU DON'T GET TO LIVE VERY LONG. HA HA!

When looking at a photograph with the Shinigami Eyes, if you can see the person's name and life span, they are alive. If you can only see their name, they are a Death Note owner. If you cannot see either, they are deceased.

I THANK YOU FOR THESE EYES.
SHING
I CAN NOW BRING JUSTICE TO THOSE WHOSE NAMES I DO NOT KNOW, AND THOSE WITH ALIASES.

It's impossible to physically tell wh has the Shinigami Eyes.

How to Use It

'he reason Ryuk reveals the Death Note rules to Light is to alleviate iis boredom. Even though he is requently asked about other rules ie has no duty to reveal them.

t takes Rem thirteen days to find a iew Kira before choosing Higuchi, o it is assumed that she returns to he Shinigami realm during this time.

3ecause Sidoh is in a situation vhere a human had taken his Death Note, he's allowed to be in the iuman world. However, because of the rules he is not able to talk to iny human about notebooks not originally belonging to him.

If a human uses a Death Note, its Shinigami owner must appear in front of the human within 39 days after he or she uses the note.

The original Shinigami owners of Death Notes don't, in principle, do anything to help or prevent the deaths brought about by the notes.

A Shinigami has no obligation to completely explain how to use the note or the rules that apply to the human who owns it.

The Shinigami must not tell humans the names or life spans of individuals he sees. This is to avoid confusion in the human world.

A Shinigami bringing a Death Note into the human world must make sure that a human uses it. Although it is unlikely that a Shinigami who has possessed a human would die, if it does happen, the Death Note brought into the human world will not lose its power.

Shinigami must not stay in the human world without a particular reason. Acceptable reasons to stay in the human world are as follows:

I. When the Shinigami's Death Note is handed to a human.
II. Finding a human to take possession of a Death Note should be done from the Shinigami realm, but if it is within 82 hours this may also be done in the human world.
III. When a Shinigami stalks an individual with an intention to kill them, as long as it is within 82 hours of possessing them the Shinigami may stay in the human world.

The Shinigami must not hand the Death Note directly to a child under six years of age (based on the human calendar). But Death Notes that have been dropped into the human world, and are part of the human world, can be used upon humans of almost any age with the same effect.

The owner of a Death Note cannot be killed by a Shinigami who is in the Shinigami realm. Also, a Shinigami who comes to the human world with the objective of killing the owner of a Death Note will not be able to do so. Only a Shinigami that has passed on its Death Note to a human is able to kill the owner of the Death Note.

If a Death Note is owned in the human world against a Shinigami's will, that Shinigami is permitted to stay in the human world in order to retrieve it. In that case, if there are other Death Notes in the human world, the Shinigami are not allowed to reveal to the humans the Death Note owner's identity or its location.

If a Shinigami's Death Note is taken away for whatever reason, it can only be retrieved from the Shinigami who possesses it at the time. If there is no Shinigami, but a human, the only way the Shinigami can get it back is to first touch the Death Note and become the one who haunts that particular human. Then they have to wait until the person dies to take it away. And they have to do it before any other human touches it.

After a Shinigami brings a Death Note to the human world and gives its ownership to a human, the Shinigami has the right to kill the human using its own Death Note for any reason, such as disliking the owner.

The following are the cases in which a Shinigami that has brought the Death Note into the human world is allowed to return to the Shinigami realm:

I. When the Shinigami has seen the end of the first owner of the Death Note brought into the human world and has written that human's name into his or her own Death Note.
II. When the Death Note is destroyed and cannot be used by humans anymore.
III. If nobody claims ownership of the Death Note, it is unnecessary to possess anyone.
IV. If, for any reason, the Shinigami possessing the Death Note is replaced by another Shinigami.
V. When a Shinigami loses track of the Death Note that he or she possesses, or cannot identify which human owns the Death Note, or cannot locate where the owner is, and therefore needs to find such information using the observation holes in the Shinigami realm.
VI. Even in cases II, III, and IV, Shinigami are obliged to confirm the death of the first owner and write down that human's name in his or her Death Note even when he or she is in the Shinigami realm.

In the Shinigami realm there are a few copies of what humans might call a "user handbook" for the Death Notes in the human world. Although Shinigami may not give the handbook to humans, it is perfectly okay for them to teach humans about its contents, no matter what that may be.

4.2 USING THE DEATH NOTE

A Shinigami can extend its life by writing human names in a Death Note, but a human cannot. A person can only shorten his or her own life by using the note.

Even the original Shinigami owners of Death Notes do not know much about them.

Shinigami must own at least one personal Death Note, which must never be lent to or written on by a human.

Shinigami may exchange and write in each others' Death Notes.

If a Shinigami decides to use a Death Note to end the life of the killer of an individual it favors, that individual's life will be extended but the Shinigami will die. The Shinigami will then disappear but the Death Note will remain. The ownership of this Death Note is usually carried over to the next Shinigami that touches it, but it is common sense that it be returned to the Shinigami King.

By manipulating the death of a human who has influence over another human's life, that human's original life span can sometimes be lengthened. If a Shinigami intentionally does this that Shinigami will die, but even if a human does the same, the human will not die.

When Light is confined by L, he forfeits ownership of the Death Not and Ryuk has no human to attach himself to. Therefore Ryuk must return to the Shinigami realm.

When Sidoh is asked by Mello to tell him about the other notebook owners, he checks a document containing rules. Is this some kind o Shinigami handbook?

After a Shinigami dies the notebook remains and becomes the property of the next being who touches it. Rem picks up Gelus's notebook after he dies and tries to carry out his will.

AND I'M FEMALE, TOO.
WELL, ABOUT THAT, YOU DON'T NEED TO PUT MUCH THOUGHT INTO IT. MY WANTING TO PROTECT YOU IS MORE LIKE A DESIRE, IT'S DIFFERENT FROM LOVE.

Ryuk is male and Rem is female. From a human point of view, it's hard to tell their gender apart, yet it appears they do have emotions relating to the opposite sex. For example, Ryuk becomes shy and embarrassed when Misa hugs him.

'he Shinigami realm contains observation holes that allow them to ook down into the human world. If Shinigami knows a person's face, t can apparently find that person nstantly just by thinking about what hey look like.

4.3 SHINIGAMI LIFE

A Shinigami cannot be killed even if stabbed or shot. However, there are ways to kill them, which are not generally known even to the Shinigami themselves.

There are male and female Shinigami, but it is neither permitted nor possible for them to have sexual relations with humans. They also cannot have sex with each other.

As long as a Shinigami has at least once seen a human and knows his or her name and life span, the Shinigami is capable of finding that human by looking down from an observation hole in their realm.

The Shinigami realm has laws that govern it. If a Shinigami should break a law, there are nine levels of punishment, with the severity starting at Level Eight and going up to Level One, plus an Extreme Level. At severity levels above Three, the Shinigami will be punished and killed. Killing a human without using the Death Note merits punishment at the Extreme Level.

Shinigami will not die from lack of sleep. They do not need sleep, so to them it is merely laziness. Shinigami in the human world shouldn't act lazy merely because they are required to possess a human.

DEATH COLUMN / The Fake Rules

Besides the rules already written in the notebook, Light adds two fake rules in order to confuse the investigation team. This causes trouble for everyone from L to Near.

If you make this note unusable by tearing it up or burning it, all the humans who have touched the note until then will die.

YEAH, WITH THIS RULE, AS LONG AS I DON'T FORFEIT OWNERSHIP, I DON'T HAVE TO WORRY ABOUT LOSING MY MEMORIES BECAUSE MY DAD DECIDES TO DESTROY THE NOTEBOOK...

⬆ Predicting that the notebook would fall into the hands of the task force, Light adds this rule to insure the Death Note is not destroyed.

If the person using the note fails to consecutively write names of people to be killed within 13 days, then the user will die.

YESTERDAY, TWO WEEK'S WORTH OF CRIMINALS WERE KILLED ALL AT ONCE.
YEAH, KIRA IS BACK.

⬆ Light creates this rule as an alibi. Because he is imprisoned for 50 days, nobody besides L suspects him after this rule is revealed.

Death Note Case Study

As one reads through the complicated rules, many questions may arise. This section will examine some of these questions by using specific scenes from the series.

CASE 01 Is It Possible for the Death Note User to Die?

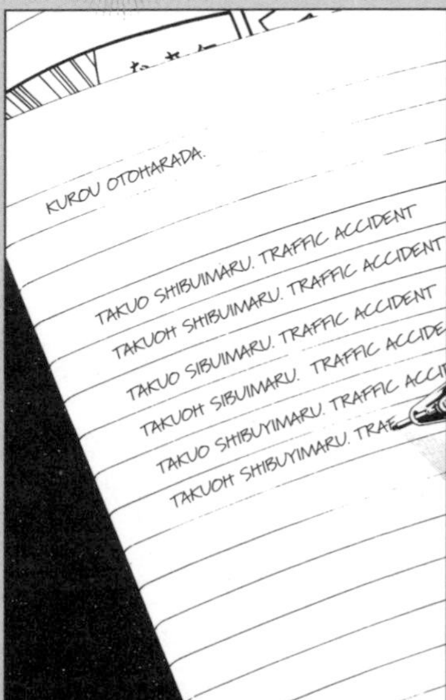

Near and Mello figure out that the 13-Day rule Light created is a fake, but there is a rule that can cause the user of a Death Note to die that comes into effect if the user misspells someone's name four times. Light misspells Shibuimaru's name six times; how does he survive? The key is that he doesn't *intentionally* misspell the name. Also, if you pay attention to the names Light writes down, the first one is the correct spelling. So it's deemed that no mistake took place and the Death Note works as it should.

I'M... OUTTA HERE, MAN!
DAMN IDIOT, WHAT WERE YOU THINK-- YAAA.. YAAA-RGH!!

↑→ Light doesn't know the proper spelling of Takuo Shibuimaru's name, so he writes down seven versions. Luckily he gets it right on the first try, and Shibuimaru dies in an accident as Light had intended.

Relevant Rule ②

If a Death Note owner accidentally misspells a name four times, the victim cannot be killed by the Death Note. However, if the owner intentionally misspells a name four times, the owner will die.

Relevant Rule ①

The Death Note will not ever affect a victim whose name has been misspelled four times.

CASE 02 Are Death Notes Sometimes Invisible?

➜The Death Note left behind by Rem's passing is visible only to Light and the task force members.

If you read the rules closely, you will see that there are situations where a notebook can be seen by humans and situations where it cannot unless specific conditions are met. For example, when a Shinigami first drops a notebook into the human world, all humans can see it. However, if the Shinigami dies, normal humans cannot see the notebook. In this case, only humans who were able to see the deceased Shinigami will be able to see the Death Note. Thus the notebook that Rem leaves behind is visible only to the Japanese task force members.

Relevant Rule ③

If a Shinigami in the human world dies and leaves a Death Note behind that is then picked up by a human, that person becomes the owner. However, in this case, only humans who can see and hear the Shinigami are able to see and touch the Death Note.

CASE 03 Can You Lose Ownership but Keep Memories?

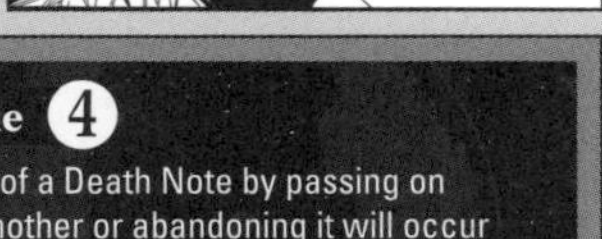

THE MURDER NOTEBOOK. IT'S A SHINIGAMI'S NOTEBOOK, AND PEOPLE WHO TOUCH IT ARE ABLE TO SEE THE SHINIGAMI.

➜It may be confusing, but Mello never has ownership of Sidoh's notebook.

When you forfeit ownership of the notebook, you lose all memories relating to it. However, Soichiro has ownership of a note during the Yotsuba Kira case and his memories remain even after losing ownership to Mello's group. This is because the first rule is overridden by a second: you will not lose your memories of a notebook as long as you do not use it. Mello also does not lose his memories, but this is because he never actually has ownership. (Ownership is with Snydar and other cronies.) In this situation, even had Mello used the notebook, he would not have lost his memories either.

Relevant Rule ④

Losing memory of a Death Note by passing on ownership to another or abandoning it will occur only when someone is actually killed using that Death Note. However, although you will not lose memory of the Death Note, you will not be able to hear or see its Shinigami anymore. You will also lose the power of the Shinigami Eyes if you had traded for them.

CASE 04 Can a Shinigami Possess Two Humans at Once?

...!
HEY, TERU, I'VE TOLD YOU EVERYTHING I NEED TO, SO I'M GOING BACK TO KIRA'S PLACE.

➡ Ryuk changes whom he stays with based on what Light wants. This does not break any rules.

Shinigami must attach themselves to the human they hand the Death Note to, but what do they do when two people have ownership? When Ryuk is asked to bring the notebook to the task force, he is attached to both Misa and Soichiro. And when a notebook is passed to Mikami, he has to attach himself to Mikami and Light. There are actually no rules dealing with multiple humans receiving Death Notes from a single Shinigami. Also, although Shinigami must possess the person who has ownership, there's no rule stating that the Shinigami has to stay with the human 24 hours a day. So Ryuk just goes with whomever Light orders him to and there are no problems.

Relevant Rule 5

The borrower of a Death Note will not be followed by a Shinigami. The Shinigami always remains with the owner of the Death Note. Also, the borrower cannot trade for the Shinigami Eyes.

CASE 05 Are There Times When a Person Written into a Death Note Doesn't Die?

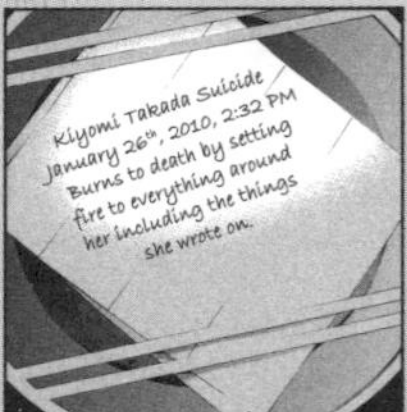

Kiyomi Takada Suicide
January 26th, 2010, 2:32 PM
Burns to death by setting
fire to everything around
her including the things
she wrote on.

➡ Had Light and Mikami written Takada's name down at the same time, we may have seen a different conclusion.

If a name is written into the notebook, the victim basically cannot escape his or her fate. However, there are two exceptions. One, if a name is mistakenly written four times in that notebook previously, and two, if the name is written simultaneously in two separate notebooks. The latter isn't likely but it almost happens when Takada is killed: after Light writes down Takada's name, Mikami does the same. Had Light and Mikami written the name simultaneously, the notebooks would have cancelled each other out and Takada would not have died.

Kiyomi Takada Suicide Burns to death by

Relevant Rule 7

If the same name is written into two or more Death Notes within 0.06 seconds, it is regarded as being entered simultaneously; the Death Notes will not take effect and the individual will not die.

Relevant Rule 6

When the same name is written in two or more Death Notes, the notebook filled in first will take effect regardless of the time of death.

CASE 06 What If a Shinigami Wants to Go Home?

NO, LIGHT. THE ONE WHO'S GOING TO DIE...
...IS YOU.
SKRITCH
SKRITCH

↑ Once Ryuk has seen enough, Light's fate is sealed.

By watching the notebook owner until their life ends and writing his or her name into their own Death Note, a Shinigami can finally return home. However, Ryuk gets tired of waiting and writes Light's name into the notebook early. This doesn't break any rules: a Shinigami is allowed to write down the name of a Death Note owner any time it wants to. When owners are not as dynamic as Light, Shinigami probably become bored with them very quickly and don't wait as long before returning home. However, when a Death Note has been taken, not given, as in Sidoh's case, different rules apply. In that case, the Shinigami must wait until the notebook owner dies or returns it.

Relevant Rule 8

After a Shinigami brings the Death Note to the human world and gives its ownership to a human, the Shinigami may have the right to kill the human using its own Death Note.

CASE 07 Will Destroying the Notebook Save a Victim?

WELL... EVEN IF THAT THEORY IS TRUE...
...THE NOTEBOOK DOESN'T EXIST ANYMORE. SO THERE'S NO PROOF.
DON'T YOU GET IT, THAT'S THE VERY PROOF OF THIS THEORY!

↑ Matsuda's theory may be correct?

In the final chapter Matsuda theorizes that Near wrote Mikami's name into the notebook. The rules show that this would be possible. Destroying a notebook doesn't prevent a victim's death. In other words, had Near written down Mikami's name, burning the notebook would only eliminate the evidence, not change Mikami's fate. If Near knew about this rule, the likelihood that Near wrote down Mikami's name is even higher. Also, at that point in time, the owner of the notebook was Mikami and not Near. So Near would not lose his memory even if had written into the notebook.

Relevant Rule 10

If the victim's name has been entered and then the Death Note is destroyed in the middle of writing the cause of death, the victim will be killed by a heart attack in fourty seconds. If the victim's name and the cause of death have been written but not the conditions of death, the victim will be killed within six minutes and 40 seconds via the stated cause of death if the cause is possible within that period of time. Otherwise, the victim will die of a heart attack.

Relevant Rule 9

Once the victim's name, cause of death and conditions of death have been written down in the Death Note, the death will still take place even if that Death Note, or the part of the note used, is destroyed before the stated time of death.

Death Note Investigation File

4 All Tricks Revealed

Many mind games and deceptions were pivotal to the outcome of the battles over the Death Note. In this section every trick, large and small (and really small), will be examined and explained.

▶Reading the Pages
- Trick Level:.......................The effectiveness rated on a scale of one to five.
- ◎ Performer:......The person who comes up with and implements the trick.
- ◎ Key Item:......................Something that is crucial in executing the trick.

01 Learning How to Use the Death Note

TRICK LEVEL ★★★★★
- ◎ Performer: Light
- ◎ Key Item: The Death Note

Light decides to kill criminals and immoral people using accidents and disease. The reason for this is to bring fear to those who would commit evil acts and to change how people behave.

IF YOU DON'T SPECIFY THE CAUSE OF DEATH, THEY ALL DIE FROM A HEART ATTACK.
THAT'S THE BEST THING ABOUT THE DEATH NOTE, RYUK.

02 Determining Kira's Location

TRICK LEVEL ★★★★★
- ◎ Performer: L
- ◎ Key Item: TV

L has a criminal unknown to the public, Lind L. Tailor, pose as L on television and promise to capture Kira. Light becomes angered by this and kills Tailor. However, this is actually a test by L to confirm Kira's power. Because Light fell for it, L learns that Kira needs to see a person's face in order to kill them. Also, L had planned to show the broadcast in different areas at different times. Thus this trick also allows L to learn the general area where Kira is located.

ALTHOUGH IT WAS ANNOUNCED THAT THIS WAS BEING TELEVISED GLOBALLY...
ACTUALLY, IT WAS BROADCAST ONLY IN THE KANTO REGION AROUND TOKYO.

03 Spying on the Police Investigation

TRICK LEVEL ★★★
- ◎ Performer: Light
- ◎ Key Item: Computer

Light kills a group of captured criminals in one-hour increments. This shows L that Kira has access to police information and causes both L and the police to start suspecting each other.

04 False-Bottomed Drawer

TRICK LEVEL ★★★★
- ◎ Performer: Light
- ◎ Key Item: Pen, Gasoline

Light converts his desk drawer into a hiding place for the Death Note. A trap is rigged to burn the notebook unless the ink cartridge of a pen is used to open the drawer.

05 Dying Messages

TRICK LEVEL ★★
- ◎ Performer: Light
- ◎ Key Item: The Death Note

Light experiments with the Death Note to see how far he can control people's actions before they die. While doing this, he makes victims write a secret message to L. This is done to confuse the investigation.

06 TRICK LEVEL ★★★★★ Learning the Name of a Tail

◎ **Performer: Light**
◎ **Key Item: The Death Note**

In order to learn the name of the FBI agent tailing him, Light comes up with a plan that involves controlling a criminal into hijacking a bus. Creating an emergency situation was the perfect way to trap the agent.

07 TRICK LEVEL ★★★★★ The Files with the Slots

◎ **Performer: Light**
◎ **Key Item: Transceiver, The Death Note**

This is the terrifying trick Light comes up with in order to kill the FBI agents. To do this, he writes down the causes of death beforehand and has Raye, who knows the people's names and faces, enter the names into the empty slots. The times of death are set up to be completely random in order to make it impossible to figure out which agent Kira has had contact with.

08 TRICK LEVEL ★★ The Real Investigation Headquarters

◎ **Performer: L**
◎ **Key Item: Hotel Suite**

After analyzing Kira's ability, L comes up with a system to keep the identities of the members of the investigation and their locations secret. This is to protect them from Kira's power.

09 TRICK LEVEL ★★ Smooth Talking

◎ **Performer: Light**
◎ **Key Item: None**

Sensing that Naomi Misora could be a danger to him, Light gets information from her through impressive conversation skills. When introducing himself, Light explains the way to write his name in order to get her to do the same.

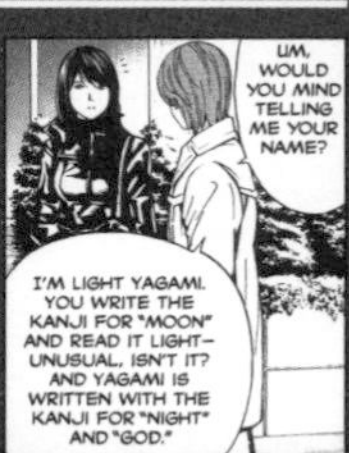

10 TRICK LEVEL ★★★★ Fake Name

◎ **Performer: Naomi**
◎ **Key Item: None**

Naomi figures out on her own that Kira needs a person's name in order to kill them. This plan to give out a fake name is simple but very effective. It's something that L began doing immediately as well.

11 TRICK LEVEL ★★★ Fake Police Badges

◎ **Performer: L**
◎ **Key Item: Police Badges**

These police badges with fake names are something that L prepares immediately. L may have thought that nobody would consider that a police officer would use a counterfeit badge.

12 TRICK LEVEL ★★★ Electric Buckle

◎ **Performer: L**
◎ **Key Item: Belt Buckle**

These are the belts that L gives to Soichiro and the other members of the team. A device is embedded in the buckle that sends a signal to Watari's phone when pressed twice.

13 TRICK LEVEL ★★★★ Hidden Cameras

◎ **Performer: L**
◎ **Key Item: Cameras, Monitors**

L plants cameras to surveil people he suspects of being Kira. He places 64 in Light's room alone! They are being monitored 24 hours a day to make sure nothing is missed.

14 Checking the Door

TRICK LEVEL ★★★★

◎ Performer: Light
◎ Key Item: Pencil Lead

Light places a pencil lead in the door hinge and checks the doorknob position so that he'll know when someone has entered his room. He doesn't even have to lock his door to keep things safe.

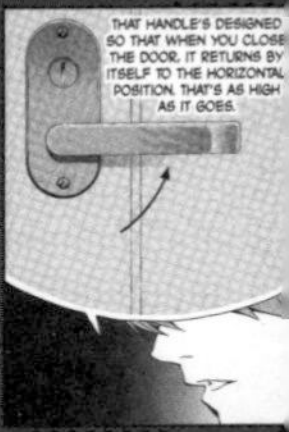

15 The Hidden Girlie Magazines

TRICK LEVEL ★

◎ Performer: Light
◎ Key Item: Book Slipcase

Light hides his magazines inside a box of reference books. He does this as a ruse to prove that he values his privacy.

16 Searching for Cameras

TRICK LEVEL ★★

◎ Performer: Light
◎ Key Item: Apples

Ryuk helps Light locate all the hidden cameras in his bedroom. Normally the Shinigami wouldn't cooperate, but Light tempts Ryuk with apples.

17 Fake News Broadcast

TRICK LEVEL ★★

◎ Performer: L
◎ Key Item: TV Station

L's plan is to pressure Kira with a breaking news headline. During this broadcast, L watches his suspect, Light, for any reaction. It isn't very effective.

18 Writing in a Blind Spot

TRICK LEVEL ★★★★★

◎ Performer: Light
◎ Key Item: Small TV, Potato Chips

If Kira continues killing criminals while Light does nothing out of the ordinary, the suspicion against Light will vanish. In order to fool the cameras planted in his room, Light actually uses a bag of potato chips with a miniature television hidden inside. To prevent someone else in the family from opening the bag, he uses a chip flavor that only he prefers.

19 L's Announcement

TRICK LEVEL ★★★★★

◎ Performer: L
◎ Key Item: None

In order to get closer to Light, L enrolls in the same university and reveals his identity. L does this because he's confident that Kira cannot kill him without knowing his name. A highly risky but very effective move.

20 Profiling with Tennis

TRICK LEVEL ★★★

◎ Performer: L
◎ Key Item: Tennis Racket

L's plan is to gauge Light's personality by playing a game of tennis with him. He tries to see if Light's reactions match Kira's. But secretly the game has another purpose.

21 Revealing Suspicion Against Light

TRICK LEVEL ★★★

◎ Performer: L
◎ Key Item: None

Reading what Light is thinking, L drops this bomb. His aim is to use Light to help solve the case while seeing if he'll slip up and reveal himself to be Kira.

22 The Print Numbers

TRICK LEVEL ★

◎ Performer: L
◎ Key Item: Photographs

These are the photographs of the messages left behind by criminals who died. It's a trap L set up to see if Light puts them in the correct order. There may be a trick to the numbers on the back as well.

23 The Fourth Picture

TRICK LEVEL ★★★

◎ Performer: L
◎ Key Item: Photographs

The last message is actually a fake created by L. He does this to see how Light would react as Kira to a picture he would know is fake.

24 Kira Videotape

TRICK LEVEL ★★

◎ Performer: Misa
◎ Key Item: Videotapes

These were the four tapes created by the Second Kira in an attempt to seek police cooperation. They were meant to be played depending on the police response.

25 Runaway Truck

TRICK LEVEL ★★

◎ Performer: Soichiro
◎ Key Item: Police Vehicle

Soichiro's plan to enter the Sakura TV building without being seen by Kira seems like a rash decision, but since the vehicle has no windows, it turns out to be a smart move.

26 The Shield of Justice

TRICK LEVEL ★★★★

◎ Performer: L
◎ Key Item: Shield

This is the wall of police officers in front of Sakura TV that is formed in order to hide Soichiro's face from Kira. The NHN announcer on the scene praises the police for standing up to Kira.

27 Watching the Video

TRICK LEVEL ★★

◎ Performer: L
◎ Key Item: Videotape

L shows Light all the investigation materials and watches his reactions. If Light doesn't infer a fake Kira, L's suspicion is lessened. If he does, L's theory is strengthened. Either way, L wins.

28 The Real Kira

TRICK LEVEL ★★

◎ Performer: L
◎ Key Item: CG Tool

This is the fake Kira's response to the Second Kira. The plan is to see how Kira or the Second Kira would react. The high quality CG work is done by Matsuda.

29 Tapes Without Traces

TRICK LEVEL ★

◎ Performer: Misa
◎ Key Item: Envelopes

Misa was tricky when she sent her videos to Sakura TV. She had a friend prepare the videotapes and envelopes so that the parcel wouldn't have her fingerprints. However…

30 The Diary Code

TRICK LEVEL ★★★

◎ Performer: Misa
◎ Key Item: Paper

The diary message that Misa creates for Light. "My friend and I showed off our notebooks in Aoyama" is the secret code; everything else is just to confuse the investigation.

35 Stealing Misa's Phone

TRICK LEVEL ★

◎ **Performer: L**
◎ **Key Item: Cell Phone**

Light and Misa must be communicating with each other. Knowing this, L steals Misa's phone, answers it quietly and hopes that Light will let something incriminating slip. What, it's not a trick…?

36 The Notebook Shuffle

TRICK LEVEL ★★★★

◎ **Performer: Light**
◎ **Key Item: The Death Notes**

In order to switch Shinigami, the notebooks are shuffled around. The aim is to have Misa's memory relating to Ryuzaki's name return so she can kill him.

37 The Fake Rules

TRICK LEVEL ★★★★★

◎ **Performer: Light**
◎ **Key Item: The Death Note**

Predicting that the notebook would fall into the hands of the task force, Light has Ryuk add two fake rules into the Death Note. Even L falls for this trick…

38 Memory Control

TRICK LEVEL ★★★

◎ **Performer: Light, Misa**
◎ **Key Item: The Death Note**

Using the rule that says those who forfeit the Death Note lose their memories, Light and Misa willfully erase their memories when imprisoned. This prevents them from confessing.

39 Soichiro's Act

TRICK LEVEL ★★★

◎ **Performer: Soichiro**
◎ **Key Item: Blank Bullets**

This is a brilliant performance by Soichiro. He acts like he's going to kill his son before dying himself. L uses this plan because he thinks Kira will be forced to use his killing powers in such a situation.

31 Hiding Ryuk

TRICK LEVEL ★★

◎ **Performer: Light**
◎ **Key Item: None**

This is the plan to move in a large group so anyone who could see Ryuk wouldn't be able to tell who he's attached to.

32 Disguise

TRICK LEVEL ★★

◎ **Performer: Misa**
◎ **Key Item: Glasses, School Uniform**

To find Light, Misa wears a disguise that consists of a school uniform, a wig and glasses. For such a spontaneous girl, this one is very well thought out.

33 Multiple Girlfriends

TRICK LEVEL ★★

◎ **Performer: Light**
◎ **Key Item: None**

Light keeps a gaggle of girlfriends to hide the fact that he has just met Misa. He doesn't want anyone to suspect that she is the Second Kira.

YOU AGREED THAT WE'D GO OUT, RIGHT?
YEAH... I DID.

34 L Part of Detective Group

TRICK LEVEL ★★★

◎ **Performer: L**
◎ **Key Item: None**

L reasons that if Light believes Ryuzaki is only one member of a larger organization, he wouldn't do anything to him. This bluff works very well.

40 Handcuffs

TRICK LEVEL ★

◎ **Performer: L**
◎ **Key Item: Handcuffs**

Not able to abandon his doubts about Light, Ryuzaki uses handcuffs to make sure he is able to monitor Light 24 hours a day. He wants to catch Light doing something incriminating.

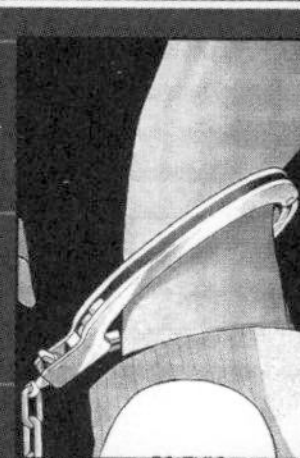

41 Testing Aizawa

TRICK LEVEL ★

◎ **Performer: L**
◎ **Key Item: None**

Lying is one of L's favorite methods to trap a suspect. Here he recommends that the investigators quit so he can see which of them still has the will to go after Kira.

YOU WERE WATCHING TO SEE WHETHER I'D QUIT THE FORCE OR NOT, WEREN'T YOU?

42 Eraldo Coil

TRICK LEVEL ★★★

◎ **Performer: L**
◎ **Key Item: None**

In order to determine when people are investigating him, L has an alter ego named Eraldo Coil, who is a master at tracking people down. Most of his enemies fall for this and try to hire Coil.

ERALDO COIL?! THE DETECTIVE WE HIRED TO FIND L? WHY IS HE CALLING ME...?

43 Conversation SOS

TRICK LEVEL ★

◎ **Performer: L**
◎ **Key Item: Cell Phone**

When Matsuda is captured by the Yotsuba employees, L fakes a regular conversation to determine the sense of urgency. He seems to be copying Soichiro's methodology, but Soichiro is obviously confused.

...IN TROUBLE AGAIN?
TROUBLE?

44 Matsuda Jump

RICK LEVEL ★★★

◎ **Performer: Matsuda**
◎ **Key Item: A Bed**

3ecause his face is seen by the iigh-ranking Yotsuba members, Matsuda is likely to be killed by Kira. Believing that the only way o save Matsuda is for him to die n front of everyone, L puts ogether this trick. The Yotsuba Eight are all invited to Misa's ffice and Matsuda "falls" off the eranda to his death but is saved y a mattress one floor down.

45 Succeeding L

RICK LEVEL ★★

◎ **Performer: L**
◎ **Key Item: None**

f Kira were to control global aw enforcement, he'd be in the ltimate position, so L figures hat if he offers the position to ight, he'll jump at it. But Light s disappointed in L's lack of aith in him.

IF I DIE, WOULD YOU TAKE OVER FOR ME?

46 Meeting with Yotsuba

RICK LEVEL ★★★

◎ **Performer: Aiber, Misa**
◎ **Key Item: None**

his is the meeting for Yotsuba o determine if they want to use Misa as a spokesperson. The ruth, however, is that Misa is athering information on Kira, nd Yotsuba is gathering information on L.

PLEASE TELL US THE TRUTH CONCERNING THAT.

47 Nurse Disguise

RICK LEVEL ★

◎ **Performer: Misa**
◎ **Key Item: Nurse Outfit**

his is the trick Misa uses o escape Mogi's watch and nvestigate Higuchi on her wn. She trades clothes with n old friend and just walks ut. Simple but effective.

48 Higuchi's Confession

TRICK LEVEL ★★★★

◎ Performer: Misa
◎ Key Item: Death Note, Cell Phone

Misa figures that if she confesses to being the Second Kira, Higuchi will do the same. With help from Rem, Misa is able to show that she still had Kira's powers and this leads to Higuchi eventually outing himself.

49 Fake Sakura TV Show

TRICK LEVEL ★★★★★

◎ Performer: Matsuda
◎ Key Item: TV

This is the big mission to figure out how Kira kills and to capture Higuchi in the act. The plan is to use Matsuda, who had supposedly died, as bait to lure Higuchi into a trap. Huguchi falls for it and even uses the Death Note on camera. But L and the team don't realize what the notebook is until later.

50 Tinted-Window Police Cars

TRICK LEVEL ★★

◎ Performer: Aizawa, Ide
◎ Key Item: Tinted Windows

In order to hide their faces from Kira, Aizawa and Ide use these special police cars. All of the car's windows are tinted so that someone from the outside can't look into the vehicle.

51 The Watch

TRICK LEVEL ★★★★

◎ Performer: Light
◎ Key Item: Watch

Light's watch has a piece of the Death Note hidden inside of it. By performing a specific action with the buttons, the bottom of the watch slides out and reveals a secret hiding place. The watch also hides a needle so he can write a name in blood.

52 The End of L and Rem

TRICK LEVEL ★★★★★

◎ Performer: Light
◎ Key Item: None

Light creates the situation where Misa draws suspicion on herself once again. The plan is to make Rem kill L to protect Misa and then have Rem die as well.

53 Data Deletion

TRICK LEVEL ★★

◎ Performer: Watari
◎ Key Item: Computer

A system set up to delete all of L's secret information in case something happens. For example, if the computer isn't touched for a period of time or a special button is pushed, all internal data is erased.

54 Countdown

TRICK LEVEL ★★★

◎ Performer: Watari
◎ Key Item: Cell Phone

This system connects L and Roger with each other. If L stops using his computer, a countdown is initiated. If it reaches zero, that means L is dead.

55 Cell Phone Number-Sharing System

TRICK LEVEL ★★

◎ Performer: Light
◎ Key Item: Cell Phone

A new cell phone technology developed in Light's police division. When a set number receives a phone call, all cell phones hooked up to this system can listen in. This is used frequently with calls from Mello.

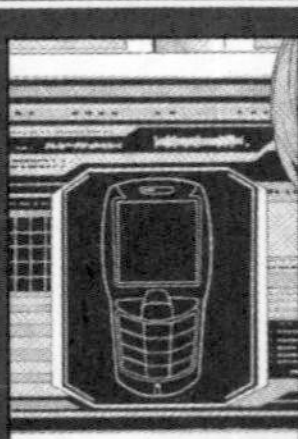

56 Hijack

TRICK LEVEL ★★★★

◎ Performer: Mello

◎ Key Item: Jumbo Jet

This is the plan used to separate Soichiro from his men and get him to the location of the trade alone. The pilot had been brought in on the plan so it wasn't exactly a regular hijacking.

57 Trade Door

TRICK LEVEL ★★★

◎ Performer: Mello

◎ Key Item: Revolving Door

This is a door used by mafia organizations for drug trafficking. The items to be exchanged are placed through holes in the glass and the door revolves when it's time to make the deal. This way, both sides get the items they want at once.

58 Missile Delivery

TRICK LEVEL ★★★★

◎ Performer: Mello

◎ Key Item: Missile

Mello uses a missile with all the explosives removed in order to transport the notebook. The main point is that it cannot be traced by radar.

59 One Man, Two Roles

TRICK LEVEL ★★

◎ Performer: Light

◎ Key Item: Voice Switching System

In order to play the roles of both L and Watari, Light comes up with this device. He can switch back and forth between two voices by merely pressing a button.

60 Searching for an Owner

TRICK LEVEL ★★★

◎ Performer: Misa

◎ Key Item: Shinigami Eyes

If someone with Shinigami Eyes looks at a photograph of a Death Note owner, they will only see their name. Using this, Misa is able to discover who the owner is on Mello's side.

61 Finding the Mafia Hideout

TRICK LEVEL ★★★★

◎ Performer: Light

◎ Key Item: The Death Note

People whose names are written into the notebook can be controlled to the extent of what is natural for them to do. Knowing the owner on Mello's side, Light uses this rule to have him reveal the location of their hideout.

62 Flying Helmets

TRICK LEVEL ★★★★

◎ Performer: Mello

◎ Key Item: Security Cameras, Shinigami

Borrowing troops from the U.S. president, Light plans to get the notebook back by force. But Mello had already planned against this possibility by sending out Sidoh, who can't be seen by other humans, to patrol the base. Mello has Sidoh remove the helmets of the troops so that their names can be written into the Death Note.

63 Protecting His Memory

TRICK LEVEL ★★

◎ Performer: Light

◎ Key Item: The Death Note

You lose your memory if you forfeit your notebook, but as long as you are touching a notebook you have used in the past, your memories will remain. Light keeps Misa's notebook on his body during this time so that he can keep his memories.

68 Hideout Explosion

TRICK LEVEL ★★★

◎ **Performer: Mello**
◎ **Key Item: Bomb Switch**

Thinking about how to escape in a pinch, Mello rigged explosives throughout the hideout. It appeared to be a suicidal plan but it's really a way for Mello to protect himself.

69 Secret Talks in the Bathroom

TRICK LEVEL ★

◎ **Performer: Halle**
◎ **Key Item: None**

Halle chooses her bathroom as the place to communicate in secret with Mello. She has been ordered to install cameras throughout her house except for the bathroom. But Near thought something was odd right away.

TAK
...
TAK
NEAR, I WANT TO TAKE A SHOWER, SO I'M TAKING THE WIRE OFF FOR A WHILE.

70 The First Representative

TRICK LEVEL ★★

◎ **Performer: Light**
◎ **Key Item: None**

To spread Kira's message throughout the world, Light selects Demegawa as his representative. His aim is to get the public on his side as quickly as possible and thus destroy Near.

71 Following Mogi

TRICK LEVEL ★★

◎ **Performer: Light**
◎ **Key Item: Hidden Cameras**

When Mogi is asked to come to New York by Mello, Light has Aizawa and Ide tail him with hidden cameras. If they can catch Mello on camera, Light will send his picture to Misa and have her kill him.

I'VE ARRIVED AT NICK ST. STATION EXIT.

72 Wrong Number

TRICK LEVEL ★

◎ **Performer: Near**
◎ **Key Item: Phone**

If Mogi was L himself, it would be dangerous for the SPK members to show their faces to him. Knowing this, Near calls L and acts like it's an accident. By doing so he is able to confirm that Mogi is not L.

SORRY, I CALLED THE WRONG NUMBER.
BIP
YES, NEAR?

64 Misa As Kira

TRICK LEVEL ★★★

◎ **Performer: Misa**
◎ **Key Item: Keyboard**

Light secretly creates a voice recording for Kira that can be controlled by a keyboard. Misa is able to use this to speak to Soichiro as Kira. It also creates an alibi for Light.

I... BELIEVED YOU TO BE...

65 Kira's Messenger

TRICK LEVEL ★★★

◎ **Performer: Light**
◎ **Key Item: The Death Note**

The notebook is sent to the task force and Ryuk is attached to the new owner. Ryuk now is bound to two notebooks. Light demands that he cooperate because of the Sidoh incident.

66 Shinigami Eyes Confirmation

TRICK LEVEL ★★

◎ **Performer: Light**
◎ **Key Item: Mafia Member Photos**

This takes advantage of the fact that the Shinigami Eyes cannot see the name or life span of a dead person. The plan here is to kill most of the mafia members with the notebook and to steal it back in the ensuing chaos.

YES, I CAN!

67 Playing Dead

TRICK LEVEL ★

◎ **Performer: Jose**
◎ **Key Item: None**

Jose, one of the mafia members, is probably able to play dead convincingly because so many other people around him are dead of heart attacks, which leave no external evidence.

73 Gift to Near

TRICK LEVEL ★★

◎ **Performer: Mello**
◎ **Key Item: Cell Phone**

Mello hands over Mogi to Near and listens in on his cell phone. This allows him to learn valuable information without any risk to himself. Though he didn't anticipate that Mogi wouldn't say a word.

74 Attack of the Crazies

TRICK LEVEL ★★

◎ **Performer: Light**
◎ **Key Item: None**

Light's plan is to use the Kira worshippers to destroy the SPK head-quarters. However, because many of the members just want to commit violence, Near was able to take advantage of their lack of unity and escape.

75 L's Legacy

TRICK LEVEL ★★★★

◎ **Performer: Near**
◎ **Key Item: Money**

Near's plan is to release the large amount of money passed down to him from L and escape in the ensuing chaos. It's a very bold move, but it could be said that the situation is such that he has no choice but to try it.

76 Near's Lie

TRICK LEVEL ★

◎ **Performer: Near**
◎ **Key Item: None**

Near lies to the Japanese task force, saying that Mogi died of a heart attack. The aim is to create doubt within the task force and get information from some of the members. This results in Aizawa breaking ranks and assisting Near.

77 Passing the Notebook to Mikami

TRICK LEVEL ★★★

◎ **Performer: Light**
◎ **Key Item: The Death Note**

Light has Misa forfeit her ownership of the notebook to Mikami. Anticipating tighter surveillance, Light has a new person play the role of Kira.

78 Fooling Matt

TRICK LEVEL ★

◎ **Performer: Mogi**
◎ **Key Item: Truck**

This is how Mogi escapes surveillance and returns to Japan with Misa. The plan is simply to slip out while a truck is blocking the way, but Matt falls for it.

I HAD THE CAMERA ROLLING ON ALL THE EXITS AND WINDOWS, BUT THEY USED THE TRUCK'S DOOR TO BLOCK THE VIEW... SHOOT...

79 The Second Representative

TRICK LEVEL ★★★★

◎ **Performer: Mikami**
◎ **Key Item: None**

Mikami chooses Kira worshipper Takada as the second Kira representative. Like Light, Mikami senses the need for a representative. This proves that Mikami is the right person for the job of Kira.

80 Talking to God

TRICK LEVEL ★★★★

◎ **Performer: Mikami**
◎ **Key Item: Cell Phone**

Asked to prove that he is god, Light mentions the date and number of envelopes he had sent Mikami. Light's brilliant memory and Mikami's quick thinking make this possible.

I CAN ANSWER THIS ONE EASILY BY PRETENDING TO NOT UNDERSTAND ANYTHING.
NOVEMBER 26TH? FIVE SHEETS? WHAT ARE YOU TALKING ABOUT?

81 Secret Notes

TRICK LEVEL ★★

◎ **Performer: Light, Takada**
◎ **Key Item: Memo Pads**

With the task force eavesdropping on them, Light and Takada pass notes between each other. The trick itself is simple and this shows just how much control Light had over the task force members.

82 The Fake Notebook

TRICK LEVEL ★★★★★

◎ Performer: Mikami

◎ Key Item: Cell Phone, Fake Notebook

In order to fool Near, Light has Mikami prepare an exact duplicate of the notebook. He later has Mikami use the notebook in public places to grab Near's attention.

83 Speaking to Yourself

TRICK LEVEL ★★★★

◎ Performer: Mikami

◎ Key Item: None

Knowing he's being watched, Light has Mikami say things to indicate there's no Shinigami attached to him. This action is meant to draw attention to the fact that Mikami's notebook is not being guarded well. Near falls for it.

IS-IT-Y-OU-SHI-NI-GA-MI.
IT'S, "IS IT YOU, SHINIGAMI."

84 Uncovering the Note Passing

TRICK LEVEL ★

◎ Performer: Aizawa

◎ Key Item: Memo Pads

Aizawa places fingernail marks on the memo pads to check if they are being used and in this way discovers that notes are secretly being passed.

85 Switching the Notebook 1

TRICK LEVEL ★★★

◎ Performer: Gevanni

◎ Key Item: The Death Note

Gevanni breaks into Mikami's gym locker and swaps the notebook pages with regular paper. Accomplishing this in a short period of time speaks very highly of Gevanni's abilities.

86 Confirming the Switch

TRICK LEVEL ★★★

◎ Performer: Mikami

◎ Key Item: Microscope

On notice from Light, Mikami is constantly checking whether the notebook has been switched. Using a microscope to examine the notebook every day, Mikami shows real dedication.

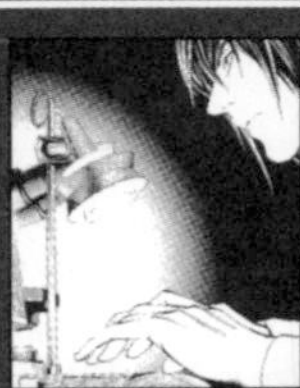

87 Killing Everyone

TRICK LEVEL ★★★★

◎ Performer: Light, Mikami

◎ Key Item: The Death Note

Having Mikami kill everyone at the Yellow Box warehouse is the final plan. Accomplishing this requires extensive preparations over a long period of time.

88 Switching the Notebook 2

TRICK LEVEL ★★★★★

◎ Performer: Gevanni, Rester

◎ Key Item: The Death Note

After switching the fake notebook, Near is also able to switch the real Death Note hidden in a bank safe-deposit box. Because of this, Light's plan backfires.

THIS IS THE REAL NOTEBOOK.

89 Writing with Blood

TRICK LEVEL ★

◎ Performer: Light

◎ Key Item: Blood, the Death Note

Distracting his opponent and writing their name down on a hidden piece of notebook paper. This is Light's final act. It is pure desperation on his part.

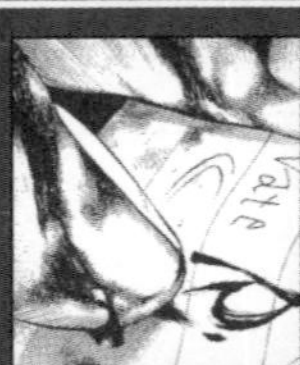

HOW TO CREATE

TSUGUMI OHBA X TAKESHI OBATA

Special Discussion

The Making of *Death Note*

33 Questions

The 13 Truths About Chapter 108

Now that everything has been revealed, both creators join us for a behind-the-scenes look at the *Death Note* series.

Ohba-sensei, did you want to become a manga creator?
Ohba: No, not at all. I didn't even think the story would get accepted. I thought it didn't fit with *Jump*... So when it was approved and I learned Obata-sensei was going to do the art, I couldn't even believe it.

When you were working on the pilot did you ever try to meet each other and discuss things?
Ohba: My editor said I didn't need to...I think it worked out all right.
Obata: Well, I did want to meet with Ohba-sensei.
Ohba: Had you told me, I would have gladly come to see you [*laughs*]. But I don't think I would have said much—I would have been too nervous.
Obata: Like, we finally meet and can only talk about things not related to the book [*laughs*]?

How did it feel when, after the pilot was published, they asked you to come up with ideas for a series?
Ohba: I was so happy. And I was thinking how the story would be more interesting as a serial.
Obata: When I read the thumbnails for the series, I thought, "Oh, so this is what Ohba-sensei wanted to do." And I felt like I would have a lot of fun drawing it.

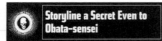

Storyline a Secret Even to Obata-sensei

Was Obata-sensei informed about future plot developments?
Ohba: Our editor didn't tell you much, did he? Just stuff like a character named L would be appearing?
Obata: I would be looking forward to your thumbnails every week, so while I was intrigued I never bothered to ask him. But honestly, how far ahead did you plan out the plot?
Ohba: Not at all.

The Pilot Chapter and Start of Serialization

I hear this is the first time you've seen each other in a while. Did you not meet in person very often?
Ohba: No. We would only meet with our editor. So I didn't even meet with Obata-sensei when we first created the pilot chapter.
Obata: I started on the pilot in the summer of 2003, then on the serialization in December of that year. We didn't actually meet until an editorial party in January of the following year.

↑ The pilot and original source. This story was more horror-based and differed a lot from the serialized version.

For the pilot chapter, Ohba-sensei brought the rough draft in to the editorial department and then Obata-sensei was brought in later, right? What did you think when you first saw it, Obata-sensei?
Obata: At first I didn't really get it. But there were Shinigami and it was dark...so I really loved the world. I really wanted to work on it.
Ohba: I was so happy to get the opportunity to work with Obata-sensei.

"So when it was approved and I learned Obata-sensei was going to do the art, I couldn't even believe it." (Ohba)

↑ The Shinigami Eyes are a plot point crucial to the story until the very end.

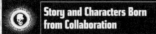

Story and Characters Born from Collaboration

Ohba: I've always wondered how you differentiate characters. Like the ICPO meeting in chapter 1; so many characters are there. Do you base them on something?
Obata: It's just…what I'm feeling at the time. Like, "Foreigners look something like this, I guess?"
Ohba: Do you have a number of character patterns in your head?
Obata: That must be the case. Different parts of actors' faces must be in my memory. So it's not like I think about it too hard. I just start moving my pen and they come to me.

Obata: That's such a lie [*laughs*]. I know you had the whole thing thought out. How else could you create such a complicated story? All right, then how much did you have planned out before the serialization started?
Ohba: Up to chapter 3…
Obata: Come on… [*laughs*].
Ohba: The first time I had difficulty was with the hiding of the Death Note in the drawer and the part with the Shinigami Eyes. I was already struggling at that point. Though it turned out that those became important plot points.
Obata: Really?
Ohba: I swear. Though I did discuss the Shinigami Eyes idea with my editor early on.
Obata: See, you did have it all planned out!
Ohba: But I didn't have any final structure to the story. With my thumbnails, I would just think about how to put Light in trouble and what would happen next. Like with Naomi: she meets Light, then what? I'm always struggling as I write [*laughs*].
Obata: Unbelievable. But you did have all the big events planned out, right?
Ohba: In some cases. I did think about adding a second Kira before we started, but…

↑ This is a scene that makes you feel the magnitude of the Kira case. There are no main characters here but it's a very important scene to show to the reader the scale of what is happening.

"There were Shinigami and it was dark…so I really loved the world." (Obata)

Ohba: Only an amazing person could say something like that. Being able to do it…without thinking?
Obata: That's the easiest way. I can't do it when I'm thinking.
Ohba: Is it more difficult to differentiate the main characters?
Obata: Yeah. Main-character types and girls are tough. There aren't that many patterns for "cool" and "cute." Especially for a handsome guy like Light, I'm limited with options. So it's hard to come up with variations.
Ohba: Weren't you the first one to bring up the idea of not having L be attractive?
Obata: Yes, I was. That's what I felt when I read the thumbnails. So what did you actually think of L's design?
Ohba: It was perfect. I loved it.
Obata: I did too. The L in your thumbnails seemed to have a lifeless face, and that inspired me.
Ohba: Then, you could have just used my exact design?
Obata: Yes. I wanted to keep it the same. It seems our tastes are very similar.
Ohba: That's true. Like with both of our ideas of Misa being Gothic Lolita. It makes me happy to know we like the same things. I get to fantasize that my design sense is on the same level as yours [*laughs*].

I heard that Obata-sensei didn't know who Kira was during the Yotsuba arc.
Obata: At first I thought it was Mido…
Ohba: I had considered that. But as I was writing it, I felt it would be too obvious and boring. So I looked at Obata-sensei's drawings of the characters and thought about each of their personalities before deciding. That's how it always is with me. With Naomi, Yotsuba, and Sidoh, things became set after I saw Obata-sensei's art.

It's like you created the characters together.
Ohba: That's why it was the toughest during the Yotsuba part. I had to come up with the plot before Obata-sensei's character designs. But without knowing what they look like, I can't imagine their actions. So I was totally confused about who was speaking which line… But once I see the character design, I think up stuff like, "This character looks like he'd want to shoot a missile at someone" [*laughs*]. But it must have been very difficult to differentiate eight characters.

"Ohba-sensei's thumbnails allow me to come up with a lot of variations." (Obata)

"Only an amazing person could say something like that. Being able to do it…without thinking?" (Ohba)

I thought, "Wow, this is amazing!" and really wanted Obata-sensei to draw more of his expressions.
Obata: What surprised me in that chapter was how L announced himself to Light. I can only blame myself for drawing him that way, but I was just thinking that because L looks like he does, wouldn't Light be constantly thinking, "There's a weirdo following me…"? And wouldn't that make it difficult for L to investigate him? I had been wondering how they would eventually meet, but I never imagined L would come out and reveal himself like that.
Ohba: When I thought about it, this was the only way it could have happened. I'm happy that it surprised Obata-sensei so much.

Did anything unexpected happen while you worked on the series?
Ohba: Raye Penber's death scene. Obata-sensei took my thumbnails and improved them.
Obata: He died so suddenly in the thumbnails I thought it was a waste…
Ohba: You made it really intense. Plus, since he looks back into the train, L is able to get a clue from watching the security video.

↑ A rare instance of Light actually showing emotion. The intensity of this scene was heightened thanks to the great art.

↑ Ooi's missile line was born from Obata-sensei's character design .

Obata: No, not at all. It was a lot of fun and allowed me to devise many variations. Having to draw eight new characters means I have to make sure to come up with something I've never used before.
Ohba: I felt really bad about it at the time.
Obata: Thanks to things like that, I was really able to release my full potential. Even if I had wanted to create my own manga with Shinigami, I doubt it would have turned out like this.
Ohba: It would have been like the "attractive human Ryuk" you mentioned before?
Obata: Yeah. Since the Shinigami in *Death Note* are just side characters, they don't need to be cool and attractive. And I never would have gone in this direction had I been working on my own. So I was very happy with the results.
Ohba: In my position, I felt I was deciding things based on my own desire to see you draw them. Like the scene with Light and L hitting each other. The reason I added it in was just that I wanted to see it drawn by you [*laughs*].

Was there something that caused you to start doing that?
Ohba : It started with the scene in chapter 19, after the college entrance exam when Light's expression goes from humiliation to laughter.

never come up with was just so much fun." (Obata)

LIGHT... YAGAMI!

↑The scene that Obata-sensei added. In the thumbnail stage, Light and Raye never came face to face.

about crazy things that would look amazing with Obata-sensei's art. Like the scene where Soichiro crashes into Sakura TV; I created that while thinking how cool it would look when completed.

Were there other scenes that were created like that?
Ohba: L's death scene. I noticed how Obata-sensei always draws L with his eyes open. So I had L close his eyes for the first time in the thumbnails. I was really excited about how it would turn out.
Obata: That was fun to draw. It's true that that was the first time I had drawn him with his eyes closed.

I...
BUT...

↑The famous scene in the middle of the series. L's eyes are finally closed...

Obata: I was worried I shouldn't have done it when I read that chapter later. I was wondering if you had to change the plot because of what I did.
Ohba: Well, I think it turned out for the best.
Obata: After that, Naomi Misora shows up, but...I was personally very sad that she had to die. I was anticipating that she might reappear at some point.
Ohba: Obata-sensei, remember later when you drew a color picture of her for a chapter cover? When I saw that wonderful picture I was also feeling that it was a waste that she died.

Enjoying the Final Art as a Reader

Ohba-sensei, I heard that you really looked forward to seeing the completed chapters every week.
Ohba: It was a lot of fun because they usually felt so different. It's weird because this is a story I came up with.
Obata: I would also turn into a normal fan when the thumbnails would arrive. I looked forward to getting them every week as well.
Ohba: Did you think about the art as you were reading the thumbnails?
Obata: Yes. Thinking about the art for these thumbnails that I could never come up with was just so much fun.

What was the most important aspect of each of your work?
Obata: Since there's so much dialogue, I focused on making my artwork as simple to follow as possible.
Ohba: Putting something important in every chapter. And as the series went along, I just started thinking

"I like to add things that are funny depending on your point of view." (Ohba)

"Thinking about the art for these thumbnails that I could

editor was that it would probably take place in America.
Ohba: Was it difficult to prepare?
Obata: The only thing I did was collect a few reference pictures. I had never been to America, so I didn't know how to make it look different from Japan. There's obviously the visual difference, but the atmosphere and feel of the location is also important. Plus I had to do color pages every week during the break, so I barely had any time.
Ohba: Sorry…
Obata: No, no [*laughs*]. I struggled with my instructions to my assistants when the series restarted. I could only tell them to make the backgrounds look "more American."

How did you collaborate in creating Mello and Near?
Ohba: I left it all to Obata-sensei. I only asked him to put a little L in them.
Obata: Oh, when Mello reappears later he has a scar, and I was finally feeling like I could draw him really well and then…
Ohba: He dies…
Obata: Maybe it's better that we didn't meet during the serialization. Had I mentioned this before, you might not have killed him, right?

And you like to add humor?
Ohba: Yes, though it's not humor so much as just that I like to add things that are funny depending on your point of view. Like the scene in chapter 92 with Misa and Takada; I put that scene in because it was something I considered funny.
Obata: The girl-fight scene?
Ohba: It's not like there was any plot development based on that dinner, so there was no actual reason for it.
Obata: While I was drawing it I figured there was a reason for the girls to be fighting, but…I see…Okay [*laughs*].
Ohba: Okay? Are you sure? Shouldn't there be more to it [*laughs*]?
Obata: No, I was just agreeing that stuff like that is what makes you so interesting [*laughs*].

The Difficult America Arc

I assume the America arc, when Mello and Near appear, was difficult from the start, but how much did you plan out at the beginning?
Ohba: I didn't have much planned out. I knew Near and Mello would show up, I knew they'd both be after the notebook, and I knew the story would take place in America. At that point, part of me was relying on Obata-sensei to make it look impressive.
Obata: The art was tough. Before I got the thumbnails, the only thing I was told by my

↑ The scar on his face left from the explosion made Mello look more intense and more human.

"His art exceeded all my expectations." (Ohba)

Obata: I felt I was able to express the negative parts of Near with those puppets.
Ohba: Yeah, you can see his dark side in the kind of puppets he used. He created them himself, right?
Obata: He bought the Kira one first and drew on it with a magic marker. Then he must have created the other ones to go along with it. And I don't think Near liked L all that much, so he made him ugly...I guess. But he liked Mello so he worked hard on that one. That was my thinking.
Ohba: So the Near in your mind doesn't like L [*laughs*]? It is true that as the story progresses, Near becomes less likeable.
Obata: Why is that?
Ohba: I think it's because right from the very start, Mello is desperate to get his hands on the notebook. Near has a different scheme. His plan is to suddenly appear later and grab it...The difference in their attitudes caused a negative reaction toward Near; perhaps he was seen as a cheat. Plus his cheeky behavior, which was meant to reinforce his childishness, may have been seen as annoying.

Who was your least favorite character, Obata-sensei?
Obata: Probably Near [*laughs*]. But I liked drawing him, so he's one of my favorite characters as well.

Thumbmails for the Climatic Final Battle

Did you two discuss how things would go in the final chapters?
Ohba: No, it was the same as always. Our editor passed notes back and forth.

"L is a character I love to draw, but he's somebody I could never have come up with." (Obata)

Ohba: You're right...I probably would have made him be the hero. But I did often ask our editor if you had said anything. He would always answer with, "No, nothing" [*laughs*].

Near's Finger Puppets

How much information related to backgrounds and props is included in the thumbnails?
Ohba: For backgrounds, I just put something like "abandoned building." So it's pretty much all left to Obata-sensei. I do put in a lot of the items myself though. I had the match tower in there but was really surprised when I saw the final art. The assistants must have worked really hard.
Obata: We went all-out for that one [*laughs*].
Ohba: On the other hand, there was nothing in the thumbnails about the finger puppets. The final scenes looked much cooler thanks to them, didn't they?

➔ One of the key items in the conclusion: Near's finger puppets. There's an interesting story behind them...

...ARE JUST A MURDERER.

WHAT YOU SEE BEFORE YOU IS KIRA...
...BUT ALSO THE GOD OF THIS NEW WORLD.

↑ Light's speech in the final chapter. His calm face becomes more and more crazed...

with. So L isn't real to me. And that's what I like about him. I put a lot of work into his death scene as well.
Ohba: Do you always work harder on a death scene if you like the character?
Obata: Yes, because in some ways it's their greatest moment. But this series itself is full of death so I always tried hard to keep up the dark image. To express that, I used a lot of religious motifs in the chapter cover pages and backgrounds...
Ohba: Sorry, I just saw them as cool...I didn't think too deeply about it.
Obata: But the apples were really important to you. They were always mentioned in the thumbnails.
Ohba: I just really wanted to use the dying message of "Shinigami only eat apples," so I needed Ryuk to be holding them. There's no other reason.
Obata: But why apples?
Ohba: Simply because the red goes well with his black body and they fit well with his big mouth.
Obata: Yes, I was told that Light would die pathetically at the end. It was something I was secretly hoping for, so when I heard about it I was very excited.
Ohba: The art was truly amazing. Obata-sensei made a lot of improvements to the thumbnails for this scene.

What were the final thumbnails like?
Ohba: They were pretty much the same as always, but I may have added some extra instructions in chapter 107 where Light dies. I would write stuff like, "Light falls down." The final version was vastly different, though.

Did you have instructions for Light's facial expressions?
Ohba: I only write in little things, so it was all Obata-sensei, who is masterful at adding expressions that fit the dialogue. His art exceeded all my expectations. I wanted to make Light look evil, but Obata-sensei made him look really evil.
Obata: Light had been a character holding in his emotions until then, so I made them really explode out. I was really intense while I drew it.

Thoughts on the Finished Work

Who was the most fun to draw?
Obata: L.
Ohba: So it was L.
Obata: But Light's fun too. The truth is, there are so many characters in *Death Note* I could never create on my own that everything about it was fun. L is a character I love to draw, but he's somebody I could never have come up

"It turned out that Obata-sensei, our editor and I were the least excited about the popularity and acclaim." (Ohba)

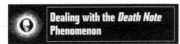

Dealing with the *Death Note* Phenomenon

***Death Note* is an incredibly popular manga, of course, and has become such a phenomenon that it's been turned into a movie and an anime and has inspired countless debates on the Internet. Did you think it would become so huge?**
Ohba: Once Obata-sensei was chosen for the art, I knew that if the series didn't sell it would be my fault. So I really wanted it to do well, but still I couldn't have even imagined this.
Obata: I didn't think so either. And our editor seemed to be thinking that it would do so-so because people have varied tastes.
Ohba: [*laughs*]
Obata: I was happy with all the attention, but it didn't change anything for me. I was just enjoying drawing something I liked.
Ohba: Honestly, I couldn't really experience the popularity. My senses were numb from doing a weekly serialization.
Obata: It's true…creating each chapter takes all your energy.

How did it feel when volume one set a record and sold a million copies in two months?
Ohba: Beyond surprised and happy.
Obata: But our editor sure was quiet even when we passed one million copies sold [*laughs*].
Ohba: I asked our editor about this. You know how they usually add a comment on the chapter cover pages saying something like, "Now on sale, super popular!!"? He felt that the phrase "super popular" just didn't fit with the feel of this series and never used it during its run. I guess *Death Note* is meant to be quietly and solemnly popular.

← Ryuk is a slave to his passion for apples. Apples play an important role in the story...

Obata: Apples have a lot of religious and psychological significance, so a person could read a lot into them being in the series if they wanted to. I assumed that that was behind it.
Ohba: No, no. I didn't think about that at all. I just think apples are cool…that's it [*laughs*]. But I figured it was good to include a lot of things that could become significant points later on. It turned out that Ryuk agreed to search for the hidden cameras in exchange for apples.

What was the reason for the apple on the final chapter cover?
Ohba: I gave no instructions for that page; it was all Obata-sensei.
Obata: As I said earlier, I had assumed that the apples represented a deep theme to Ohba-sensei. But it turns out there was nothing behind them…
Ohba: Oh, no. I'm disappointing him…

↑ Light commits murder in the very first chapter of the series. This is unusual and surprising content for a popular story.

Obata: True... [*laughs*].
Ohba: I think it turned out that Obata-sensei, our editor and I were the least excited about the popularity and acclaim. To us, working hard every week to create something that more people would enjoy was more important.
Obata: To me, too, the art is the most important. I think that's just our personalities.
Ohba: Also, the only person we have to talk to is our editor. We'd meet and talk but it would just end with us saying stuff like, "It sold a million," "Isn't that great?," or "Yeah."

Were you aware of all the commentary about the series?
Ohba: Not much during the serialization, though I did see a magazine article. But...it was too difficult for me to understand [*laughs*]. People were talking about some really serious stuff.
Obata: It's true, some people may have been taking the series a little too seriously. The other day I saw a critic on television talking about *Death Note,* but it was so complicated that I didn't understand [*laughs*].
Ohba: *Death Note* was never meant to be such a noble piece of work.
Obata: Yes, we just want people to enjoy reading it, right?
Ohba: Debates about Light being good or evil, or about the merits of our Internet society; these types of deep philosophical themes are totally different from the *Death Note* we first imagined. "Life and death," "good and evil"...as I said in the interview, we never put much thought into it. We just wanted it to be entertaining.

Private Life: Workspace

Obata: I once heard from our editor that Ohba-sensei's workspace was really nice...
Ohba: I just can't work if my room is a mess. So I gave my room a real Western, fairy-tale feel. And I have art on the walls.
Obata: Oh, that's nice.
Ohba: That's why I never leave: it's so comfortable.
Obata: What kind of art do you have up?
Ohba: A French artist named Jean Jansem. I have one of his lithographs.
Obata: You look at the painting when taking a break from work?

DO YOU REALLY THINK THAT KIRA IS EVIL?

↑ The debate over good and evil sometimes found its way into the series. The answers are always left up to the reader.

"To me, too, the art is the most important." (Obata)

but I don't read any of them." (Ohba)

Private Life: Movies and Novels

Do you like movies?
Ohba: I do watch a lot. I especially like Akira Kurosawa movies.
Obata: What's your favorite genre?
Ohba: I'd say comedy. And I like Japanese movies more than American ones. Like *Crab*

Goalkeeper. And, though it's not Japanese, *Shaolin Soccer*.
Obata: So you like Asian movies.
Ohba: Yeah, seems like I'm watching a lot of them lately. But I also love Charlie Chaplin. I own all his movies on DVD. You like suspense and horror movies, right? Like *The Exorcist*?
Obata: Yes. In terms of Japanese movies, stuff like *The Ring* and *School Ghost Stories*.
Ohba: But I heard you're afraid of ghosts.
Obata: Yes [*laughs*]. I like to be scared.
Ohba: But I can imagine you watching the movies and thinking, "Oh, that was a good angle!"
Ohba: Yes, I do. It's very nice. I of course have your lithographs as well, Obata-sensei. Are there any painters you like?
Obata: I have a few current illustrators that I like. Akihiro Yamada (illustrator for the *Twelve Kingdoms* novels) and Hajime Sorayama (illustrated Aerosmith's *Just Push Play* CD cover). And Alfons Mucha. I like art that makes great posters. I like them because they are pretty to look at. I'm not so fond of abstract art.
Ohba: So you also like looking at realistic art as well as drawing it?
Obata: Either way, I never really think about putting art up. When it comes to decorating a room with art, like you do, doesn't that take a special sense?
Ohba: Looking at the amazing art you draw, you definitely have the artistic sense to decorate your room!
Obata: I'm also bad at cleaning up, so my room is always a mess.
Ohba: In contrast, I'm probably a clean freak. I even wash my coffee cup between refills.
Obata: Wow, what a difference between us! I never wash my cup and sometimes I'll unknowingly down a cup of coffee that's been sitting out for two or three days...
Ohba: Eww [*laughs*].
Obata: Then I just refill it with new coffee. My desk usually always has a half-full cup on it.
Ohba: When do you clean your room?
Obata: I haven't used my vacuum cleaner in about three years. One time my editor realized this and started cleaning. But he gave up midway [*laughs*]. Your workplace is really clean, right?
Ohba: I usually clean once a day, at least once every three days. I can't take it if I see dust or eraser shavings.

"My editor recommends me things

Obata: I'm really bad with scary things, like photos of ghosts or pictures of hell—I really believed in that stuff when I was a kid. My childhood fears affect me even now.
Ohba: I actually don't believe in that stuff very much.
Obata: I figured that when you didn't want to come to the purification [*laughs*].
Ohba: I told our editor that if I were going to go to something like that, I'd go by myself…
Obata: But you never went, right?
Ohba: But hey, I do go to a nearby temple for New Year's.
Obata: Well, that's just to ring in the new year [*laughs*].
Ohba: Yeah, but I also ask to be purified during that visit [*laughs*]. I do remember how in the commentary section of the books, you once wrote about not wanting to be cursed for drawing Shinigami.

THE DEATH NOTE…
IS THE BOND BETWEEN LIGHT THE HUMAN AND RYUK THE SHIN-IGAMI.

↑ Ryuk's design was inspired by that famous movie?

Obata: I do think about that stuff. So I'm actually not that interested in the story. I'm all focused on the camera work.
Ohba: Have you gotten ideas from movies?
Obata: In terms of character design, a little bit from *The Matrix*.
Ohba: Ryuk is inspired by Tim Burton?
Obata: Yes, *Edward Scissorhands*.
Ohba: I love *Edward Scissorhands* too! I like most of Tim Burton's movies.

Do you read many novels?
Ohba: I actually never read anything.
Obata: I read from time to time. I like stuff from Natsuhiko Kyogoku. I like stories about demons and exorcists. I had assumed you were a big reader, Ohba-sensei. Especially mystery books.
Ohba: I'm terrible with kanji. My editor recommends me things but I don't read any of them. When I read, I'll start thinking about something else or start analyzing the story. I just lose track of the thing I'm reading. Sorry for not having a more interesting answer.
Obata: Yet there's so much text in your thumbnails [*laughs*].

Private Life: Fears

Obata: Recently I was pretty sick. I was thinking maybe it was a curse from having drawn *Death Note*…So I went to get my fortune read with tarot cards and the first card to come up was Death.
Ohba: That's pretty interesting [*laughs*].
Obata: I was really worried I was going to die. Though I got better quickly once I took some medicine [*laughs*].
Ohba: Oh yeah, didn't you go to a purification ritual when the series just started?
Obata: Yes, our editor took me.
Ohba: I was invited too, but…Obata-sensei, you seem to have a strong belief in the supernatural.

"The first card to come up was Death…" (Obata)

Similar but Different

Is there anything important you've learned about each other from talking today?
Ohba: Because of our similar taste with the manga, I thought we were very much alike. But now I see that in terms of private life and personality, we're pretty different.
Obata: We have similar tastes. But perhaps a different…style [*laughs*]?

What about you, Obata-sensei?
Obata: Ohba-sensei is very interesting.
Ohba: Perhaps we're both really weird [*laughs*]? We're comrades but not comrades…something like that?
Obata: Also, I've reconfirmed that Ohba-sensei is a mysterious person. I really wonder what you're usually doing [*laughs*].
Ohba: I'm not doing anything. I like doing nothing [*laughs*]. You could say my hobby is spacing out.
Obata: Are you doing anything while doing that? Like listening to music?
Ohba: I'm really just spacing out. Though I do look outside.
Obata: Does that help you think up new ideas?
Ohba: Not at all [*laughs*]. I actually have to think to come up with stuff. When I'm spacing out, I'm just spacing out.

⬆ Many Shinigami besides Ryuk appear in the series.

Obata: You hear about it a lot, you know? Someone draws a picture of a demon and bad things happen to them. Demons, Shinigami, they're pretty much the same thing. What are you most afraid of?
Ohba: I think I'd want to see a ghost if I could. Humans are the scariest things to me. That, and the prospect of having absolutely no work.
Obata: So, realistic things [*laughs*]?
Ohba: And also tight spaces. I don't like Ferris wheels. I'll ride elevators but I'm always thinking about if it gets stuck.
Obata: Everyone can't help but imagine getting trapped in one of those.
Ohba: I'd almost rather you be able to open the door on a Ferris wheel.
Obata: No, no, that would be dangerous [*laughs*]! I actually like tight spaces. My room's so packed with stuff that it's gotten really tight, but that makes me feel more comfortable.
Ohba: What about large crowds? That makes me really uncomfortable…
Obata: I'm totally fine with it. So I like hanging around in town. I guess I'm the outdoors type, at least in my mind. I'd travel a lot if I could. I can even sleep on the side of the road in a sleeping bag.
Ohba: We have a lot of similarities in our work, but our private lives are vastly different, aren't they?

"Honestly, how far ahead did you have the story planned out?" (Obata)

"I didn't have all of the ideas in my head at the beginning." (Ohba)

Ohba: How was it when you were creating *Cyborg Grandpa G*?
Obata: I was constantly stuck. You're saying it was the same with *Death Note*?
Ohba: Basically. That's why my own memory is that it turned out much better than I was expecting [*laughs*].
Obata: What [*laughs*]?!
Ohba: I admit that I did make sure the rules worked and things were consistent, but I didn't plan everything out. I didn't have all of the ideas in my head at the beginning.
Obata: How do you get these ideas? Adrenaline…?
Ohba: It might be. When I come up with a solution, I get pumped up and burn through a large chunk of story. So for some of the big chapters, I finished the thumbnails very quickly.
Obata: So when you think up a new idea, it's usually already complete?
Ohba: When I'm on a roll, it usually is.
Obata: So there's very little planning in developing the plot?
Ohba: Yes [*laughs*].
Obata: I'm really not feeling satisfied but…all right. I'll let you keep that mystery a mystery [*laughs*]. Once again, congratulations for completing the series.
Ohba: Same to you. Thank you so much for the wonderful art!

↑ *Death Note* was filled with plot twists, but how much of it was calculated?

Obata: So to you, an idea is something you need to think up.
Ohba: Yes, and it's very painful.

The Real Truth Behind *Death Note*

Obata: Sorry to return to a previous question but… Honestly, how far ahead did you have the story planned out?
Ohba: This again [*laughs*]?
Obata: You keep saying that you didn't think ahead at all, but I have my doubts. I'm thinking that everything was "exactly as planned"!

He doesn't believe you, does he?

Ohba: In a weekly serialization, it's impossible to plan every chapter out and have them go exactly as you want. It may be possible in a single novel but not in a weekly manga.
Obata: But you could have several plot points that you spread throughout the story.
Ohba: That's true. But my basic style was to put Light in a jam and then think of the way to get him out of trouble. So sometimes I got really stuck. I spent weeks on some of the thumbnails.
Obata: So you're saying that even the writer of *Death Note* didn't know what was going to happen next? Come on, you have to be lying [*laughs*]!

The Making of *Death Note*

Examining the work process using the thumbnails.

The Making of *Death Note*, as explained by the creators.

Ohba-sensei's thumbnails and Obata-sensei's art came together to create *Death Note*. What was the basic process behind it all?

The General Creative Process

The process started with Ohba-sensei and then moved to Obata-sensei. Both creators also listened to advice from their editor.

Ohba-sensei's Part

Rough Draft of the Story

First is the preparation that will serve as the basis of the work, when all the content to be included in the overall story and the flow of the story—broken down into panels—is determined. In Ohba-sensei's case, too many elements get crammed in and there's too much to fit on the pages.

The Making of the Thumbnails

The draft goes through a few rounds, until all the elements are decided on. At this point, the panels are split up, and the dialogue, monologue, and everything else is solidified. In case specific art is needed, that is also included in the thumbnails.

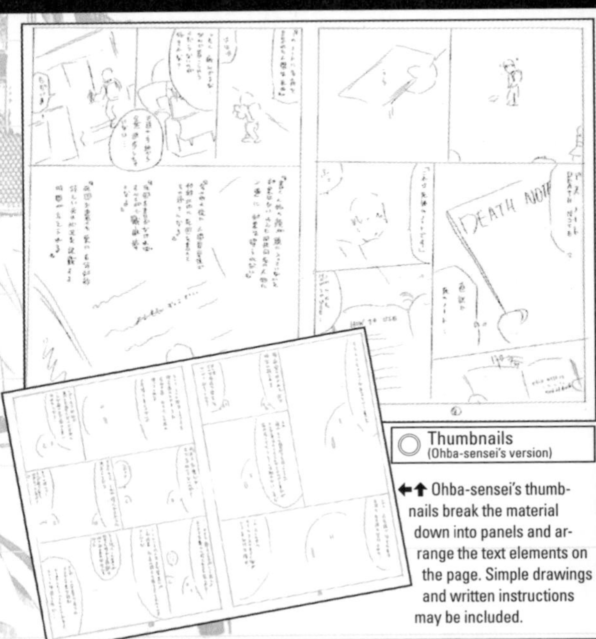

Thumbnails (Ohba-sensei's version)

←↑ Ohba-sensei's thumbnails break the material down into panels and arrange the text elements on the page. Simple drawings and written instructions may be included.

Comparing the Thumbnails and Final Art

Now that you know the basic process, how were some of your favorite scenes drawn? Let's take a closer look at some of Ohba-sensei's thumbnails.

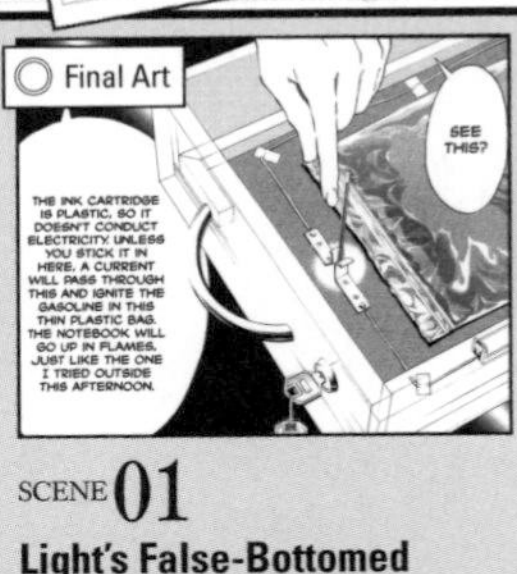

SEE THIS?
THE INK CARTRIDGE IS PLASTIC, SO IT DOESN'T CONDUCT ELECTRICITY UNLESS YOU STICK IT IN HERE. A CURRENT WILL PASS THROUGH THIS AND IGNITE THE GASOLINE IN THIS THIN PLASTIC BAG. THE NOTEBOOK WILL GO UP IN FLAMES, JUST LIKE THE ONE I TRIED OUTSIDE THIS AFTERNOON.

Final Art

Thumbnails (Ohba-sensei's version)

SCENE 01

Light's False-Bottomed Drawer

→ The details of Light's false-bottomed drawer. The details in the thumbnail version are rather precise.

Lettering Is Inserted, and It's Complete!!

The pages are handed in to the editor and the dialogue, special effects and other type are set. And then it's done!

Drawing Begins

Once the contents are determined, the drawing commences. During this process, it's not uncommon for the design of new characters and items to be decided upon. This is when Ohba-sensei's thumbnails come to life.

Processing Ohba-sensei's Thumbnails

Ohba-sensei's thumbnails are worked on in terms of camera angles and character expressions. In order to really grasp the concept behind Ohba-sensei's thumbnails, Obata-sensei uses them as a model in creating his own.

Obata-sensei's Part

◯ Thumbnails (Obata-sensei's version)

◯ Incomplete Inks

⬆ Here are the new thumbnails based on Ohba-sensei's version. When more elaborate drawings are inserted, the overall feeling of the artwork is expanded.

⬅ The page in the middle of the inking stage. At this point, the contents are almost completely set, but expressions, composition and other elements are sometimes only decided after consulting with the editor.

SCENE 03 Near's Dice Tower

➡ Both creators talked about the dice tower previously. Does this panel convey Obata-sensei's of endurance?

◯ Final Art

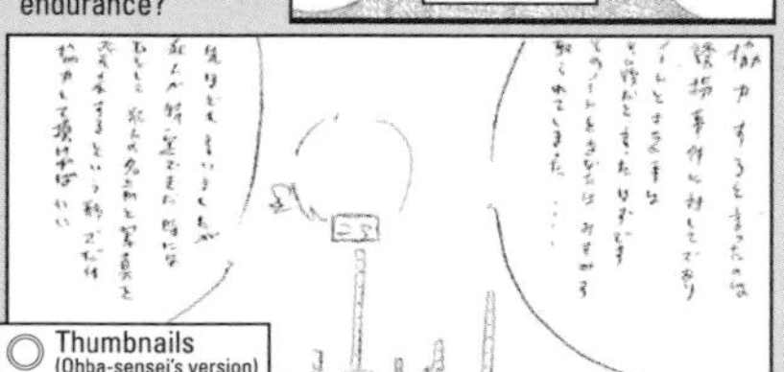

◯ Thumbnails (Ohba-sensei's version)

SCENE 02 L's Snack Time

◯ Thumbnails (Ohba-sensei's version)

◯ Final Art

⬅ Pudding with bites taken out. Even the smallest of details is included.

Tsugumi Ohba × Takeshi Obata

Tsugumi Ohba-sensei
×
Takeshi Obata-sensei

33 QUESTIONS

We asked both creators to answer a special survey. These 33 questions cover everything from the series to their private lives. Reading this may reveal some unexpected facts!

The survey wherein both creators reveal the truth!

↑ L was loved by both creators. Unfortunately for him, that love didn't affect the plot of the series.

Q01 Tell us your three favorite human characters and why?

-OHBA-
①L. Besides Light, I think he was my strongest character.
②Teru Mikami. Besides Light, I think he was my second strongest character.
③Soichiro Yagami. Besides Light, I think he was my third…yada yada.

-OBATA-
①L. Appearance, personality, everything. I could never come up with such a strange character and he fits the series so well. He was so fun to draw.
②Light Yagami. I don't know whether it was because I liked him or because I was happy to be able to draw such an evil character in a children's magazine.
③Watari. I like older characters, and he seemed to be hiding a lot of ability. I think he had depth.

Q02 Your favorite Shinigami and why?

-OHBA-
Ryuk. If I didn't say Ryuk here, his whole character would be in vain [*laughs*].

-OBATA-
Rem. Because she was both a Shinigami and a good person.

Q03 Your three favorite scenes and why?

-OHBA-
①The scene in chapter 19. That was the most exciting part of the story for me.
②L's death in chapter 59. I was in shock and couldn't eat for three days.
③Light's death in chapter 107. I knew it was coming, but it was drawn so much more powerfully than I was imagining.

-OBATA-
①When Light and L meet in chapter 19. I never imagined L would reveal himself like that. ②L's death in chapter 59. ③The scene of the girl praying at the end of chapter 108. I wanted to end the series with something beautiful.

TSUGUMI OHBAxTAKESHI OBATA 33 QUESTIONS

Q04 Tell us your favorites lines and why?

-OHBA- What Light said to Naomi Misora in chapter 14: "Because I'm Kira." I was thinking "Why are you telling her?!" but that's also what I like about it.

-OBATA- L's confession in chapter 19: "I am L." Who knew he'd say it himself...?

Q05 Your favorite trick and why?

-OHBA- The notebook hiding place in chapter 4 and the way Light checks if someone's been in his room in chapter 16. Mainly because it took a lot of time and effort to come up with the hiding place and because both times, I felt like yelling, "You're going too far!" to Light.

-OBATA- How L uses Lind L. Tailor to figure out that Kira is in the Kanto region. This scene made me think about how great this manga was. Plus you could see how L would do anything to win.

Q06 Which character was difficult to create?

-OHBA- Matt. I didn't even know what kind of person he was.

-OBATA- Misa. The notion of doing anything for the person you love was hard to comprehend and I felt like she was controlling me while I was drawing her.

↑ Because she has so many expressions—from goofy to serious—she required a lot of artistic variation.

Q07 What scenes/plot points did you really struggle over?

-OHBA- The time between chapters 59 and 60. It was very difficult to come up with a new arc in such a short amount of time. And also, keeping the right pace once I decided I wanted the series to end at 108 chapters.

-OBATA- Rather than the really flashy scenes, the hardest stuff for me was the conversational dialogue or the changes in Light's expressions in the Yellow Box warehouse. And it was very difficult when Light suddenly lost his Death Note memories.

Q08 Who do you think is the smartest character?

-OHBA- L. Because the plot requires it [*laughs*].

-OBATA- Near. Because he cheats.

Q09 Who is the most evil character?

-OHBA- The mafia boss (Rod Ross) with Mello. He's the head of the mafia so he must be pretty darn evil.

-OBATA- I don't know...

Q10 Who is the most good character?

-OHBA- Sachiko and Sayu Yagami. I can't sense any evil or twistedness from these two at all.

-OBATA- Soichiro Yagami.

Q11 Who is the most pitiful character?

-OHBA- The Yagami family. Light is ruined because he picked up the notebook. Soichiro dies while on duty. I felt sorry for Sayu and Sachiko, who survive.

-OBATA- The people of the Yagami family.

Q12 If you had to say what the most important thing in *Death Note* is, what would it be?

-OHBA- The human whose name is written in this note shall die.

-OBATA- Impossible to say.

Q13 What was your basic weekly schedule during the series?

-OHBA- When I could finish things in a week, the basic pattern was to think about things for five days and then pencil it out and insert the dialogue in one day. Then I'd fax it to my editor and spend the final day making corrections.

-OBATA- Thumbnails, layout, pencils: one day. More penciling, inking: one day. My assistants come to work: four days. The final touches: one day. That would be the basic week. Though when we had to do color pages it would take an extra day or two and mess with the schedule.

Q14 Was your work schedule consistent or would it change a lot depending on the chapter?

-OHBA- Sometimes I could do a whole chapter in three to four days while other times it took me close to a month.

-OBATA- It was consistent except when I had to do color pages.

Q15 During the serialization, was there anything you would remind yourself to always focus on?

-OHBA- To add something funny in every chapter, even if it would get edited out. And to use interesting ideas as soon as I thought of them.

-OBATA- To keep my deadlines and to draw the art in a way that brings out the greatness of the script.

Q16 Do you have some kind of item you need to have when you work?

-OHBA- A pencil and eraser. If you meant something else, then not really.

-OBATA- Even if I skip meals, I can't skip my coffee. I listen to music while doing color work. My Aeron chair. Movie DVDs.

Q17 Did anything help or shock you while you were working?

-OHBA- The most helpful thing was my editor's advice. What shocked me was that the series was more popular than I had anticipated.

-OBATA- Fashion magazines were helpful to me when creating the character designs. Also, a book of jewelry accessories, for drawing the Shinigami.

Q18 Did you know about the discussions on the Internet about future plot twists? What did you think of them?

-OHBA- I heard that there was a lot of online discussion going on, but I didn't have time to see any of it. Also, I didn't want it to affect me, so I chose not to check it out. But I'm very happy to have people discussing my work, no matter the method.

-OBATA- I don't know much about the Internet, but I'm happy that people were discussing the series.

Q19 How do you write the comments for the collected volumes?

-OHBA- It's the thing I least liked doing and I would pretty much just write something up really quickly before it was due. I'm sorry.

-OBATA- I'm so bad at it that I'd rather not write anything, but I try my best. I thought the ones for volumes 2 and 12 were pretty good.

YOU GUYS ARE ALL PRETTY PATHETIC SHINIGAMI...
HEH HEH HEH, LIKE YOU CAN TALK. ALL YOU DO IS GAMBLE WITH ME EVERY-DAY.
YEAH, THIS IS HOW SHINIGAMI ACT THESE DAYS. TIMES HAVE CHANGED FOR THE SHINIGAMI REALM...

Q20 What are your favorite manga series and genres?

-OHBA-

My favorite manga is *Death Note*. My favorite genre is comedy.

-OBATA-

Kazuhiro Fujita's *Ushio and Tora*, anything by Yosuke Takahashi, dark one-shot stories.

MISA-SAN, PLEASE STOP WITH THE TOTAL OVER-ACTING.
WHA?!!

↑ The comic elements in the story must come from Ohba-sensei's enjoyment of humorous stories.

Q21 What made you want to create manga? And how old were you when you started?

-OHBA-

A friend encouraged me when I was 18.

-OBATA-

I've wanted to draw art for a living ever since eighth grade.

Q22 What did you want to be when you were a child?

-OHBA-

A gymnast.

-OBATA-

Someone who creates stuff.

Q23 Do you have a creator who inspires you or whom you admire?

-OHBA-

Not a creator, but my editor. He advises me with such a serious face that I can't help but be affected [*laughs*]. I admire how hard he works.

-OBATA-

Kazuo Umezu. One manga that inspired me was Shotaro Ishinomori's *Cyborg 009*.

Q24 Are there any current *Weekly Jump* creators that you keep your eye on?

-OHBA-

I follow all the *Weekly Jump* creators. If I have to name one, I'd say Daiamon-sensei, who did a lot of *Death Note* parodies in his comedy series.

-OBATA-

All the *Weekly Jump* mangaka.

Q25 How do you view your readers?

-OHBA-

Since I was once a reader, I'd say as comrades?

-OBATA-

The people who support me.

Q26 Is there a character in *Death Note* who you could say is most similar to you?

-OHBA-

Near, since I don't leave my house very much, or maybe Light, because I did well in school…

-OBATA-

Matsuda.

TSUGUMI OHBA TAKESHI OBATA 33 QUESTIONS

Q27 Do you have any hobbies besides manga?

-OHBA- First off, manga isn't my hobby [*laughs*]. My hobby is going to pet shops, staring at the animals and saying, "They're so cute!!"

-OBATA- I like cars and motorcycles.

⬆ Cars and bikes, of course, but *Death Note* even had helicopters and jet planes in it.

Q28 What are you most interested in these days?

-OHBA- I'm very excited about the movie *Death Note: The Last Name.* I've also been into traditional Japanese sweets.

-OBATA- Traveling. I want to see ancient ruins.

Q29 What was the first thing you did after *Death Note* ended?

-OHBA- Nothing out of the ordinary. Sorry.

-OBATA- I watched all the DVDs I had been meaning to watch.

Q30 Why do you think *Death Note* appeals to so many readers?

-OHBA- Perhaps because it's a story not usually seen in *Jump* and because it had Obata-sensei's realistic art.

-OBATA- Perhaps because it didn't seem like a typical *Jump* manga—although it actually was, really.

Q31 How do you feel about your creation being turned into movies, anime, novels, video games, etc.?

-OHBA- Very happy. I'm grateful to all those involved.

-OBATA- I look forward to all of them. I'm very happy.

Q32 If you were to create another series, what kind of genre and story would it be?

-OHBA- A really normal sports manga or maybe fantasy (though I doubt I could do it).

-OBATA- Either something really fantastic or something really realistic.

Q33 Do you have any comments for your readers?

-OHBA- Thank you for reading my series, especially those who read all the way to the very end.

-OBATA- This series can be enjoyed in various mediums, so please check out the movie and anime as well.

The 13 Truths About Chapter 108

The Two Creators Reveal the Final Mysteries

Chapter 108, "Finis," the final chapter in the *Death Note* saga, is filled with many unanswered mysteries. We'll now have both Ohba-sensei and Obata-sensei reveal the truths behind them!

The Secrets Buried in Death Note's Final Chapter!!

MYSTERY 01 How did you come up with the final chapter?

-OHBA- I first came up with the idea of followers surrounding Kira's grave. I figured that even if Kira died, there would still be those who worshipped him. But I realized it would cause problems if everyone knew that Kira had died. Plus, we discussed how it could be distasteful to have to see the Yagami family grave [*laughs*]. The final idea of the long line of followers was something I developed with my editor at the end of 2005 when we decided on how to end the series.

-OBATA- I had heard from the editor that it would be a scene with Kira worshippers surrounding his grave. At that point I thought it was a little lacking...but the thumbnails looked really good and I was excited when drawing it. I wanted to set the mood, so I had them all wearing hoods.

MYSTERY 02 When did you decide to end the series at 108 chapters?

-OHBA- When I decided how to end it, I also came up with the idea of ending it at chapter 108. I then kept that in mind when creating the thumbnails. So from around the time that Takada reappeared, the plot and chapter numbers were already set. I had also already plotted out the Yellow Box warehouse scene, so it was really difficult to end it at exactly 108 chapters. The number represents the 108 earthly desires in Buddhism.

I'M GOING TO DIE IN A FEW MORE SECONDS!
NO, I DON'T WANT TO DIE! I DON'T WANT TO DIE! I DON'T WANT TO DIE!

MYSTERY 03 What was the importance of the apple for the chapter cover?

➡ Apples often appeared during important parts of the story. They served as plot devices and are a motif that represents the series.

-OBATA-

I had believed that the apple was a very important aspect of the *Death Note* lore, so I figured that it was the only way to go. And the final set of chapter covers all featured "things": close-ups of the watch, the orbs used to look into the human world, and the apple. I tried to draw all the important objects.

MYSTERY 04 Who's the man who first appears in the chapter?

-OHBA-

That's Ryo, the bullied kid who was waiting for a ride in chapter 1. He should be an adult by now...

⬆➡ The street scenes in chapter 108 are similar to those in chapter 1. The schoolgirls are different but act the same.

MYSTERY 05 Why did you make Aizawa the NPA chief?

⬇ In the end, Aizawa took over for Soichiro. This would've been unimaginable earlier in the series.

-OHBA-

If I were going to choose from the surviving members, it would have to be Aizawa. I didn't want to use some new character in the final chapter. Though now that I think about it, Aizawa might be perfect since he has connections with both the police and L (Near). Since he knows both organizations, he's a good choice as leader. If it were Mogi, he'd probably lean toward L's side.

MYSTERY 06 Matsuda's theories were correct?

-OHBA-

It can be taken either way, and I haven't decided if it's right or wrong. I want the readers to decide on their own. The only thing I can clearly say about this is that Light ordered Mikami to "not take out the notebook until the end." And also Yamamoto, the new character who gets teased by Matsuda, is someone I added in at the thumbnail stage and isn't significant. I just used him to show Matsuda bossing someone around [*laughs*].

WELL... EVEN IF THAT THEORY IS TRUE...
...THE NOTEBOOK DOESN'T EXIST ANYMORE. SO THERE'S NO PROOF.
DON'T YOU GET IT, THAT'S THE VERY PROOF OF THIS THEORY!
YOU IDIOT!
I TOLD YOU NOT TO MAKE ANY UNNECESSARY MOVES UNTIL TODAY...

⬆ Mysteries remain even in the final chapter. So the truth is…?

⬅ Light's orders reveal his conceit.

MYSTERY 07 Why do the Kira worshippers appear at the very end?

-OHBA-

Although Light was evil, he had many who supported him. It would have been fine to have him end in his pathetic state, but I decided to redeem him a little bit by showing that even though he died, he did become the god he wanted to be for a select group of people. But, as he told Ryuk, what he really wanted was to be a living god, so even though he has followers he would not have been happy with the fact that he died. So there's a little irony in there too. Well, the fact that I went back and forth with this part shows how much love I had for the character of Light. Though L is still number one [*laughs*].

ONCE THIS CASE IS OVER, LET'S GO DRINKING AGAIN, YAMAMOTO.
HUH? AGAIN... NOT AGAIN, MATSUDA.

⬆ Matsuda's become a bit of a troublemaker. Yamamoto's face says it all.

➡ The Kira case was the most terrible murder spree in human history. But there were also those who were saved by it.

⬇ Light's use of the word "reign" here reveals that what he really wanted to do was rule.

OVER WHICH I PLAN TO REIGN LIKE A GOD FOR A LONG TIME.

God not only accepted him, but even granted him godly powers.
He too had become a god.

⬆ The crescent moon in the night sky…This is a very metaphoric scene.

⬅ Mikami and other Kira worshippers called him "God."

MYSTERY 08 Was the final scene based on the name "Light Yagami"?

-OHBA-

Praying to god at night under the moon…it's perfect, right? It's definitely based on Light's name, but it wasn't something I had planned from the beginning. I came up with it while I was creating the thumbnails for the final chapter. It turned out to be something for fans to figure out, so I liked it very much.

⬆ A young female worshipper praying for the return of Kira. When the series ended, there was a flurry of discussion among fans about who she was.

MYSTERY 09 Who is the girl who appears at the end?

-OHBA-

She's merely one of the followers who worship Kira. In the thumbnails, I just had her hands in the praying position with her face covered; Obata-sensei made it into the final version. It's not Misa; since she doesn't appear in the final chapter, some people may have thought it was her…

-OBATA-

It's not really anyone. In the thumbnails, it was a woman whose face was hidden. I thought that could work well too, but I think I personally wanted to draw something pretty in the final chapter. There's no real motif, I just tried to capture the scene.

MYSTERY 10 What's the meaning of the English sentence on the final page?

-OHBA-

It simply means that this story of the Death Note is concluded.

➡ "This story" refers to the Kira case surrounding Light. Meaning it's a different story from the pilot chapter…?

HEH, HEH...

I DON'T KNOW WHY, BUT I'M IN A DELUXE SUITE AT THE TEITO HOTEL. MUST BE THEIR WAY OF APOLOGIZING OR SOMETHING. IT'S GREAT!

⬆ Misa is released right before the Yellow Box warehouse showdown. This panel above is her final appearance.

H-HEY... I'M NOT... I...

↑ They were the perfect family up until Sayu's kidnapping…

↓ Due to her husband's job, Sachiko was prepared for hardships.

I'M SORRY, SACHIKO...
...

MYSTERY 11 What happened to the two survivors of the Yagami family?

-OHBA-

I didn't have the chance to include Sayu and Sachiko in the final chapter. I would guess that someone like Aizawa told them that Soichiro and Light sacrificed themselves to defeat Kira so that they wouldn't know the truth that Light was Kira. And the truth of the Kira case will never be revealed to the world. That's because the task force members and the people on Near's side will not tell anyone the truth.

SO YOU'LL GET TO SEE WHAT THE EXCEPTION TO THE RULE IS LIKE, RYUK.
HYUK, HYUK! THAT'S A LUCKY BREAK FOR ME.

↑ Light suffered a pathetic end. This line reveals his arrogance.

THERE'S NO WAY LIGHT WOULD KILL MISA. AND WHY WOULD YOU GO SO FAR FOR ME?
I DON'T EXACTLY WANT TO BE LOVED BY A SHINIGAMI... AND IF LIGHT DIED, I COULDN'T LIVE ON WITHOUT HIM...

→ A scene from the Yotsuba Kira arc. This line would hint at her future.

MYSTERY 12 Why didn't Misa appear in the final chapter?

-OHBA-

Again, I just couldn't come up with a situation to fit her in. Misa had lost her memories as Kira but still loved Light. And since those who use the notebook suffer misfortune, someone like Matsuda probably let it slip that Light had died. Misa then fell into depression and committed suicide…something like that.

→ It may have been locked away in a safe, but there was plenty of opportunity to switch it.

AND THE NOTEBOOK AIZAWA BROUGHT DOWN FROM THE JAPANESE INVESTIGATION HEADQUARTERS.
ARE THEY REAL?

DEATH NOTE

← The Shinigami notebook that brought chaos to the human world. The time could come when it once again falls into the hands of a human…?

MYSTERY 13 Did Ryuk return to the Shinigami realm?

-OHBA-

Yes, he did. However, since the notebook at the task force headquarters was burned right after Light's death, it was never determined whether it was real or not. My theory is that Light secretly replaced it with a fake and was hiding it. So some of Light's bluffs at the end may not have been total lies. If so, there would still be a notebook remaining in the human world and when it is found, Ryuk may once again come down…?

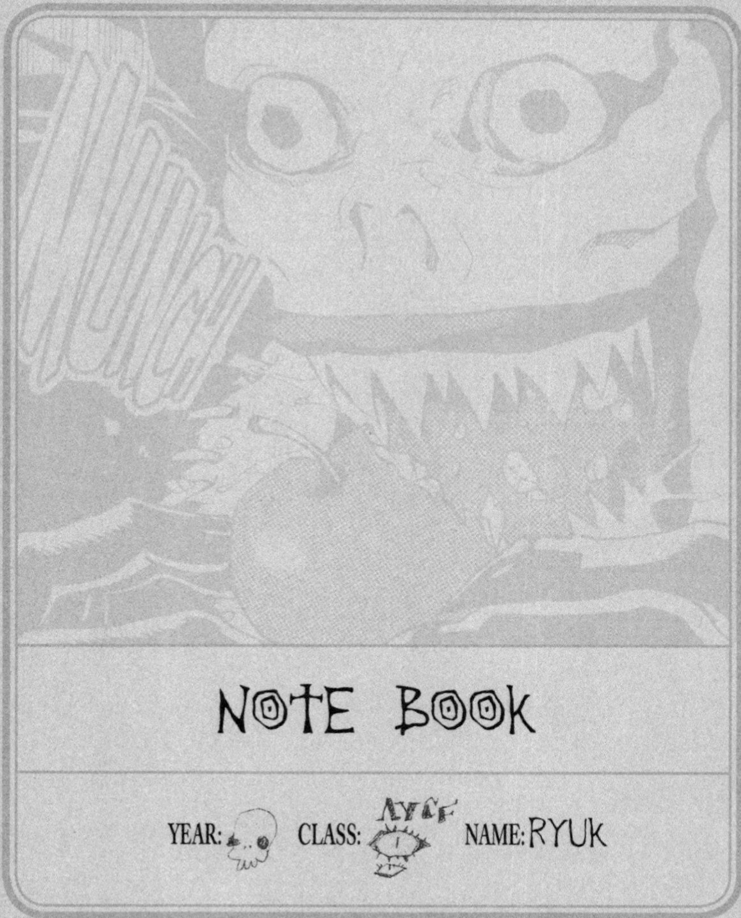

Ryuk's Human Observation Journal

***Death Note* Four-Panel Comics**

***Death Note* Pilot Chapter**

The Shinigami Ryuk was a big troublemaker in the human world. Now we present to you a special collection of what might have been his strange notes. The following pages contain original bonus material and other extras. This data was very seriously researched. Supposedly.

THE NEW WORLD ACCORDING TO LIGHT YAGAMI

Light is always talking about a "new world." The term sounds cool in itself, but what is his actual vision? Here's a look inside his fantasy-filled head!

A happy world where (only) the chosen can live in peace.

The new world that Light envisions is a peaceful place devoid of crime...That's all well and good, but it seems you won't be allowed to live in it if you aren't chosen by Light and don't worship him.

The new world that Kira strives for: now revealed!

No more crime!
CRIMES OF PASSION AND THE LIKE WILL NEVER STOP, BUT SOON NOBODY WILL COMMIT PRE-MEDITATED CRIMES OR ACTS THAT MAKE OTHERS SUFFER.

↑ An incredibly peaceful world. Is it just me or does everyone seem to have dead eyes? Aw, it must be my imagination!

The grand scheme! The hierarchy of the new world!

This is the hierarchy of ordinary citizens who Light imagines will live in the new world. And, of course, everything is decided by Light.

Those whom Light wishes to protect. Well, I guess it'd obviously include his little sister..

Including: Sayu Yagami and others.

Crime is absolutely out of the question—even if it's committed on Kira's request. Now isn't that convenient?

Including: Teru Mikami, Kyomi Takada, Kuro Otoharada and others.

These folks are glad they follow Kira! The God Squad!

Kira's the Ally of the Weak!

Mr. TM (civil servant)

I'm always being bullied by my afro-haired superior. I believe Kira is fighting for all of us underdogs.

Ratings Through the Roof!

Mr. HD (TV producer)

The new "Kira Show" is a huge hit! And my salary's nothing to complain about, either! Thanks, Lord Kira!

Spurred on by Revenge for her Parents!

Ms. MA (celebrity)

I finally got closure over my parents' death! Now I'm going to find Kira. I'll also become an idol along the way.

The Scoundrels Who Threaten Me! On the New World's Blacklist

The hateful enemies standing in the way of Kira's plans. As long as they're around, the new world will never arrive.

L

An argumentative young man with an insatiable lust for sweets. He's been against Kira since he first appeared. Generally, I don't like this guy.

Mello & Near

L's successors. I feel sorry for L that his successors are immature kids who can't even get along.

SPK Members

Though established by America, they turn into an illegal organization thanks to the vice president. Always be careful about what job you accept.

Misa Amane

A scary criminal and the self-proclaimed girlfriend of Kira. Although she contributes to the creation of the new world, that's that, and this is this!

Every one wore a refreshing smile upon their faces.
And he was not wrong. A few days later, he saw before him a peaceful classroom.
Smiles, everyone!

⬆ The natural smiles of the young. But the best smile has to be God's!

I INTEND TO SUGGEST THIS TO THE OTHER WORLD LEADERS IN THE NEXT WORLD SUMMIT.
...HAVE DECIDED TO ACCEPT KIRA, AND WILL DO NOTHING TO STAND IN KIRA'S WAY.

The world will revolve around God!

⬆ Even a huge country like the U.S. turns submissive! Though I don't care much for his enunciation.

These are the people Light's trying to make the new world for. As if they asked for it.

Including: Soichiro Yagami, Sachiko Yagami and others.

They aren't really needed but they might as well hang around... Is that what he means?

Including: Touta Matsuda, Shuichi Aizawa, Kanzo Mogi, Hideki Ide and others.

Lord Kira!!
Lord
Lord Kira!!
Lord Kira!!
Lord Kira!!
But he fails in the end anyway.
Lord Kira!!
Lord Kira!!

Passionate cheering from so many people, we couldn't fit it all!

Money, Status and Power!

Mr. ET (company employee)

Constantly mocked by my coworkers, I've suddenly been promoted to an important position. Though I still get made fun of...

INSIDE L'S BEWILDERING BELLY

Every time L appears in the story, there's always food next to him. This has caused many confused readers to ask: "Just how much does he eat?" I decided to look into the matter myself.

really none of your concern. I mean it.

The insatiable L!

I checked out just how much he does eat!

"A drink in one hand and some sweets on the table." That's L's basic style. I really think he drinks too much coffee and tea!

DATE	FOOD	WAY OF EATING
12/31/2003	Coffee	Put in dozens of sugar cubes and drained the cup
1/12/2004	Chocolate	Peeled off the wrapper, melted it inside mouth
	Coffee	Waited a while after stirring in sugar, then drank it cold
4/07/2004	Coffee	Didn't drink it, gave to assistant
4/18/2004	Cake	Ate half of it, was distracted by the Second Kira's tape, and forgot about it
	Black tea	Drank at same time as eating cake, let it go cold before drinking
4/23/2004	Cake	Ate until satisfied, ate the strawberry last
	Black tea	Drank it after eating the strawberry from the cake
5/12/2004	Chocolate	Ate it quickly without letting it melt in mouth
	Black tea	Drank it while still hot
5/25/2004	Cake	Left it during a meeting but didn't forget to eat it afterward
	Coffee	Drank it while eyeing the abandoned cake on the table
5/27/2004	Donut	Ate it normally
	Coffee	Added three cubes of sugar and drained it
5/28/2004	Coffee	Drank it while hot
	Black tea	Tea went cold, so gave it to Watari
5/31/2004	Black tea	Drank it while eating a fruit sandwich
6/01/2004	Hors d'oeuvre	Ignored it
	Champagne	Ignored it
	Black tea	Drank it normally
	Ham on melon	Avoided the slices of ham on top and ate only the melon
7/20/2004	Jelly	Ate it right away when he entered the room
7/23/2004	Coffee	Downed it while watching Light, Soichiro and Misa
8/02/2004	Cake	After eating his own piece, ate Misa's too
	Black tea	Downed it along with the cake he stole from Misa
10/02/2004	Cherry	Tied the stem in a knot with his tongue then ate the whole thing
	Black tea	Drank every last drop after it went cold
10/08/2004	Cake	Ate it normally
	Tea	Drank it with no incidents
10/09/2004	Ohagi*	Ate it with the paper wrapping but spat paper out afterward
	Black tea	Downed it after his ohagi
10/15/2004	Anmitsu†	Ate even the syrup
	Black tea	Drank it in one gulp while Light was on the phone with Namikawa
	Coffee	Put tons of sugar in it and drank it before sugar completely dissolved
10/24/2004	Coffee	Drank it exceedingly normally
10/25/2004	Bean jelly	Played around by stacking sugar cubes on it before eating
	Coffee	Tossed in five cubes of sugar and drank it
	Sugar cubes	Stuffed a bunch in his mouth and sucked on them
10/28/2004	Coffee	Drank it without a hitch
	Banana	Peeled it and ate it normally
	Coffee	Put it in a water bottle and drank it outdoors
10/29/2004	Coffee	After it went cold put a ton of milk in it and drank it
11/04/2004	Ice cream	Ate it in minutes
	Coffee	Gulped it down after eating ice cream
	Pudding a la mode	Ate the cherry last
	Coffee	Had another cup after the first
11/05/2004	Chocolate snack	Mashed it with his fingers and nibbled on the edges but was unable to finish it due to his death
	Coffee	Only had a couple sips but had to leave the rest due to death

*Sweet rice cakes †Mixed fruit and jelly cocktail

the best!

So Shocking! Scenes of L Preying on his Food!

L-kun's eating style is anything but typical! Looks like even Wammy-san, who can usually do anything, wasn't able to teach him table manners. It must be tough to raise someone.

Ham on melon

Eat the ham too! The ham!!

Cherries

THEN PLEASE CHOOSE.

No! Not such a typical high school girl trick!

"You know what they say about people who can knot cherry stems with their tongues... They're good kissers!" "Omigod! You're so dirty!!" is what this leads to. But the tongue action isn't the only thing that makes for a good kisser!

Ohagi

THIS NEXT FRIDAY SHOULD BE VERY INTEREST-ING.

At least take off the wrapper!!

Did he eat the wrapper because he didn't want to get his hands dirty? If he pulled something like this in front of a parent, he'd get a beating for sure.

Sugar cubes

Sure, he likes sweet things, but this is too much! If you're going to eat sugar cubes straight-up, why even buy candy? Why not just get some high-grade sugar?

What, you can't afford to buy real candy?!

Banana

Ahh, we were hoping you'd eat the skin too!

He bites it with his teeth showing! Wait . . . That's surprisingly normal. I think it was wrong for him to defy everyone's expectations.

Well, as long as you don't get fat, maybe it's okay?

Bean jelly abuse!

Warning!

No playing with your food!

Food is for eating, not for playing. Maybe Wammy-san should've paid more attention to that? At least that's what I think.

Me and Light's Love Love Diary! ♡

This is Misa's super special diary, where I've recorded the journey from when I first had my dramatic encounter with Light, all the way up to marriage [squeal]! Looking back on everything now, a lot of stuff sure happened.

Love Memory 1

Kira became my boyfriend!

When I met Light at Aoyama, Misa's heart was struck by Cupid's arrow! I think Light felt the same way, too, because he went out with me in no time!

I sent a love letter!

⬅ I think he noticed how much passion I put into it!

I got his name thanks to the Shinigami Eyes!

⬆ Name confirmed with the Shinigami Eyes! What a cool name…

MAKE ME YOUR GIRL-FRIEND.

My pushy proposal

⬅ I couldn't wait any longer, so I went to Light's house. Would he be interested in me as his girlfriend?

She's like a stalker…

Love Memory 2

I dazzled Light with my array of outfits!

I put on tons of different outfits to show Light a good time! I thought he'd be happy, but he was always so quiet. Light, you really have to open up!

Light, look!
Look at me!
Come on!
Come on!
Huh? Oh, yeah.

➡ This was my best shot! What do you think, Light?

⬅ I think this really appealed to Light's more serious side!

⬅ Schoolgirl uniform's a must! This had to hit the strike zone!

MISA AMANE'S PURE LOVE MEMORIAL

"I'll do anything for Light!!" Misa will often yell out serious things like that seemingly without a care in the world. Let's take a look at this diary, which chronicles her burning passions.

Misa crushes all of her rivals!

The meddlesome girls I needed to keep an eye out for. Light already has a girlfriend, so get a clue and give up!

Kiyomi Takada

⬆ She only met Light at work, so Misa wins!

GOSH, I HAVEN'T BEEN TO SPACELAND SINCE JUNIOR HIGH. THIS IS GONNA BE FUN!
PLUS, I GET YOU ALL TO MYSELF TODAY, LIGHT...

Yuri

⬆ Misa wins for having a more mature charm!

YOU'VE SEEN ME WITH SHIHO AND EMI. I'LL HAVE TO KEEP THIS UP AND MAKE SURE SHE STAYS TOTALLY INFATUATED WITH ME.

Other Sluts

⬆ Girls who weren't even shown automatically lose!

Damn!

I'VE WON!!
MISA CAN SEE RYUGA'S REAL NAME!

I saw L's name!

⬅ Misa's greatest feat! At least, it should have been. Sorry, Light...

Love Memory 3

I'll risk my life to serve you!

Because I'm Kira's girlfriend, of course I helped with creating the new world. Misa's a helpful girl!

LIGHT! HIGUCHI IS KIRA!

Got a confession out of Higuchi!

⬅ Got evidence against Yotsuba Kira! Was I a help to Light again today?

Checking up on the mafia!

⬆ I spent a lot of late nights looking for the owner of the Death Note for Light. There might've been some times I felt overwhelmed.

Yeah, good work.

Roommates

➡ For a while, Light was so busy that we hardly ever saw each other. But it's okay, because I know how he feels.

LIGHT, ARE YOU DONE FOR THE DAY?!

Love Memory 4

Light and I, together at long last!

Finally, Light proposed to me! Now I can go back to being a regular girl, and live happily ever after with Light!

And then...

I'M RETIRING TO BECOME YOUR WIFE?
YEAH, I'LL MARRY YOU, SO QUIT YOUR JOB.

...the proposal!

⬅ Light asked me to quit my job as an actress. Does this mean he wants to be with me every day?!

Misa's going to be so happy!
SHOULD I KILL MISA RIGHT NOW...?
IF THE ENEMY HAS THE EYES NOW, THEN THERE IS A CHANCE THAT THEY'LL SEE MISA'S PICTURE AND REALIZE THAT SHE'S THE OWNER OF THE DEATH NOTE,

The sad scarface... The eternal #2 of Wammy's House

Mello likes a good match! Let's look back on his showdown record!!

From fated rivals to the average joe, Mello's victory is decided with every match! Here are some comments from the challengers themselves!!

Mello throws down a lot of fights during our story, but the real question here is: what's his success rate? I couldn't stop wondering, so I did some investigating.

ROUND★1 VS Near (At Wammy's House)

Ever since he could remember, Mello lived for challenges. Every day was a struggle against Near... I'm sure he'll be rewarded for his efforts one day.

⬆ It was during a great downpour when his anxiety about his future began. Would he search for a job first?

Gains: The right to succeed L (renounced)

Losses: House he grew up in, friends

Defeat...

I'll just use this defeat as fuel to get stronger!

ROUND★2 VS Japanese Task Force

Mello's magnicent debut battle against the world! Going up against the lame Japanese police is a little disappointing, but it's the perfect warm-up for taking down Near!!

➡ It's only mafia money, so might as well spend it. Actually, he spends more on chocolate...

Victory!!

I beat Near to it!

Gains: Death Note

Losses: Hostages' lives, underlings (a few), necessary expenses (funds for the missile, etc.)

ROUND★3 VS U.S. Government

On a roll, he takes on the entire country. His hideout is discovered, but since he was about to move anyway, it's not a problem.

⬆ Victory thanks to flying helmets! Shinigami sure are useful guys!!

Gains: Sidoh's cooperation

Losses: The old hideout, contact with the president

This Shinigami's pretty handy.

Victory!!

ROUND★4

VS

Japanese Task Force

Gains: Facial scar (the true sign of a man)

Losses: The Death Note, underlings (all of them), bed

↑ He let Soichiro live; that gray hair's just too cute...

← Cool as a cucumber even during an explosion.

These average joes get pissed and come back for revenge. Overwhelmed by their numbers, Mello's surrounded by the enemy! It's a bit of a pinch but he escapes dashingly!! However, he loses the Death Note and his buddies...

ROUND★5

VS

Near (In the SPK HQ)

Gains: Picture of self, friend (Halle)

Losses: Space to rent (Halle's house)

The real battle starts here!!
A tie!

→ Mello rejects a tempting proposal. A capable man won't lose to seduction!

You can't catch the snake without entering its hole. He goes to the SPK HQ to spit in his rival's face! They exchange light greetings, take a commemorative photo, and go home satisfied.

ROUND★6

VS

Kira

Gains: The foundation for Near's victory

Losses: Buddy (Matt), own life

....
....
Defeat
...

AND I CALLED YOU AS SOON AS I GOT THE CHANCE.
WELL, AS LONG AS YOU CAN CALL US, WE CAN TRACE THE CALL. EVERYBODY'S WORKING HARD TO HELP YOU. YOU KNOW WHAT YOU'RE SUPPOSED TO DO UNTIL THEY COME TO RESCUE YOU, DON'T YOU?
YES. I'M GOING TO STAY PUT AND MAKE NO FALSE MOVES, LIKE YOU SAID.

↑ Loses one of his last few buddies and ends up alone again.

If he can just beat Kira, he'll be the ultimate winner! "That's right, let's go to Japan! First I'll nab his girl and make him suffer even more!!" I'm not sure if that's what he's thinking, though...

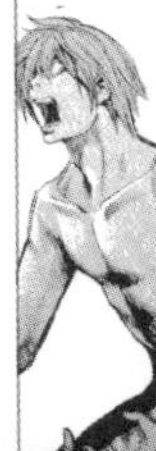

← It's not so much sleeping at the wheel as the eternal sleep. The curtain closes here on the competitive life of Mello.

As long as you believe that, what's the big deal?
Since Kira also dies...I'd say that makes us even.

Though he seems pathetic, Mello actually wins two rounds. When he yells, "I won more times than I thought," his face is brimming with pride.

Mello's Record

2 wins

1 draw | **3 losses**

The top-secret memo Ryuk found in the SPK! It's actually Near's toy list?!

?!
I have to get all of this...?

This mission, assigned to Rester, is quite a strenuous endeavor! Good luck, Rester! Don't fail us, Rester! Is he seriously the commander around here?!

To: Commander Rester
Re: A list of the things I want you to source. Thank you in advance for your efforts.* (I've included estimated prices.†)

	$5
☐ Deck of cards	$60
☐ Matches (20 sets)	$121
☐ Dart set	$1,080
☐ Dice (3,600)	$450
☑ Plastic models (15)	$75
☐ Plastic model-building tools (file, glue, etc.)	$234
☑ Block diorama	$240
☐ All types of monster & alien figures (12)	$260
☐ Train set (including automatic trains)	$250
☐ Tarot cards	$150
☐ Secret base set	$115
☐ All types of robots (5)	$25
☐ Die in a die	$30
☑ Finger puppet kit	$23
☐ Inflatable pool	$98
☐ Radio-controlled rubber duck (2)	$26
☐ Tower figurine	$2
☐ Paper for building towers	
☑ NHN shooting game set	¥9,980
(With block dolls)	¥20,790
☐ Christmas tree	
☐ All types of Christmas presents	¥58,800
(game consoles, baseball game board, etc.)	¥16,000
☐ Marble roller coaster	¥5,250
☐ Mini New Year's pine decoration	¥5,000
☑ Kagami mochi & mikan	¥3,000
☐ Mask-building set	

Near

I nabbed a memo sheet from the SPK.

NEAR'S SHOPPING LIST

A curious Ryuk managed a solo sneak-in of the SPK main building! There, he discovered a top-secret document...or so he thought.

Heh heh!
As soon as possible, please.

A sneak peek at Near's collection!!

* Item names are all Near's terms.
† Prices were all calculated by Near based on 2009 market averages in L.A. and Tokyo.

SPECIAL

Blank Puzzle with L Logo

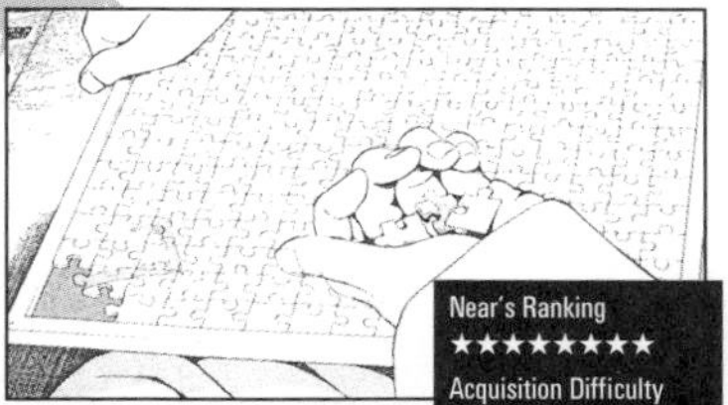

Near's Ranking
★★★★★★★★
Acquisition Difficulty
☆☆☆☆☆☆☆☆

Fate: Stored at Wammy's House.

Wammy's House's deluxe and exclusive premium item. I've never seen one myself, but it seems Near likes it plenty.

Plastic Models

Near's Ranking
★★★★★
Acquisition Difficulty
☆☆

Fate: Smuggled into Japan from America, stored in Near's toy box.

Bringing plastic models and robots even during an emergency escape... All that work disguising him put to waste...

Block Diagram

Near's Ranking
★★★
Acquisition Difficulty
☆☆

Fate: Left behind at the New York HQ?

The scope of his toys has increased gradually... Actually, these things might be necessary to our investigation.

Finger Puppet Kit

Near's Ranking
★★★★★★
Acquisition Difficulty
☆☆☆☆

Fate: After the Kira case is solved, the Near and Mello dolls are stored in Near's toy box. Were the others trashed?!

Kits are pretty hard to find, so I had to put in a special order at a huge toy store. Will he make puppets of us SPK guys too?

NHN Shooting Game Set

RIGHT NOW, THEY'RE BOTH IN A ROOM WE BOOKED NEAR NHN.

PLEASE CONNECT ME TO THEM.

Near's Ranking
★★★★★★★
Acquisition Difficulty
☆☆☆☆☆☆

Fate: Stored in Near's toy box. A number of the block dolls are damaged and lost.

These are really popular in Japan. I had to wait in line outside a big toy store to get mine.

Kagami Mochi & Mikan

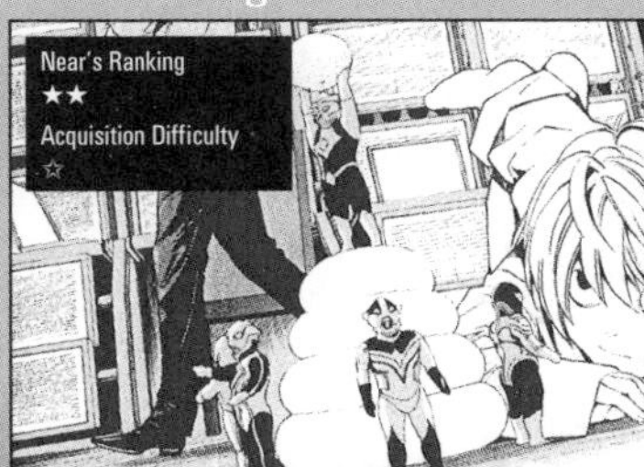

Near's Ranking
★★
Acquisition Difficulty
☆

Fate: Eaten as New Year's treats...?

In accordance with Japanese New Year's customs, I bought them from a supermarket. Is this the correct way to display them?

Hyuk hyuk... Is the SPK actually a romper room or something?

Please answer honestly.

Who do you resemble most?! *Death Note* Character Type Diagnoses!!

Maybe it's a personal thing, but people on the edge really go nuts over *Death Note.* Analyze yourself to see whom you resemble. And it might be helpful to really get into it while you're at it.

START FROM ①

1 If you picked up a Death Note you...

- Would use it ⇒ Go to ②
- Would not use it ⇒ Go to ④
- Would not pick it up ⇒ Go to ⑤

2 What do you think of Shinigami?

I AM ON YOUR SIDE.
ON MY SIDE...? THIS THING...? EWW...

- Scary ⇒ Go to ③
- Cute ⇒ Go to ⑤
- Reminds you of yourself ⇒ Go to ⑥

PHEW, IT'S OVER AT LAST. THAT SURE WAS INTENSE AGAIN TODAY. MAN, IT'S TOUGH TO HAVE TO LISTEN TO THESE CONVERSATIONS FOR HOURS...
YOU SEEM AWFULLY HAPPY THOUGH, MATSUDA.

3 Which would you belong to?

- Japanese Task Force ⇒ Go to ⑤
- SPK ⇒ Go to ⑦
- Shinigami realm ⇒ Go to ⑧

4 Whom do you like from the following?

SO WHAT ARE YOU GOING TO DO?
LIVE IN THE BATH-ROOM?

- Rester ⇒ Go to ⑤
- Halle ⇒ Go to ⑥
- Gevanni ⇒ Go to ⑩

5 Are you hiding things from your family?

JEEZ... TRICKED BY THE COVER, AGAIN...

- Yes ⇒ Go to ⑨
- No ⇒ Go to ⑫
- They already know ⇒ Go to ⑬

PROFESSOR RYUK PRESENTS RELATIVELY ACCURATE CHARACTER TYPE DIAGNOSES

Ryuk's thorough human observation skills have been trained by keeping a watchful eye on humans for years. Now you can analyze yourself based on these diagnoses of different character types!

DEATH NOTE
※Names have been changed to protect the innocent.

The Shinigami Realm
HUH?!
MY DEATH NOTE'S GONE!!
GYA HA HA!! YOU LOST IT AGAIN? HOW LAME!
YOU CAN'T GET A NEW ONE UNLESS YOU REPORT TO THE OLD MAN... THE SHINIGAMI KING.
THIS IS WHY YOU'RE STILL A C-RANK SHINIGAMI.
HEH HEH HEH.
THIS IS MY STYLE.
RUSTLE
YOUR STYLE?

Taro Kagami Age 13
A NOTE-BOOK ...?
DEATH NOTE
IT'S BRAND NEW. NOTHING'S WRITTEN IN IT YET.
PERFECT. I LOST MY OLD DIARY, SO I'LL USE THIS ONE INSTEAD.
"DEATH"...?
DEATH NOTE
I KNOW WHAT "NOTE" MEANS BUT WE HAVEN'T LEARNED THIS OTHER WORD IN ENGLISH CLASS YET...
I'M HOME.

HAAH ...
MAYBE WRITING IN MY DIARY'LL MAKE ME FEEL BETTER.
FLIP
FLIP
Month-XX Day-XXth
Today when I went to school, A-ta Suzuki and B-rou Tanaka bullied me
TARO, DINNER-TIME!
'KAY...
AUGH!
WHAT'S WRONG, A-TA?
UGAH!
B-ROU, ARE YOU OKAY?!

The Next Day
'MORNING!
RATTLE
RUSTLE
RUSTLE
I HAVE SAD NEWS FOR EVERYONE.
I'M SURE SOME OF YOU ALREADY KNOW BUT...
SUZUKI-KUN AND TANAKA-KUN SUDDENLY PASSED AWAY LAST NIGHT...
IT SEEMS BOTH SUFFERED FREAK HEART ATTACKS...
HUH? NO WAY...
MUTTER
THEY DIED?
MUTTER
THE TWO GUYS WHO BULLIED ME YESTERDAY..
WH- WHY?
SO TODAY YOU MAY LEAVE AFTER HEARING THE PRINCIPAL'S ADDRESS TO THE SCHOOL.
CHATTER
CHATTER

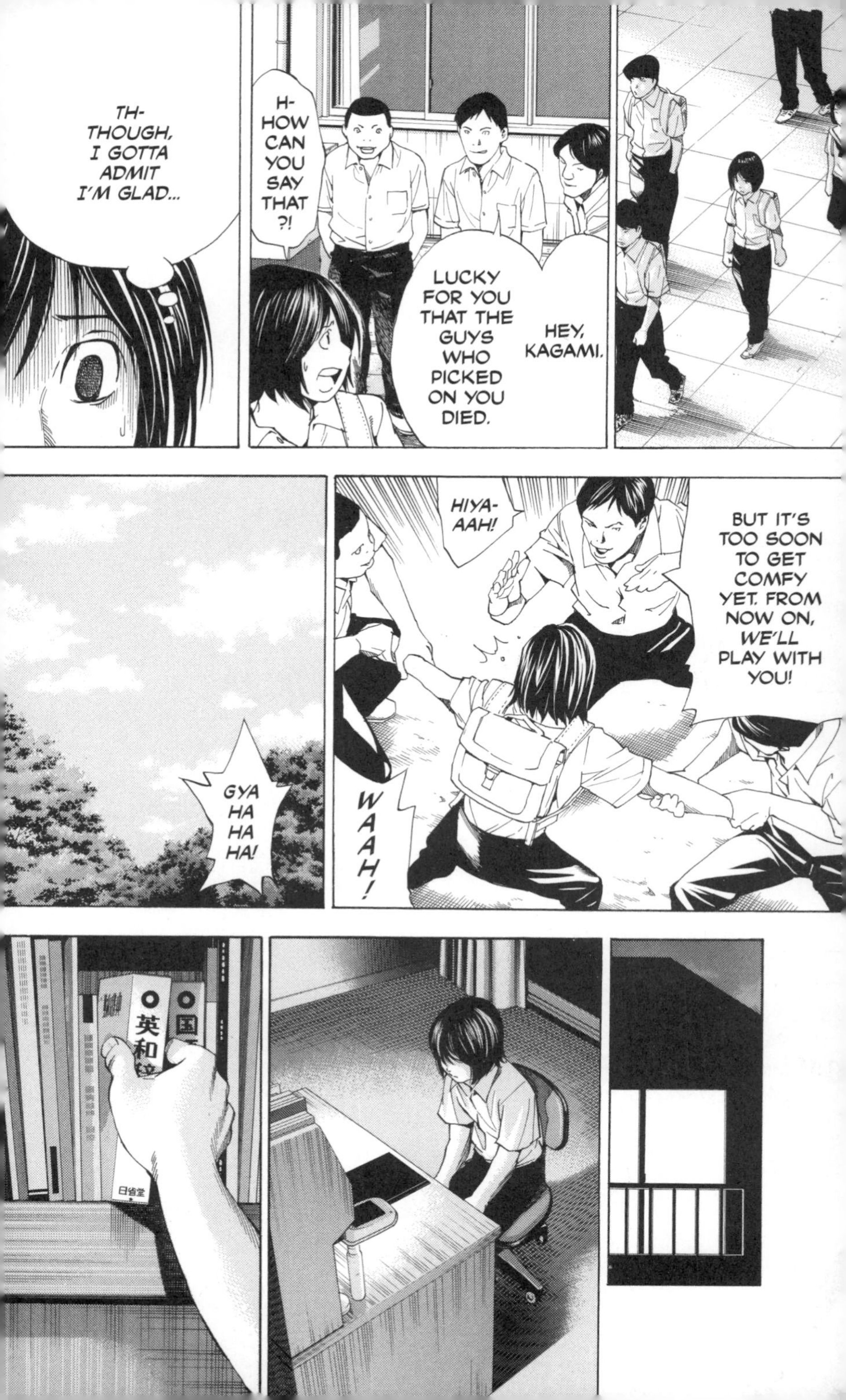
HEY, KAGAMI.
LUCKY FOR YOU THAT THE GUYS WHO PICKED ON YOU DIED.
H-HOW CAN YOU SAY THAT?!
TH-THOUGH, I GOTTA ADMIT I'M GLAD...
BUT IT'S TOO SOON TO GET COMFY YET. FROM NOW ON, *WE'LL* PLAY WITH YOU!
HIYA-AAH!
WAAAH!
GYA HA HA HA!
英和
日省堂

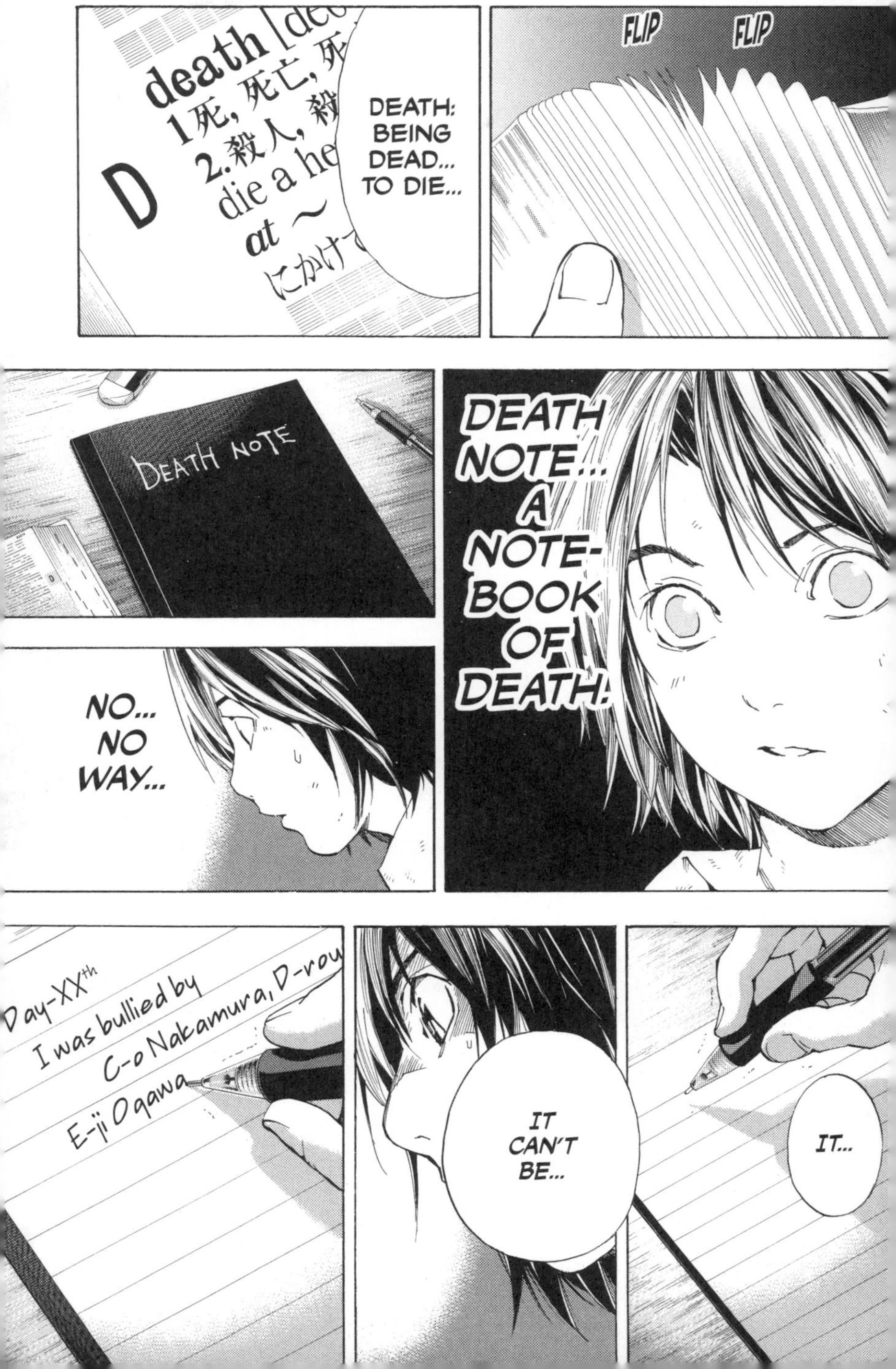
FLIP FLIP
death [dea
1死, 死亡, 死
2.殺人, 殺
die a he
at ~
にかけて
DEATH: BEING DEAD... TO DIE...
DEATH NOTE... A NOTE-BOOK OF DEATH.
DEATH NOTE
NO... NO WAY...
IT...
IT CAN'T BE...
Day-XXth
I was bullied by
C-o Nakamura, D-rou
E-ji Ogawa

PSST
PSST
PSST
...
PSST
BUT, FOR BOTH OF THEM TO HAVE HEART ATTACKS...
IT'S JUST TOO WEIRD TO BE A COINCIDENCE.
KLAK
LAST NIGHT... NAKAMURA-KUN AND YAMAZAKI-KUN HAVE...
CHATTER
CHATTER
I'M GETTING SCARED...
NO WAY... IT CAN'T BE...
IS THIS CLASS CURSED?
IT...
IT WAS THE NOTE-BOOK!

DASH
I HAVE TO HURRY HOME AND HIDE THAT NOTE-BOOK.
IF MOM FOUND IT...
OH! THAT'S MIURA-KUN.
UH-OH... THE POLICE!!
OH YEAH... MIURA-KUN WAS BULLIED BY THOSE FIVE KIDS TOO, SO...
...THE POLICE MUST SUSPECT HIM...

中村医院
THANKS FOR YOUR HELP.
BUT INSPECTOR, THEY ALL HAD HEART ATTACKS... I DON'T THINK WE HAVE A CASE HERE.
YES, BUT TO HAVE FIVE KIDS ALL IN THE SAME SCHOOL, LET ALONE THE SAME CLASS, DIE IN TWO DAYS? SOME-THING'S UP...
TA-TARO?
DASH
KLAK
DEATH NOTE
KI HI HI HI HI...

AAAAAH!!
SHI–
SHINI-GAMI ...?!
COME ON. IF THAT NOTEBOOK CAN EXIST...
...THEN A SHINIGAMI SHOULDN'T BE THAT SURPRISING.
YEAH, I'M RYUK. A LOSER FROM THE SHINIGAMI REALM WHO LOST HIS DEATH NOTE IN THE HUMAN WORLD.

...
YEAH, IT'S JUST AS YOU'RE THINKING. THE PEOPLE WHOSE NAMES ARE WRITTEN IN THERE WILL DIE.
OH. SO YOU WANNA RETURN IT?
W-WELL, DIDN'T YOU COME FOR THIS?
HYUK HYUK HYUK. YOU SURE YOU WANNA GIVE IT UP?
IF YOU HAVE THAT, YOU CAN ERASE ANYONE WHO GETS IN YOUR WAY. EVER.
BESIDES, I ALREADY GOT A NEW ONE, SO I DON'T CARE EITHER WAY.

NOK-NOK
TA-TARO?
HO-HOLD ON, MOM!
DON'T WORRY. ONLY YOU CAN SEE AND HEAR ME.
Y-YES?
THE POLICE ARE HERE. THEY WANT TO TALK TO YOU...
THE POLICE ?!
DID YOU... DO SOMETHING BAD, TARO?
OF COURSE NOT!
FIVE KIDS IN MY CLASS DIED, SO THEY'RE JUST ASKING EVERYONE FOR INFORMATION.
I DIDN'T DO ANY-THING, DON'T WORRY.
OKAY, THEN.

GOOD EVENING. ARE YOU TARO-KUN?
...
Y-YES. AND YOU GUYS ARE...?
WE'RE DETECTIVES FROM THE XX DIVISION.
YOU DON'T HAVE ANYTHING TO BE AFRAID OF.
SEE? HERE'S MY POLICE BADGE.
...
UH... UMM ...
DO YOU GUYS HAVE SOMETHING OTHER THAN A BADGE TO PROVE YOU'RE DETECTIVES?
HAH HAH. YOU GOT US. IT'S TRUE A BADGE ALONE DOESN'T PROVE WE'RE REALLY WITH THE FORCE.

SEE? THAT'S MY NAME AND PICTURE. AND THE "INSPECTOR" THERE MEANS DETECTIVE.
CHIEF INSPECTOR
YAMANAKA
N-SUKE
HYUK HYUK HYUK!
FLAP
YOU IMPRESS ME. YOU'RE GOING TO MEMORIZE THEIR NAMES... AND THEN WRITE THEM IN THE NOTEBOOK. GOOD THINKING.
YEAH, THEY ALL BULLIED ME A LOT...
I SEE ...
W-WAIT JUST A SECOND!
NOW NOW, MA'AM.

IT SEEMS LIKE YOU SUSPECT MY SON...!
NOT AT ALL, ACTUALLY.
ALL FIVE VICTIMS DIED OF HEART ATTACKS WHILE IN THEIR VERY HOMES WITH FAMILY PRESENT.
SUCH A SITUATION HAS A ONE-PERCENT CHANCE OF BEING SUICIDE, SO WE'RE GOING HOUSE TO HOUSE TO ASK ALL THEIR FRIENDS MORE ABOUT THEM.
THEY DIED FROM HEART ATTACKS BECAUSE YOU DIDN'T WRITE THE CAUSE OF DEATH NEXT TO THEIR NAMES.
FOR EXAMPLE, IF YOU WROTE "(SO-AND-SO) DIED IN AN ACCIDENT," HE'D HAVE DIED IN SOME ACCIDENT. IF YOU WRITE NOTHING, THEY JUST DIE OF HEART ATTACKS.
THANK YOU FOR YOUR HELP.
MY, HOW DREAD-FUL...FIVE CLASS-MATES IN TWO DAYS... NOW I'M WORRIED ABOUT YOU.
HAH HAH, YOU WORRY TOO MUCH, MOM. I'LL BE FINE.

TAKAGI, WOULD YOU SAY THAT KID WAS ACTING STRANGE?
HUH? YOU THINK HE WAS?
YEAH... HIS FACE WAS PALE AND HIS EYES KEPT DARTING AROUND.
TRUE, BUT MOST KIDS GET LIKE THAT JUST FROM HEARING THE WORD "POLICE," YOU KNOW?
...
YEAH... THAT'S A GOOD POINT...
...
HOW-EVER, TAKAGI...
YES?
...EARLIER YOU WERE SAYING WE DON'T HAVE A CASE, BUT...

THEN YOU'RE SUSPECTING MAN-SLAUGHTER ...?
...THIS IS MOST DEFINITELY A CASE. THERE'S NO WAY FIVE CLASSMATES ALL DYING OF HEART ATTACKS COULD JUST BE A COINCIDENCE.
I'M NOT SAYING THAT YET.
CLICK
FIVE PEOPLE ALL IN THE SAME VICINITY DYING FROM THE SAME CONDITION. THAT IN ITSELF IS A CASE.
WE COULD SOLVE IT BY SIMPLY WRITING IT OFF AS A "COINCI-DENCE," BUT SUSPECTING THERE'S SOMETHING BELOW THE SURFACE IS OUR JOB.
YOU DO THIS FOR 25 YEARS AND YOU COME ACROSS DOZENS OF CASES YOU KNOW ARE MURDERS BUT THAT JUST CAN'T BE SOLVED...
...
!

TAKAGI, YOU UP FOR SOME OVERTIME?
HUH? UH, SURE, I GUESS...
POLICE BUREAU XX DIVISION
DATA ROOM
LOOK FOR A CASE BACK IN 1978 OR '79 THAT HAPPENED AT THE YAMASHITA BRANCH OF TAKARA BANK.
ON IT.
I'M NOT GETTING ANYTHING ON THE COMPUTER.
!
HERE WE ARE...

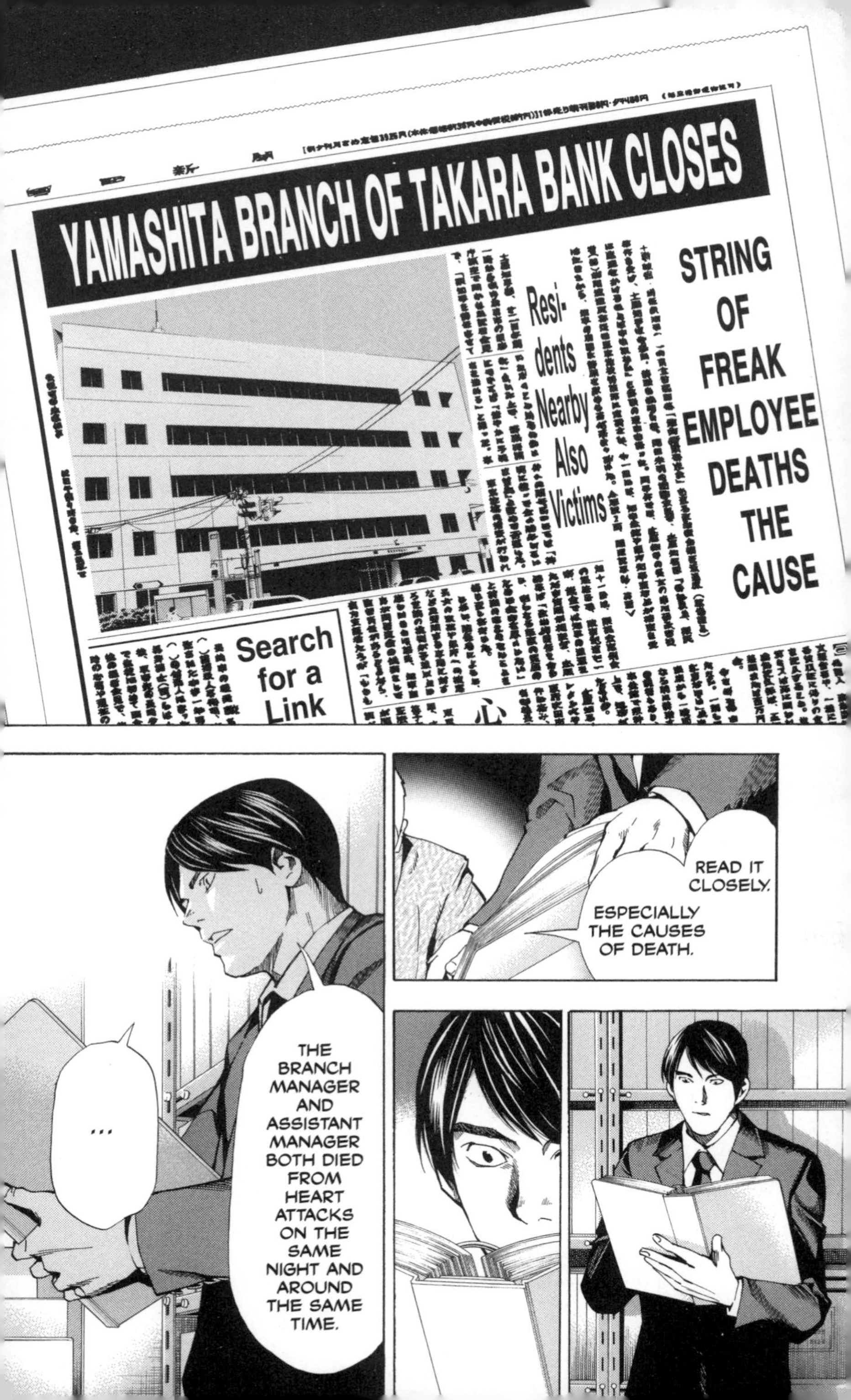

YAMASHITA BRANCH OF TAKARA BANK CLOSES
STRING OF FREAK EMPLOYEE DEATHS THE CAUSE
Resi-dents Nearby Also Victims
Search for a Link
READ IT CLOSELY.
ESPECIALLY THE CAUSES OF DEATH.
THE BRANCH MANAGER AND ASSISTANT MANAGER BOTH DIED FROM HEART ATTACKS ON THE SAME NIGHT AND AROUND THE SAME TIME.
...

WELL? DOESN'T THAT RESEMBLE THE CASE WE HAVE HERE? PEOPLE FROM THE SAME AREA DYING OF HEART ATTACKS SIMULTANEOUSLY.
...
BUT...THAT WASN'T THE END OF IT. OTHER PEOPLE FROM THE SAME BRANCH ALSO DIED SUDDEN DEATHS...
YEP.
AND THE FINAL DEATH WAS AN EMPLOYEE WHO COMMITTED SUICIDE...
STRING OF FREAK EMPLOYEE DEATHS
Residents Nearby Also Victims
IT WAS ONLY LATER THAT WE LEARNED THAT OTHER PEOPLE ASSOCIATED WITH THE SUICIDE VICTIM HAD ALSO DIED UNDER STRANGE CIRCUMSTANCES.
WH-WHAT DOES IT ALL MEAN...?
GOOD QUESTION. THE CASE WAS NEVER SOLVED.

IF WHAT-EVER HAPPENED TO ALL THOSE PEOPLE IN THE TAKARA BANK CASE IS WHAT WE'RE DEALING WITH NOW...
...THEN THERE'S A GOOD CHANCE THAT MORE KIDS IN THAT CLASS AND OTHER PEOPLE ARE GOING TO START DYING TOO.
LET'S CALL IT A NIGHT.
WE CAN PICK UP AGAIN TOMOR-ROW.
CLICK
TAKAGI!!
Y-YES, SIR?!

NOW, THIS IS JUST A "WHAT IF"!
WH-WHAT IF WHAT, SIR?
WHAT IF...
...YOU HAD THE ABILITY TO KILL PEOPLE JUST BY *THINKING* IT? WHAT WOULD YOU DO?
HUH ?!
C-COME ON...
Hah hah!
THERE'S NO WAY...

IF IT WERE ME, I'D PROBABLY START KILLING OFF ANYONE WHO WAS IN MY WAY...
WHA ...?!
THAT'S WHY IT'S A "WHAT IF."
YEAH, BUT...
KLAK KLAK
THEN, SO NOBODY WOULD SUSPECT ME, I'D KILL A LOT OF OTHER PEOPLE WHO WEREN'T RELATED TO ME.
THEN, IF SOMEBODY *STILL* SUSPECTED ME, I'D KILL THEM TOO.
THIS IS THE INSPECTOR'S THEORY OF THE TAKARA BANK CASE? HE'S NUTS!
SO I GUESS I'D HAVE TO KILL EVERY DETECTIVE...
YEAH...

...
INSPEC-TOR!
IF I HAD THAT ABILITY...
...I'D KILL ALL THE PEOPLE WHO I THOUGHT THE WORLD WOULD BE BETTER OFF WITHOUT. THEN I'D CREATE A WORLD OF PEACE WITH ONLY THOSE WHO HAD GOOD HEARTS LEFT.
... I SEE.
WELL, THAT'D AUTOMATI-CALLY CUT OUT THE MAJORITY OF MAN-KIND.
...
KLAK

WHAT'RE YOU THINKING WHILE YOU HOLD THAT NOTE-BOOK SO CLOSE?
...
WHAT IF... I COULD MAKE A PEACEFUL WORLD...?

HYUK HYUK HYUK! YOU'RE AWFULLY YOUNG TO BE THINKING ABOUT TAKING ON ALL THE EVILS OF THE WORLD.
NO, NOT ON THAT LARGE A SCALE. BUT I CAN'T HELP THINKING WHAT GOOD COULD COME FROM THIS NOTE-BOOK...
THAT'S THE SPIRIT! I THOUGHT YOU WERE A YELLOWBELLY, BUT NOW I LIKE YOU, TARO. I'LL HELP YOU OUT WITH WHATEVER YOU DO.
BUT THE NOTEBOOK DOESN'T WORK UNLESS YOU KNOW THE FACE OF THE PERSON WHOSE NAME YOU WRITE DOWN.
NAME AND FACE...

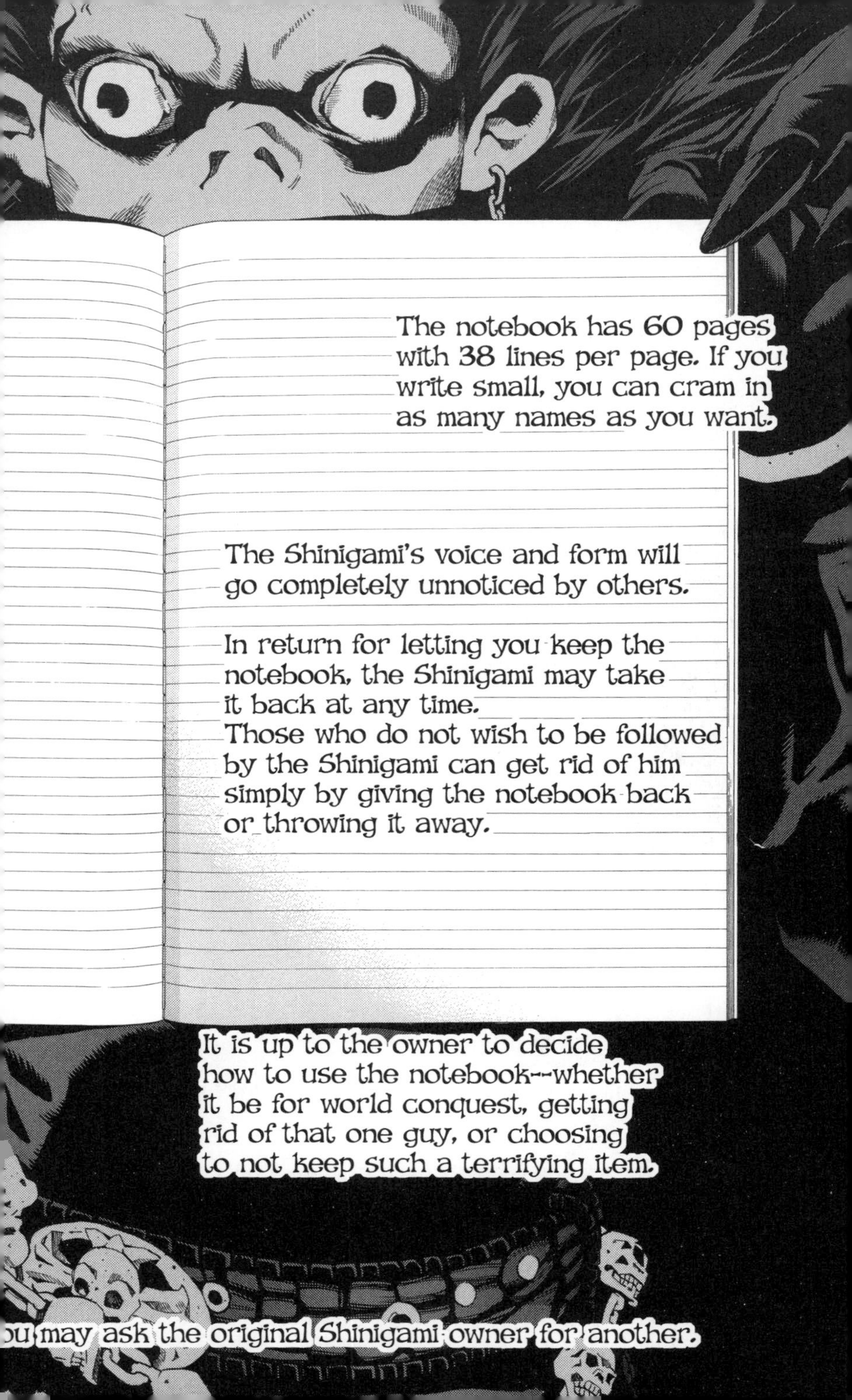

The notebook has 60 pages with 38 lines per page. If you write small, you can cram in as many names as you want.
The Shinigami's voice and form will go completely unnoticed by others.
In return for letting you keep the notebook, the Shinigami may take it back at any time.
Those who do not wish to be followed by the Shinigami can get rid of him simply by giving the notebook back or throwing it away.
It is up to the owner to decide how to use the notebook--whether it be for world conquest, getting rid of that one guy, or choosing to not keep such a terrifying item.
ou may ask the original Shinigami owner for another.

Death Note Rules

This notebook can only be used by the one who found it. If the owner throws it away or loses it, the right of ownership is automatically transferred to whoever next picks it up.

One must know the face of the person whose name is written down for there to be an effect. That way, people with the same names will not be affected all at once.

If you write a cause of death after the name like this: (Name) died from (cause), then that will happen.

You can write with any pen: the color doesn't matter. If you use a sticker with a name printed on it, there will be no effect. Please write directly onto the notebook. It would be a good idea to change your handwriting as much as possible.

These letters cannot be erased.

If the cover is destroyed, the notebook cannot be used.

Be careful not to let other people see it.

You will not die if you write your own name here, but it is not recommended.

When you run out of room to write in the noteboo
How many Death Notes would you need?

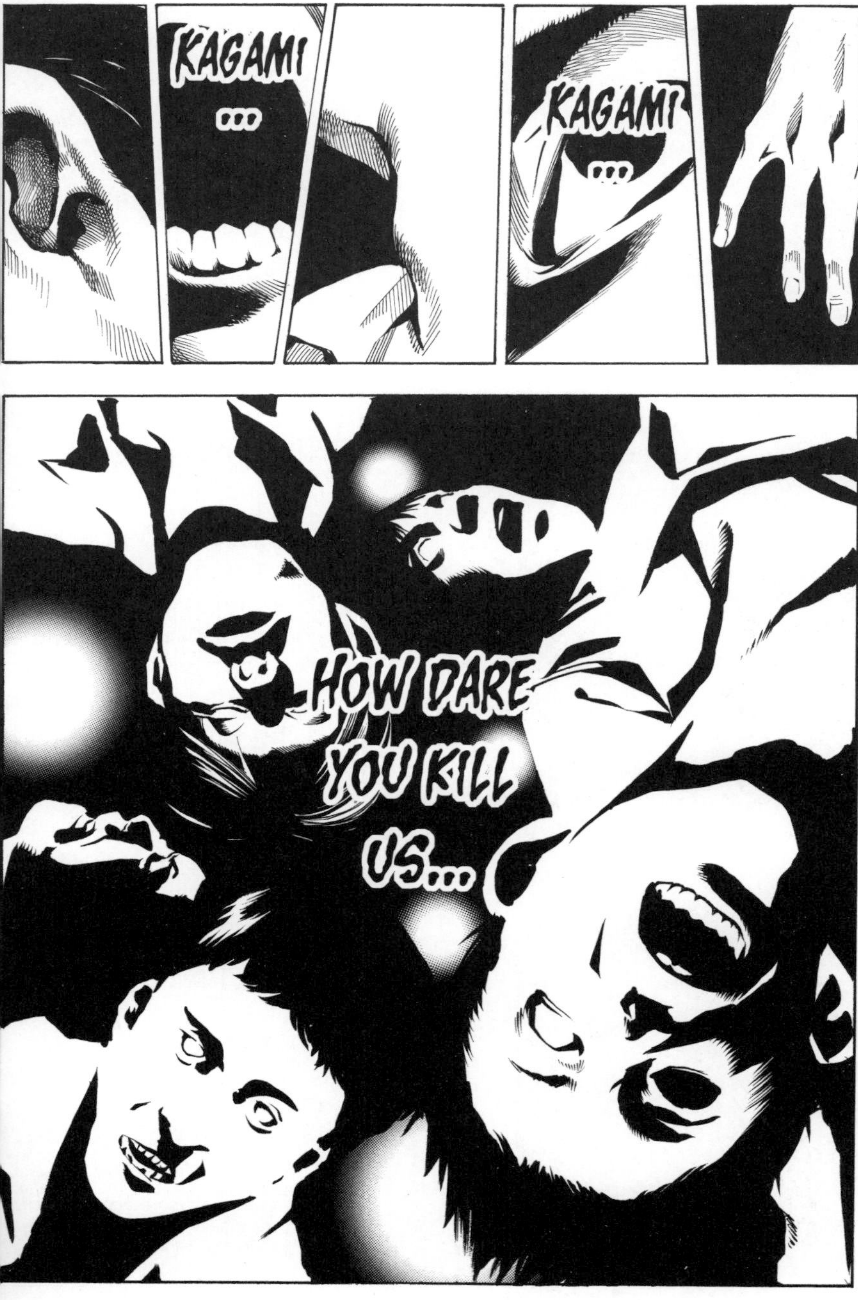
KAGAMI...
KAGAMI...
HOW DARE YOU KILL US...

UWAAAAH!!
BA!
HFF HFF
DREAMS LIKE THAT ARE A NATURAL PART OF THE PROCESS.
AFTER ALL, YOU'VE KILLED FIVE PEOPLE IN TWO DAYS. ANY AVERAGE PERSON WOULD FEEL THIS...
I-I DIDN'T *KILL* THEM! I DIDN'T MEAN TO!
YEAH? THEN HOW ABOUT YOU USE THIS? THE DEATH ERASER.
HUH? WHAT IS THAT?
IF YOU ERASE A NAME IN THE NOTE-BOOK WITH THIS, THAT PERSON WILL COME BACK TO LIFE—SO LONG AS HE HASN'T BEEN CREMATED YET.

POLICE
KLAK
INSPEC-TOR!
THE FIVE KIDS HAVE COME BACK TO LIFE!
WHAT ?!
IT'S TRUE! TWO NIGHTS AGO, AROUND NINE O'CLOCK, THEY ALL CAME BACK TO LIFE. ALL FIVE ARE BACK IN SCHOOL TODAY.
THAT'S IMPOSSI-BLE!
HEART ATTACK VICTIMS WHO ALL DIED WITHIN TWO DAYS OF EACH OTHER... ALL COME BACK TO LIFE ON THE SAME DAY...
RATTLE
THAT DOES IT! WE'RE GOING TO HAVE A TALK WITH THOSE RESUR-RECTED BOYS NOW!
BUT SIR, THEY'RE IN THE MIDDLE OF CLASS.
ALL THE BETTER! THERE'S SOME-THING GOING ON IN THAT CLASS!!
INSPEC-TOR!

PARDON US. I'M YAMANAKA FROM XX STATION.
CHIEF INSPECTOR
YAMANAKA
N-SUKE
POLICE
AND I'M TAKAGI.
INSPECTOR
TAKAGI
POLICE
WE'D LIKE TO HAVE A WORD WITH THE FIVE BOYS WE HEARD HAD COME BACK TO LIFE.
HUH? RI-RIGHT NOW?
YES. RIGHT HERE, RIGHT NOW.
...
YEP, I SAW THIS COMING. *HYUK HYUK.*
RATTLE
SUZUKI, TANAKA, AND...
CHATTER
CHATTER
THE MOMENT THEY MENTION THEY'VE ALL BULLIED YOU, THE FIRST ONE WHO'LL BE SUSPECT-ED IS...
THAT DAY, WE...

UUH!!
GAH!
UUH!!
WH-WHAT'S HAPPENING?!
AAAAH!!

TAKAGI, CALL AN AMBULANCE!
Y-YES, SIR!
GAH!
UUH!
DAMMIT...
THUD
DID YOU...
HUH? NO! IT WASN'T ME! I DON'T EVEN HAVE IT HERE...
After the deaths of five students and two detectives by freak heart attacks...
...the school had to be closed for a while.

The Next Day
WHAT COULD HAVE HAPPENED? WHY DID THOSE KIDS AND THE DETECTIVES DIE?
YOU SURE YOU DIDN'T WRITE IN THE NOTE-BOOK AGAIN?
I TOLD YOU, I LEFT THE NOTE-BOOK IN MY DRAWER AFTER THAT!
SEE?
HMM ...
CHECK IT OUT. THE PRESS IS FREAKING OUT TOO.
XX MIDDLE SCHOOL
FIVE STUDENTS COME BACK TO LIFE
TWO DETECTIVES ALSO DIE OF HEART ATTACK
STUDENTS
SINCE TWO GUYS ON THE FORCE WERE INVOLVED, THE POLICE ARE PROBABLY GETTING DOWN TO BUSINESS WITH THE INVESTI-GATION NOW.
TURN ON THE TV. THEY'RE EVEN HOLDING PANEL SHOWS.
CLICK
HUH?!

LOOK WHAT THEY TITLED IT! HAH!
HYUK.
THE CURSED CLASS
I DON'T BELIEVE THE INCIDENTS WILL STOP HERE.
HUH? WHAT DO YOU MEAN?
Journalist
Gen Suzuki
Former City Police Official
Keiji Shitayama
IT HIT ME AFTER WATCHING THE WORLD NEWS.
SINCE LAST NIGHT, HEINOUS CRIMINALS ALL OVER THE WORLD HAVE BEEN DYING ONE AFTER ANOTHER.
THAT'S CERTAINLY A POINT OF DEEP INTEREST.
Journalist
Gen Suzuki
Former City Police Official
Keiji Shitayama
Mystery Author
Akihiko Yajuuin
PLUS, THEY ALL DIED OF THE SAME THING: HEART ATTACKS!
Journalist
I CAN ONLY ASSUME THAT MEANS THERE'S ANOTHER DEATH NOTE OUT THERE.
SO SOME-ONE ELSE IS WRITING IN THE OTHER DEATH NOTE, EH?
PROBABLY SOMEONE WHO DOESN'T REALIZE THAT IF YOU DON'T WRITE A CAUSE OF DEATH, THEY ALL DIE OF HEART ATTACKS.

WAIT A MINUTE, RYUK...
ARE YOU SAYING THAT...?
YEP, I DROPPED MY OTHER DEATH NOTE.
HYUK HYUK HYUK. OOPS.
CLINK
I WONDER IF THIS IS GOD'S DOING...
OOH, GOD, HUH?
GOD'S DOING? PLEASE! MAYBE IF JUST EVIL PEOPLE DIED. BUT FIVE CHILDREN AND TWO HONEST POLICEMAN ARE DEAD, SIR!

WH- WHERE DID YOU DROP IT, RYUK?
WHO KNOWS? I'VE ONLY EVER BEEN HERE AND AT THE SCHOOL.
EVEN IF YOU FORCED A CONNECTION BETWEEN THE CRIMINALS' DEATHS, IT ALL STARTED AT ONE SCHOOL.
Mystery Author
Akihiko Yajuuin
YOU MUST HAVE SOME WAY TO TRACK IT DOWN. I MEAN, YOU FOUND ME, DIDN'T YOU?
NOT UNLESS I CHECK FROM THE SHINIGAMI REALM.
SUPPOSING, JUST SUPPOSING, I WAS MAKING THIS CASE INTO A NOVEL...
...I WOULD MAKE THE MAIN CHARACTER A YOUNG BOY WITH SPECIAL POWERS.
A BOY? WHY A YOUNG BOY?
BECAUSE THE FIRST TO DIE WERE BOYS.
A BOY, HUH? BUT WHY WOULD HE KILL OTHER KIDS?
Journal
Gen
WELL, THAT BRINGS UP THE POSSIBILITY OF BULLYING OR...
City Police Official
Shitayama
UUGH!

...
!
WHAT IN THE WORLD...
WHAT THE--?
HUH?
IDIOTS. THAT'S WHAT THEY GET FOR SAYING ALL THAT ON TV, FOR CRYING OUT LOUD.
BUT WHY'S THAT MYSTERY AUTHOR OKAY?
MUST BE BECAUSE HE USED A PEN NAME. THEY WON'T DIE UNLESS YOU WRITE THEIR REAL NAME.
PAAA
WE ARE NOW EXPERIENCING TECHNICAL DIFFICULTIES
BUT NOW IT'S CONFIRMED. WHOEVER FOUND THAT OTHER NOTE-BOOK WAS AFRAID OF THE TRUTH BEING REVEALED AND SO WROTE DOWN THOSE SEVEN NAMES...
EVEN THOUGH I WAS THE ONE WHO WAS BULLIED...

I'VE GOT IT!
WHERE'RE YOU GOING, TARO?
DASH
I KNOW WHO HAS THE OTHER NOTE-BOOK, RYUK!
OH, REEEALLY?

ARE NOW
ERIENCING
CHNICAL
FICULTIES
DIE!
DIE!!
SKRCH
SKRCH
A-ta Suzuki, B-rou Tanaka
C-o Nakamura, D-rou
E-ji Ogawa
N-suke Yamanaka
Takagi
Keiji Shitayama
Gen Suzuki
AKIHIKO YAJUUIN
SKRCH
ALL OF YOU, JUST DIE!!
MIURA-KUN!

GRIP
Takagi
ji Shitayama
n Suzuki
IHIKO YAJUUIN
Taro Kaga
MIURA-KUN, STOP!!
BUMP
DON'T STOP ME! AFTER I WRITE YOUR NAME, I'LL WRITE MY OWN AND DIE!
IT'S NOT YOUR FAULT! I DID IT ALL!
I WAS THE ONE WHO FIRST WROTE THEIR FIVE NAMES!
HUH?

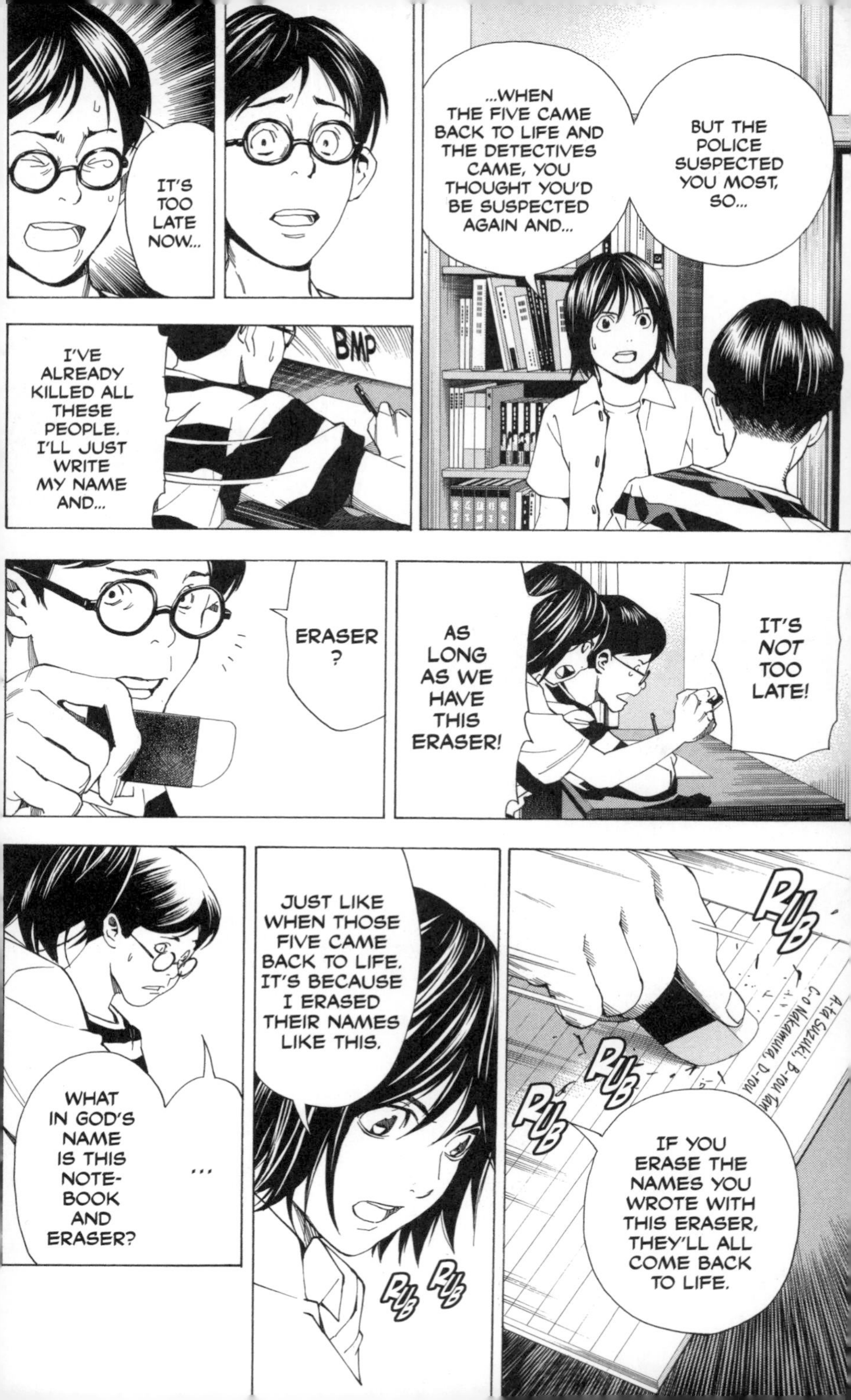
BUT THE POLICE SUSPECTED YOU MOST, SO...
...WHEN THE FIVE CAME BACK TO LIFE AND THE DETECTIVES CAME, YOU THOUGHT YOU'D BE SUSPECTED AGAIN AND...
IT'S TOO LATE NOW...
BMP
I'VE ALREADY KILLED ALL THESE PEOPLE. I'LL JUST WRITE MY NAME AND...
IT'S NOT TOO LATE!
AS LONG AS WE HAVE THIS ERASER!
ERASER?
RUB
RUB
RUB
A-ta Suzuki, B-rou
C-o Nakamura, D-rou
IF YOU ERASE THE NAMES YOU WROTE WITH THIS ERASER, THEY'LL ALL COME BACK TO LIFE.
JUST LIKE WHEN THOSE FIVE CAME BACK TO LIFE. IT'S BECAUSE I ERASED THEIR NAMES LIKE THIS.
RUB
RUB
WHAT IN GOD'S NAME IS THIS NOTE-BOOK AND ERASER?
...

DEATH NOTE
WE HAVE TO TAKE THIS NOTE-BOOK TO THE POLICE.
HUH ?!
OUR ONLY CHOICE IS TO TELL THE TRUTH AND GET THEM TO UNDER-STAND.
POLICE BUREAU XX DIVISION
HUH? YOU WANT TO SPEAK WITH INSPECTOR YAMANAKA AND DETECTIVE TAKAGI?

I'M SORRY, BUT YESTER-DAY...
...THEY BOTH PASSED AWAY.
NO, THEY SHOULD HAVE COME BACK TO LIFE BY NOW.
HUH? WHAT'RE YOU KIDS TALKING ABOUT?
LOOK, AT LEAST TELL US WHICH HOSPITAL THEY WERE TAKEN TO.
I GIVE UP.
IT'S PRETTY SCARY, BEING DEAD 'TIL JUST A MOMENT AGO...
NOW THAT WE GOT KILLED, THIS CASE IS DEFINITELY...
HMM?
YOU KIDS ARE...
?!
INSPECTOR, YOU'RE ALL RIGHT?!
? ?
PLEASE LISTEN TO WHAT WE HAVE TO SAY.

AH HA HA HA…
CONFERENCE ROOM
YOU EXPECT ME TO BELIEVE THAT RIDICULOUS STORY?
IT'S TRUE.
PEOPLE WHOSE NAMES ARE WRITTEN IN THIS NOTE-BOOK DIE.
YOU WON'T CONVINCE ME, SO QUIT WASTING YOUR BREATH! WE'VE HAD ENOUGH OF YOUR LITTLE GAMES. GO HOME!
NO, WAIT. HEAR THEM OUT.
INSPEC-TOR...
I WAS THE ONE WHO WROTE THOSE FIRST FIVE BOYS' NAMES IN THE NOTEBOOK.
BUT I DIDN'T THINK THEY'D DIE, SO WHEN THEY DID I FREAKED AND ERASED THEIR NAMES WITH THE ERASER THAT CAME WITH IT. THEN THEY CAME BACK TO LIFE.
NOW AN ERASER THAT CAN BRING BACK THE DEAD?! I'VE HAD JUST ABOUT ENOUGH OF YO–
TAKAGI, BE QUIET!

I WAS SO SCARED OF EVERYTHING THAT'D HAPPENED THAT I THREW AWAY THE NOTEBOOK IN THE CLASSROOM GARBAGE.
THAT'S WHEN MIURA-KUN PICKED IT UP...
I FOUND IT IN THE HALL-WAY.
THEN IT MUST'VE BEEN THE JANITOR WHO DROPPED IT THERE.
YOU GUYS WERE SUSPECT-ING MIURA-KUN FROM THE START, WEREN'T YOU?
YES, IT'S TRUE THAT WHEN THE FIVE BOYS DIED, HE WAS THE FIRST ONE WE APPROACHED.
THEN YOU ASKED THEM, AFTER THEY'D COME BACK TO LIFE, WHO THEY'D BULLIED. ALL RIGHT IN FRONT OF MIURA-KUN.
I WAS SO SURE YOU'D CALL ME OUT RIGHT THEN AND THERE.
I THOUGHT MAYBE IF I WROTE THEIR NAMES IN A NOTEBOOK CALLED THE "DEATH NOTE," WELL...
BUT THEN IT REALLY HAPPENED TO ALL FIVE OF THEM...
...

AFTER THAT I REALIZED THAT I'D BE THE MOST LIKELY SUSPECT FOR SURE.
SO I WROTE DOWN THE NAMES I'D SEEN ON YOUR BADGES...
...
I JUST CAN'T BELIEVE ANY OF THIS...
IF WE PROVE THAT THIS NOTEBOOK REALLY WORKS, WILL YOU FORGIVE US?!
RATTLE
WELL, IF ALL YOU'VE SAID IS TRUE, YOU'RE NOT GUILTY OF ANY CRIME.
I'LL TAKE FULL RESPONSI-BILITY.
THEN, MIURA-KUN, WRITE MY NAME IN THE NOTE-BOOK.
ONCE THEY'VE CONFIRMED I'M DEAD, ERASE IT.

AND AFTER MY NAME, WRITE "PEACE-FUL DEATH."
HEART ATTACKS LOOK PAINFUL.
YOU ...!
A-ARE YOU SURE?
SKRIT
SKRIT
Taro Kagami, peaceful
death

THUD
HE...
THIS ISN'T A TRICK...
HE'S DEAD.
UWAAH!!
USE THE ERASER!
RUB RUB RUB

YOU OKAY, KID?!
IF YOU STILL DON'T BELIEVE ME, YOU COULD TRY ANOTHER PERSON... MAYBE SOMEONE SENTENCED TO DEATH.
THAT WON'T BE NECESSARY. I BELIEVE YOU.
LISTEN, TAKAGI. DON'T TELL ANYONE ABOUT THIS NOTE-BOOK.
UNDER-STOOD, INSPEC-TOR.
SAME GOES FOR YOU TWO.
FOR SOMETHING THIS TERRIFYING TO EXIST IN THIS WORLD...
CRACKLE CRACKLE
And thus, one of the Death Notes turned into ashes right before their very eyes... forever remaining their secret.

I THINK THOSE FIVE GUYS WILL BE TOO AFRAID TO BULLY ANYONE NOW.
YEAH...
THANK YOU, TARO.
I WAS ABOUT TO KILL YOU WITH THAT NOTE-BOOK...
REAU XX DIVISION
TARO-KUN?
I SAW THE WHOLE THING, TARO.
THAT WAS SOME PRETTY SMART THINKING. *HYUK HYUK HYUK.*
SO HOW WAS IT...
...THE LAND OF THE DEAD?

Seven Years Later
DEATH NOTE
上映中
CHATTER
CHATTER
入場券売場
The hot thing today is that Death Note stuff...
HEY, DID YOU HEAR? THE STORY ABOUT THE REAL DEATH NOTE?
書店
MONTHLY RUMOR MAGAZINE
Death Note
特集!!
¥600
UNLIKE IN THE MOVIES AND TV, IT'S JUST A NORMAL NOTE-BOOK...
OOOOH. THAT MAKES IT EVEN SCARIER!
UWASA MAGA
RUMOR MAGAZINE
特別付録
Death Note
特集
THESE RUMORS ARE SOMETHING ELSE.

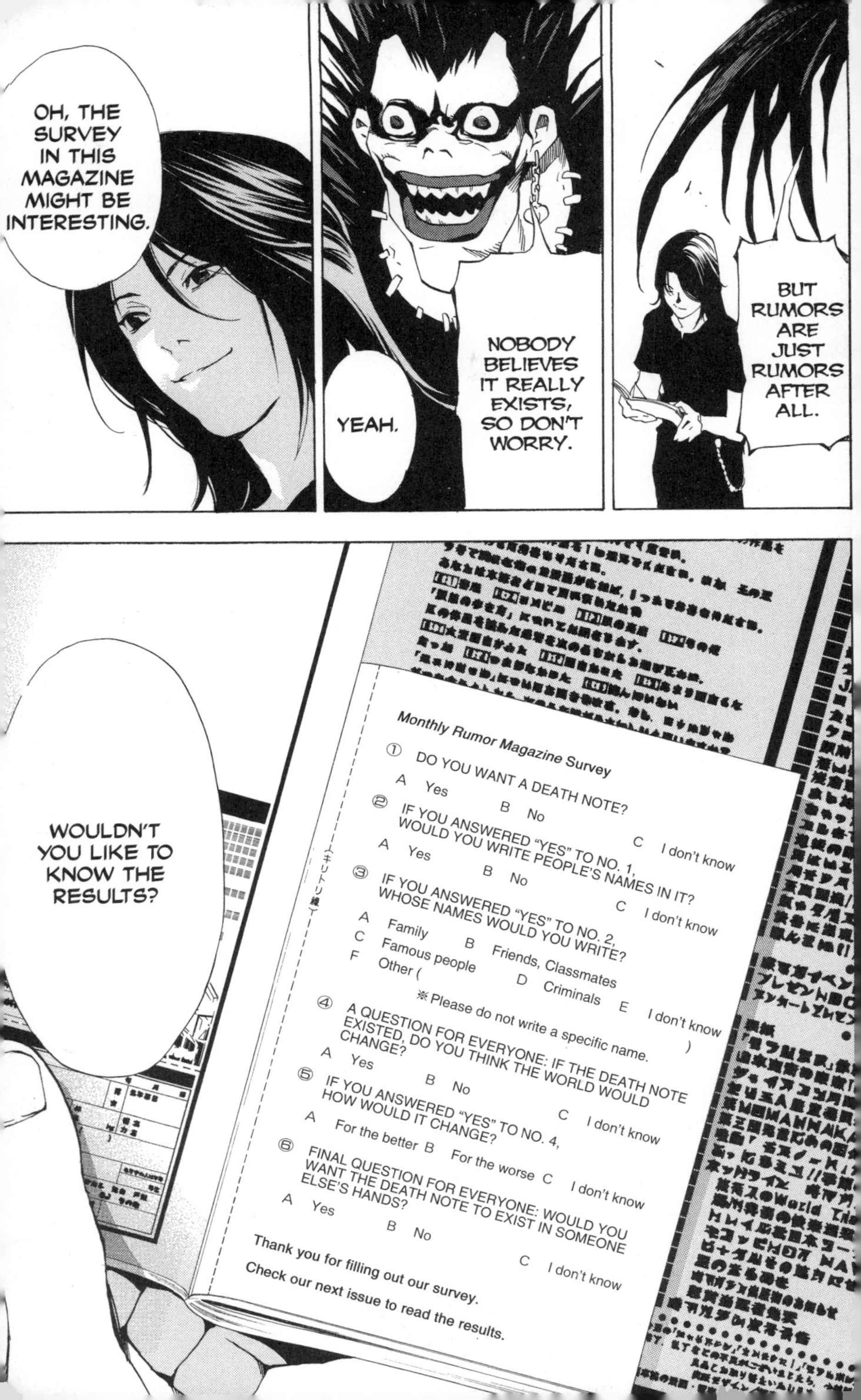
BUT RUMORS ARE JUST RUMORS AFTER ALL.
NOBODY BELIEVES IT REALLY EXISTS, SO DON'T WORRY.
YEAH.
OH, THE SURVEY IN THIS MAGAZINE MIGHT BE INTERESTING.
Monthly Rumor Magazine Survey
① DO YOU WANT A DEATH NOTE?
A Yes B No C I don't know
② IF YOU ANSWERED "YES" TO NO. 1, WOULD YOU WRITE PEOPLE'S NAMES IN IT?
A Yes B No C I don't know
③ IF YOU ANSWERED "YES" TO NO. 2, WHOSE NAMES WOULD YOU WRITE?
A Family B Friends, Classmates
C Famous people D Criminals E I don't know
F Other ( )
※Please do not write a specific name.
④ A QUESTION FOR EVERYONE: IF THE DEATH NOTE EXISTED, DO YOU THINK THE WORLD WOULD CHANGE?
A Yes B No C I don't know
⑤ IF YOU ANSWERED "YES" TO NO. 4, HOW WOULD IT CHANGE?
A For the better B For the worse C I don't know
⑥ FINAL QUESTION FOR EVERYONE: WOULD YOU WANT THE DEATH NOTE TO EXIST IN SOMEONE ELSE'S HANDS?
A Yes B No C I don't know
Thank you for filling out our survey.
Check our next issue to read the results.
(キリトリ線)
WOULDN'T YOU LIKE TO KNOW THE RESULTS?

DEATH NOTE 13™
デスノート

HOW TO READ

SJ Profiles

Created by
Tsugumi Ohba & Takeshi Obata

Art by
Takeshi Obata

Original Japanese Edition

Cover Design/Ken Yokoyama
Banana Grove Studio Design Staff/Kenichi Hayashi, Masako Shiratai,
Yoko Iwasa, Masayuki Tanibayashi, Emi Nakano, Yuki Aikawa, Takashi Akiba

English Edition

Translation & Adaptation/Akira Shiwawa
Lead Design/Sam Elzway
Graphic Design/Gerry Serrano
Editorial Assistance/Pancha Diaz & Andrew McKeon
Editors/Leyla Aker & Eric Searleman
Editorial Director/Masumi Washington

Printed in China

Published by
VIZ Media, LLC
P.O. Box 77010
San Francisco, CA 94107

10
First printing, February 2008
Tenth printing, July 2017